INTERNATIONAL

POLITICAL ECONOMY

AND GLOBALIZATION

(2nd Edition)

Published by

World Scientific Publishing Co. Pte. Ltd.

5 Toh Tuck Link, Singapore 596224

USA office: 27 Warren Street, Suite 401-402, Hackensack, NJ 07601

UK office: 57 Shelton Street, Covent Garden, London WC2H 9HE

British Library Cataloguing-in-Publication Data
A catalogue record for this book is available from the British Library.

INTERNATIONAL POLITICAL ECONOMY AND GLOBALIZATION
(2nd Edition)

ISBN-13 978-981-281-872-0
ISBN-10 981-281-872-3

Typeset by Stallion Press
Email: enquiries@stallionpress.com

Printed in Singapore by Mainland Press Pte Ltd

INTERNATIONAL

POLITICAL ECONOMY

AND GLOBALIZATION

(2nd Edition)

S Javed Maswood

American University in Cairo, Cairo, Egypt

 **World Scientific**

NEW JERSEY · LONDON · SINGAPORE · BEIJING · SHANGHAI · HONG KONG · TAIPEI · CHENNAI

PREFACE

When the publisher suggested a second edition of International Political Economy and Globalization, I naively assumed that it meant little more than adding new material at the end of each chapter to extend the coverage to include later developments. I committed to an ambitious target date for submission of the revised manuscript and the effort involved was considerably more than initially anticipated. This edition not only updates the previous edition but also includes a basic structural redesign. The initial exercise of minor revisions led to important questions about the structure and organization and, consequently, most of the chapters have been extensively modified and large sections have been completely rewritten. This reflects not only my intellectual maturity and development but also the influence and input of my students at Griffith University. It is to them, that I owe, a collective sense of gratitude. The University supported me by providing teaching relief so I could concentrate on the task of my revised book project. I would like to thank my research assistant, Caitlin. Mullins, who provided valuable help in the collection and preparation of the statistical tables and the bibliographic searches. I would also like to thank my editors at World Scientific for cleaning up the final manuscript that was submitted with many formatting errors. Finally, I am grateful to my wife and my two boys for their patience and understanding.

Javed Maswood
Associate Professor
Department of Political Science
American University in Cairo
Cario, Egypt

Contents

List of Tables

LIST OF FIGURES

LIST OF ABBREVIATIONS

AIDS — Acquired Immuno-Deficiency Syndrome
BIBF — Bangkok Inter Bank Facility
CAP — Common Agriculture Policy (of the European Union)
CB — Currency Board
CIS — Confederation of Independent States
CMEA — Council for Mutual Economic Assistance (Comecon)
DR — Doha Round (of the WTO)
DSB — Dispute Settlement Body
EOI — Export Oriented Industrialization
EU — European Union
FDI — Foreign Direct Investment
G4 — Group of 4
G7 — Group of Seven
G20 — Group of Twenty
GATS — General Agreement on Trade in Services
GATT — General Agreement on Tariffs and Trade
GDP — Gross Domestic Product
GSP — Generalized System of Preferences
IBRD — International Bank for Reconstruction and Development
(World Bank)
IMF — International Monetary Fund
MFA — Multi Fibres Agreement
ODA — Official Developmental Assistance
OECD — Organization for Economic Cooperation and Development
OPEC — Organization of Petroleum Exporting Countries

PAMSCAD — Program of Action to Mitigate Social Costs
of Adjustment
SDT — Special and Differential Treatment
SOEs — State Owned Enterprises
SI — Structural Impediments
UR — Uruguay Round (of the GATT)
URAA — Uruguay Round Agreement on Agriculture
TRIMs — Trade Related Investment Measures
TRIPS — Trade Related Intellectual Property Rights
WTO — World Trade Organization

Chapter One

INTRODUCTION

International political economy (IPE) is a study of interactions between states and markets at the international level. More specifically, IPE is a study of how political and economic variables facilitate or obstruct international economic transactions. IPE assumes that pure markets, unencumbered by political intervention and regulation, do not exist and that it is impossible to demarcate the empirical contents of economics and politics.

Through much of the postwar period, the discipline of international politics was narrowly focused on issues of international security and conflict. This was understandable in the context of a Cold War between the United States and Soviet Union. However, in the 1970s, an easing of Cold War tensions created an opening for non-security issues to emerge on the disciplinary agenda. At the same time, a series of international economic crises, including the collapse of the Bretton-Woods monetary regime, quadrupling of oil prices, and stagflationary pressures in the West, led to a better understanding of linkages between politics and economics. For example, the sharp hike in oil prices, in 1973, was part of an attempt by Arab members of the Organization of Petroleum Exporting Countries (OPEC) to use an economic resource as a weapon to realize their political objectives. Similarly, growing economic interdependence globally has diminished the policy autonomy of states, with obvious political consequences. Economic interdependence was an important new development in the 1970s. The main impact of interdependence was to leave national economies more sensitive and vulnerable to external developments. More recently, scholars have labelled contemporary developments as globalization, a progressive replacement of segmented national economies with an undifferentiated global economy.

The difference between globalization and interdependence is that while the latter was essentially an exchange-based linking of economies, the former includes an integration of economies through production and financial networks. The evolving seamless global economy is dominated by large multinational corporations and would not have been possible without revolutionary new developments in information and communications technology (ICT), which made it possible for corporations to overcome the tyranny of space and time. Yet, as we shall see below, technology alone does not provide an explanation for the establishment of global production and financial networks. The new reality is still in a process of "becoming", but it is useful to trace its origins.

Globalization incorporates both an inclusionary expansion and a transformation of production processes. Inclusionary expansion followed the collapse of non-market economies and removal of the East–West economic divide. During the Cold War, economic exchange between the two blocs was limited and eastern bloc countries had limited access to western multilateral agencies, like the GATT. In the late 1980s, GATT for example, had approximately 90 member countries but by 2007 the membership base of World Trade Organization, successor to the GATT, had expanded to include almost all the countries. Globalization is also defined by a rapid transformation of economic activity, the movement towards a single global market and global production strategies. The globalization of production, distribution and marketing of goods and services,[1] is the key to understanding the contemporary international political economy.

End of the Cold War

Although not hermetically sealed, the postwar international political economy was divided into two separate groupings, one dominated by the United States and the other by the Soviet Union. The western liberal international economic order was premised on principles of non-discrimination and decentralized market-based decision-making. By contrast, the eastern Soviet-dominated economic regime (Council for Mutual Economic assistance, or CMEA) was based on the principle of centralized decision-making. Because of this difference in organizing principles, CMEA members were not considered eligible for membership in western institutions, like the GATT.

The CMEA was founded by the USSR, Poland, Czechoslovakia, Hungary, Romania and Bulgaria in January 1949 and until the early 1960s, it was an agglomeration of East European countries. Mongolia, in 1962, was the first non-European country to be granted full participation in the CMEA. Others, like Cuba and Vietnam, became participating members in the 1970s.

In its early years, CMEA was essentially a mechanism for extending Soviet control over the other members through coercive policies. But according to Michael Marrese, the Soviets soon realized that the allegiance of East European countries could not be secured effectively via the stick alone and resorted to a new policy that employed a combination of the carrot (trade subsidization) and the stick (the threat of armed intervention).[2] Thereafter, East European countries posted significant economic gains as the Soviet Union provided them with raw materials at below world market prices and purchased their (allegedly shoddy) manufactured goods at above international market prices.[3] This enabled the Soviet Union to demand political loyalty and subservience in exchange for economic privileges but proved detrimental to the Soviet economy, which was essentially subsidising living standards in East Europe, Cuba and elsewhere through the supply of cheap minerals and fuels, and monetary aid.

The collapse of communism was precipitated by Soviet economic reforms and a retraction of the Brezhnev Doctrine. Economic reforms were introduced in the Soviet Union, in the mid 1980s, in response to a worsening economic crisis. Soviet economic malaise was largely, a product of intensified Cold War rivalry in the early 1980s that diverted economic resources away from productive sectors to military programs, and exposed vulnerabilities and inefficiencies of a command economy. The reform agenda quickly snowballed and led to the abandonment of communism. The Brezhnev Doctrine emphasized socialist unity and the right of the Soviet Union to intervene elsewhere in defense of socialism. Its retraction removed the spectre of Soviet military intervention in East European countries in defense of socialism, as had happened in Hungary in 1956 and in Czechoslovakia in 1968, when they initiated reforms and began to gravitate out of the Soviet sphere of influence. Following retraction of the Brezhnev Doctrine, the centralized economic and political structures of East European countries gave way to a greater reliance on market mechanisms and political competition.

At the height of Cold War confrontations, some East European countries were allowed conditional membership of the GATT, for instance, in order to entice them away from Soviet domination and weaken eastern bloc integrity. Yugoslavia became the first East European country to join GATT in 1966 and later similar conditional membership was extended to Poland, Hungary and others. The conditions on Polish membership required it to increase annual imports from GATT member countries by 7 percent to compensate for a similar annual increase in exports anticipated out of Poland's participation in the GATT.[4] This condition was felt necessary to prevent a trade imbalance arising from the fact that, in East European economies, import and export decisions were made by state authorities rather than by market forces. Following the collapse of communism, East European countries and others joined the WTO as normal members. In early 2008, Russia was the only major country still outside the WTO but its membership application was in the final stages of negotiations and expected to be approved soon.

Global Production Networks

The fall of communism created a unitary global political economy, but the formation of global markets, transcending national borders, was more significant to the emergence of globalization. A definition of globalization includes not only the integration of the world through a process of economic exchange in finished goods and commodities, but also the development of global production network where trade is increasingly intra-firm trade, and in parts and components rather than finished products. An example of global manufacturing is the Ford Escort, which is produced in the United Kingdom by an American automobile company with components and raw materials sourced from 11 countries.[5] Other instances of globalization include American companies which handle telephone inquiries through operators in the Caribbean, or Swiss Air which has some of its accounting done in New Delhi.[6] Global manufacturing processes have increasingly liberated firms from national control, a development that has prompted analysts to suggest that the world economy is 'in control', superseding the macroeconomics of nation-states on which much of the economic theory, whether Keynesian, monetarist or Marxist, still anachronistically focuses.[7]

Globalization of production was facilitated by revolutionary advances in communications and information technology. But its causation can be traced to a combination primarily of, trade liberalization in the postwar period, neo-protectionism in the 1970s and 1980s, and the Plaza Accord of 1985. While globalization is a logical extension of the process of liberalization and interdependence after the Second World War, it has also been profoundly shaped by the illiberal forces of neo-protectionism and by exchange rate adjustments in the 1980s. The latter two instigated Japanese manufacturing investment in a number of developed countries. Neo–protectionism in important consumer markets, encouraged Japanese manufacturers to establish production facilities in their export markets to retain market share. This explains the rapid surge in investment in the United States, for example, in the automobile industry. Whereas, prior to the restrictions on Japanese automobile exports in 1981, Japanese car manufacturers had relied exclusively on exports to service consumer demand in the United States.

Appreciation of the Japanese Yen, following the Plaza Accord of September 1985, accelerated globalization further because it forced Japanese manufacturers to seek cheaper production platforms in East Asia. This development was instrumental to the emergence of regional production networks and ultimately, to global production networks — a core element of contemporary globalization. It is interesting that although globalization was at least partly, a response to the imperative to lower production costs, the net result of globalization has been to increase transaction costs for firms. According to John Dunning, the advent of globalization has led to an increase in the relative significance of transaction to production costs of doing business.[8]

The Reality of Globalization

Economic globalization has not developed uniformly across all aspects of international economic relations. It is most pronounced in trade and financial relations but not in labor market relations. Labor remains relatively confined to national jurisdictions even though there are attempts, led by some of the advanced economies to standardize labor market conditions globally, and by developing countries to expand mobility of workers across borders. Attempts to standardize labor market conditions have not attracted majority support. Developing countries in particular, fear that harmonization presumably at a higher level of labor regulations, will erode their competitive advantage and prove detrimental to their growth prospects. Developing countries also argue that globalization without easier labor mobility puts them at a disadvantage because of foregone potential benefit of savings and investment capital repatriated by expatriate workers. There is no logical reason why globalization should not extend to labor mobility but there is little realistic probability of significant change, given prevailing western preoccupation with border security and protection.

On the other hand, western countries and multilateral agencies have relied on incentives and sanctions to pressure developing countries to pursue trade and financial liberalization and to deepen their participation in the global economy. Influenced by a "Washington Consensus" to transform developing countries in line with policy prescriptives grounded in neo-liberal economics, such as privatization, deregulation, liberal trade, tariff policies, etc., multilateral agencies like the International Monetary Fund (IMF) and the World Bank (WB) have used their lending programs to extract such commitments from developing countries. Conditional lending by IMF and WB has been defended as essential to better growth performance in developing countries but in some case, atleast premature liberalization has led to economic distress. For instance, the Asian financial crisis of 1997 was partly a result of premature financial liberalization before domestic financial institutions had acquired the capacity to withstand unforgiving global market forces. Whatever the merits of globalization, in the aftermath of the Asian crisis, it is recognized that developing countries should defer large-scale liberalization until they acquire appropriate institutional capacity. Thus, Ha-Joon Chang writes "The more recent economic success stories of China and increasingly India, are examples that show the importance of strategic, rather than unconditional, integration with the global economy based on a nationalistic vision".[9]

Globalization is reflected in the rapid increase in share of trade (exports plus imports) in the Gross Domestic Product (GDP) of a country, increasing share of intra-firm trade and of trade in components and parts (as indicators of global production networks), a rapid increase in the flow of capital across borders, and foreign direct investment. For example, in the 10-year period between the mid-1980s and mid-1990s, the share of trade in GDP for the developing countries increased from 33 percent to around 43 percent. For the high income developed countries, the same ratio increased from around 24 percent to about 33 percent.[10] World trade growth has also, throughout the postwar period, outpaced the growth in production. Average annual growth of world merchandise trade between 1950 and 1994 was around 6 percent compared to world output growth of 4 percent. The value of world merchandise trade in 2005 was approximately US$10.1 trillion, an increase of 13 percent over 2004. Similarly, (foreign direct investment FDI) flows increased from US$115 billion in 1990 to about US$1.2 trillion in 2006. FDI may still be only a fraction of world merchandize trade but FDI flows have contributed to economic globalization through a web of global production networks.

Foreign direct investment for instance, is geared not only to consumption demand in the host country, as suggested by the product-cycle theory but is also, increasingly, a part of a global production and marketing strategy. This has, consequently, increased the share of intra-firm trade in total world trade and is a testimony to the role of multinational corporations (MNCs) in the global economy. At the beginning of the 1990s, there were approximately 35,000 MNCs, the largest 300 of which accounted for one-quarter of all developing countries' corporate assets.[11] This was a clear reflection of the growing importance of MNCs in developing countries and the push by these firms to gain cost advantage by shifting some productive activities to low-cost countries.

Reflecting the prominent role of MNCs, the share of intra-firm trade, as opposed to arms-length trading, is substantial. According to OECD statistics, nearly 40 percent of total United States goods trade in the late 1990s was intra-firm. But if we look at a specific bilateral relationship, it is worth noting that 73 percent of United States imports from Japan was intra-firm import.

There are of course sceptics, who are less convinced of the reality of globalization. Richard Harris for example, argues that globalization is still a ways off because of the natural limits posed by politics, culture, language, and distance.[12] Even less sympathetic to globalization is Bairoch, who finds that globalization is not the significant new development that it is claimed to be. He argues that, historically periods of high internationalization (globalization) have alternated with periods of low internationalization and that contemporary globalization is simply an aspect of this long-term cyclical trend (see Table 1.1). This leads him to conclude that, even for a country like the United States, where the case for globalization seems to be most obvious, the process is not a new one.[13] This view is shared by Paul Krugman who writes that, "historians of the international economy date the emergence of a truly global economy to the forties — the 1840s, when the railroads and steamships reduced transport costs to the point where large-scale shipment of bulk commodities became possible."[14]

The statistical evidence presented above, however, conceals important undercurrents of change in the contemporary period. As the example

Table 1.1:   Merchandise exports as percentage of GDP.

	Western developed countries	United States	Western Europe	EEC (12 members)	Japan
1890	11.7	6.7	14.9	—	5.1
1913	12.9	6.4	18.3	—	12.6
1929	9.8	5.0	14.5	—	13.6
1938	6.2	3.7	7.1	—	13.0
1950	7.8	3.8	13.4	12.9	6.8
1970	10.2	4.0	17.4	16.7	9.7
1992	14.3	7.5	21.7	21.1	8.8

Note: The figures are three year averages, except for 1950.
Source: Bairoch (1996).

of the Ford Escort demonstrates, manufactured products are no longer traded, largely as, consumer goods or capital goods, but increasingly as intermediate goods. This feature of contemporary trading patterns has produced a much higher level of economic integration than in the past. Globalization cannot be conflated to an increase in exports and imports and globalization of production processes has injected a unique new dimension to the contemporary period. Robert Boyer and Daniel Drache acknowledge that, "today's globalization is qualitatively and quantitatively different from previous periods."[15]

Significantly, globalization has blurred distinctions between trade and investment. It is a fact that many countries, while encouraging foreign investment, also impose performance criteria to force foreign firms to comply with local content requirements or minimum export requirements. Both have major implications for international trade and it became obvious that investment issues could not be dealt with separately from trade issues, or that GATT, as the machinery to deal with trade, could not ignore investment issues. The earliest proposal, however, was to develop a separate and independent regime on investments. In 1970, Goldberg and Kindleberger, for example, recommended establishing a new body, similar to GATT, to formulate a set of rules and dispute settlement procedures for foreign investment flows.[16] Instead, when the Uruguay Round opened, foreign direct investment was brought under GATT purview. Thus one obvious consequence of globalization has been to push GATT, and its successor the World Trade Organization, into new areas.

Globalization and the Nation State

The impact of globalization on state autonomy has attracted considerable attention. It is suggested for example, that globalization has rendered states obsolescent and unable, to preserve traditional patterns of international relations in the face of global market forces. Even if this is debatable and the state system unlikely to disappear, globalization has complicated the task of national economic management. In many instances, global economic forces are beyond the control of national government, even when governments act collusively. In practical terms, globalization has raised the costs of bad governmental policies, such as fiscal deficits, over-regulation of the economy, and labor market rigidities.[17]

The existing literature on globalization and the nation state can be classified into two groups. The first emphasizes the transformation or the "transformational potential" of globalization.[18] Ruggie, for example, argued that globalization not only enhanced the role of multinational and transnational corporations within the international political economy but also unleashed forces, which could alter the way we conceptualize world politics and international political economy, especially in regards to territoriality and state sovereignty. He argued that the relationship between transnationalism and contemporary state system was not unlike that between medieval trade fairs and feudal authority structures. While the feudal lords encouraged trade fairs as a source of revenue, these fairs also contributed significantly to the demise of feudal authority relations,[19] and in initiating the capitalist revolution.

If true, globalization has initiated a transformation of world politics, away from a system of segmented, although interlinked, political and economic units to one of the political segmentation alongside a single global economy. This raises questions on the emerging relationship between nation states and a single global economy. Kenichi Ohmae, for example, highlights the expanded horizon of producers and consumers alike and popularized the concept of a "borderless" economy. He heralded the emergence of a "nationalitiless" global market with a significantly diminished role for national governments. He relegated the government to the backseat, not the driver's position, and its role to ensuring that the country benefited fully from the best-performing corporations and producers in the world, at the lowest possible cost to their people on a long-term basis.[20]

The second view is exemplified by, for example, Kapstein, and Hirst and Thompson. Kapstein argues that, despite globalization, there has been no significant change in contemporary structures and that states have retained full economic and political sovereignty.[21] He argues that throughout history, states have shown a remarkable ability to adapt to changing circumstances and there is no reason to assume that they will not adjust to the challenges of globalization and remain pre-eminent on the international stage. Similarly, according to Hirst and Thompson, globalization is not yet an extant reality.[22] Unlike advocates of global-ization, they assert a basic continuity in international political economy. Hirst and Thompson argue that the international economy was equally integrated at the beginning of the 20th century. While satellite commu-nication had brought markets closer together, it had not fundamentally altered their operation; and that there are few true MNCs, with most companies still operating in a small number of countries, or at most regionally.

The truth probably lies somewhere in-between these two positions. Economic liberalization and advances in communications technology facilitated the process of globalization, but operating within a global mar-ket still requires coordination of market-segmented regulatory policies. It would be an exaggeration to conclude that globalization has produced a unitary regulatory structure, despite a general trend towards economic lib-eralization and more relaxed entry conditions to foreign capital in many developed and developing countries.

In the global economy, the significance of non-state and societal actors has increased. Multinational corporations, for example, have become major new players and played an important part in the Uruguay Round negotiations. Alongside the growing influence of MNCs, there has been a concomitant rise in the role and influence on non-governmental organiza-tions (NGOs) in various aspects of global trade negotiations.

Critics of Globalization

As a recent development in international political economy, globaliza-tion has its defenders and critics both in the West and in developing countries. One of the most respected and prominent defenders of glob-alization is Jagdish Bhagwati, Professor of Economics at Columbia University. He has always been an advocate of free trade; and global-ization to him is the logical progression of free trade and is hence desir-able. He is not insensitive to the possibility that globalization may create losers in the process but all systems produce winners and losers and, for Bhagwati, in the case of globalization the winners win more than what the losers lose and it is, therefore, theoretically possible for the winners to buy off, or to compensate the losers so that no one is necessarily worse off. Western critics, however, point to the following dysfunctional aspects of globalization:

- **Hollowing out:** Another term for hollowing out is deindustrialization and it was first used to explain what was happening in Japan in the late 1980s, after the Plaza Accord. Until the early 1980s, Japanese manufacturers had shown no interest in establishing production facilities off shore but started doing so following the automobiles crisis with the US and many Japanese car manufacturers established plants in the United States and later in Canada, UK and elsewhere. But the Yen shock was the major push to set up manufacturing in Southeast Asia and the region was integrated into the Japanese economy through production networks. This allowed them to maintain their export profile, remain profitable but also led to concerns within Japan of a "hollowing out" of the Japanese economy. Hollowing out implies a growing vacuum where all the manufacturing activity (the basis of industrial economies) is moved offshore to leave only a shell in the home country. Indeed, the reality is that most industrial economies that are based on manufacturing will have to shift to, and are increasingly shifting to services and knowledge-based industries. Critics of a services based economy lament that hollowing-out and deindustrialization will create economies where workers are reduced to flipping hamburgers be this is a gross simplification of the reality.

- **Race to the bottom and loss of income guarantee:** This term implies that because of global interconnectedness, success for any economy is dependent on its ability to remain globally competitive and not to have its products priced out of competition either as a result of domestic inflation, or a ballooning out of wages and the cost structure. So for every economy, it is important to keep prices in control and to remain competitive. For many companies, this has meant relocating production to cheapest practical production platforms or to countries where the cost structures are most advantageous. Today, wages are low in China, India and more of the developing countries and there is a discernible trend to relocate production facilities in these countries, leading to an export of jobs or to a lowering of wages to the levels of developing countries. The fear is that wages will be bargained down in Australia, United States and developed countries to the level of wages in developing countries in other words a race to the bottom, that will undermine western life styles and standard of living. The reality is that jobs that have migrated overseas from developed countries are low-paid and unskilled and the question is whether this is necessarily a bad thing. Skilled professional jobs are unlikely to be relocated overseas but it is important to stay open and receptive to opportunities overseas.

- **Democratic deficit:** This is also called the democratic discontent. As a result of global market forces, governments in democratic countries are torn between demands made by the global economy and by competing demands of their own citizens. Increasingly it looks like governments want to cater to demands and imperative of global market forces rather than of their own citizens. This flies against our common assumptions that, in a democracy elected politicians are answerable only to their domestic constituents and will do whatever is demanded of them by citizens. Critics believe that under globalization, markets have become dominant and governments make policies to suit the interests of corporations and MNCs that dominate these markets. Of course, governments have always been mindful of external realities but the assertion is that, globalization has severely eroded governmental capacity to respond to popular demands, i.e. governments do not simply favour corporations over citizens but are forced to do so. In Australia, for example, a Liberal–National coalition government, deregulated workplace conditions in the early 2000s and justified these as essential to international competitiveness and global competition despite significant popular distaste for these reforms. In the 2007 federal elections this was an, important electoral issue and led to a change of government. Even if the new Labor government had a seeming mandate for a complete overhaul of workplace reforms, it chose not to abandon all the reform measures introduced by the previous government. Democracy has never been absolute but the issue is how to balance democratic demands with international imperatives, despite some expectation that elected representatives should meet the demands of their constituency rather than the needs of the global economy.

Table 1.2:   Benefits of globalization.

Financial globalization	Trade globalization
Adds to domestic savings	Adds to consumer Choice
Reduces cost of capital	Lowers production costs
Technology transfer	Increases consumer welfare
"Disciplines" economic policy	Improves trade competitiveness

Theoretically speaking the globalization (liberalization) of trade and financial markets is beneficial for many reasons, stated in Table 1.2.

Among the many defenders of globalization are Biil Gates of Microsoft and Steve Jobs of Apple Computers. They equate globalization with the ICT revolution and find that new technologies have given developing countries an opportunity to access global markets and boost exports with the help of the world wide web. They see computers as one of the best tools for development in poor countries and advocate putting a computer in every home to create equality of opportunity. On a theoreotical level, Bhagwati puts forward a strong intellectual case for globalization, emphasizing that, globalization through increased trade opportunities, offers the best hope for poverty reduction in developing countries. This is because of a two-stage process where trade produces growth and growth reduces poverty. But Bhagwati also added a cautionary note that growth can lead to immiseration if export growth reduces international prices. The immiseration effect is more likely if there is excessive reliance on a single or small number of commodities and the solution to this potential trap is diversification and a broader export profile. Bhagwati argues that while government policy can help developing countries profit from globalization, bad policies may actually worsen existing conditions. Bhagwati illustrated this by comparing divergent economic performance of pre-liberalization India with that of East Asian economies, including China. The latter group of countries did well by taking advantage of trade opportunities and linking into the global economy whereas India remained relatively stagnant because it pursued isolationist practices until the early 1990s. But since economic liberalization in India, annual growth rates have been nearly comparable to that of mainland China.

A dissenting view is that of Daniel Cohen who, taking a historical perspective, pointed out that the earlier ICT revolution of railways and telegraph poles in the 19th century did not help bridge the gap between the rich and poor countries. Instead of allowing the poor people access to global markets or, in other words, dispersing wealth across countries, the ICT revolution of the 18th and 19th centuries simply concentrated wealth in a few countries, led to monopolization of production, and widened the gulf that separated the rich and poor countries. Karl Marx and others certainly thought that the spread of railways and telephone and telegraph by the colonial powers would create a levelling of economic conditions but this did not happen. It did not happen in the 19th century and may not happen in the 21st century. Indeed historical evidence shows that regardless of technological breakthroughs, the reality has been one of a widening gap between developed and developing countries. Paul Bairoch says there was rough income parity among all countries of the world in 1750 but that by 1950 the disparity was 1:8 and increased to 1:13 by 1970.

On the other hand, Mike Moore, former Director General of the World Trade Organization argues, like Bhagwati, that all systems produce winners and losers and that "the right way to alleviate the hardship of the unlucky few [is] through social safety nets and jobs retraining rather than by abandoning reforms that benefit the many". However, structural adjustment is easier said than done, as even developed countries have discovered.

Just as in the West, there are proponents and opponents of globalization in developing countries. Whether globalization is harmful or beneficial for developing countries, the reality is that they had little choice but to embrace it, because of their dependence on foreign aid and capital flows from developed countries, and multilateral agencies like the World Bank and IMF. Both these agencies have large lending programs for developing countries. Both are also heavily influenced by policies of the US government and the US Treasury that, developing countries must qualify for loans by deregulating, liberalization and privatization of their economies. This linkage among the US Treasury, World Bank and IMF in order to spread the message of liberalization is known as the Washington Consensus and has been used to force, encourage and coerce developing countries to participate in the globalization

Table 1.3: Income disparity between countries (1975 Dollars).

Year	Developing countries	Developed countries
1900	110	640
1913	120	775
1929	130	930
1952–1954	150	1360
1960	210	1780

process. Williamson coined the phrase in 1990 "to refer to the lowest common denominator of policy advice being addressed by the Washington-based institutions to Latin American countries as of 1989".[23] These policies included:

- Fiscal discipline;
- Tax reform (to lower marginal rates and broaden the tax base);
- Interest rate liberalization;
- A competitive exchange rate;
- Trade liberalization;
- Liberalization of inflows of foreign direct investment;
- Privatization;
- Deregulation (to abolish barriers to entry and exit); and
- Secure property rights.

Later, the policy measures that defined the Washington Consensus were expanded to include non-economic criteria and Danii Rodrik dubbed this the Augmented Washington Consensus,[24] which now included:

- Corporate governance;
- Anti-corruption;
- Flexible labor markets;
- "Prudent" capital-account opening;
- Independent central banks/inflation targeting;
- Social safety nets; and
- Targeted poverty reduction.

The phrase "Washington Consensus" has become a lightning rod for dissatisfaction. As the phrase's originator, John Williamson says: "Audiences the world over seem to believe that this signifies a set of neo–liberal policies that have been imposed on hapless countries by the Washington-based international financial institutions and have led them to crisis and misery. There are people who cannot utter the term without foaming at the mouth."[25]

But, as Williamson also states:

> Some of the most vociferous of today's critics of what they call the Washington Consensus, most prominently Joe Stiglitz... do not object so much to the agenda laid out above as to the neoliberalism that they interpret the term as implying. I of course never intended my term to imply policies like capital account liberalization...monetarism, supply-side economics, or a minimal state (getting the state out of welfare provision and income redistribution), which I think of as the quintessentially neoliberal ideas.[26]

Joseph Stiglitz, former Chief Economist of the World Bank and a strong critic of the Washington Consensus argues that it is time to move beyond the narrow goal of economic growth to the more expansive goal of sustainable, equitable and democratic development". His main issue with globalization is not that it is necessarily harmful to developing countries but that its practice of indiscriminate liberalization has been harmful to developing countries that do have, but not yet possess a strong and internationally viable manufacturing capacity. If liberalization happens prematurely, the nascent domestic industry is more likely than not to collapse in face of more competitive producers. This is what has happened in Mozambique in 1991–1992 when it was forced to liberalize raw cashew-nut exports by IMF. Earlier Mozambique had imposed a ban on export of raw cashew-nut in 1975 and this led to the development of a domestic cashew-nut processing industry that grew to employ about 10,000 workers. But after liberalization of raw cashew-nut exports, about 8500 workers (in 2001) had lost their jobs as the industry could not compete with foreign processors of cashew-nuts such as India and the local processing industry collapsed. The problem is premature liberalization and quick liberalization on grounds that is more

Table 1.4:   Changing share in world merchandising exports (1983–1998)%.

Region	1983	1988	Change
East Asia & Pacific	5.5	10.2	+85
Latin America & Caribbean	5.6	5.2	−7
MENA	6.8	1.9	−72
South Asia	0.8	1.0	+25
SubSahara	2.8	1.4	−50

likely to be done poorly. At an aggregate level, if liberalization was meant to raise a country's level of international economic interaction, then to some extent this has happened. For instance developing countries have increased their share of world trade from 19 percent in 1971 to 29 percent in 1999. But the picture is not uniform and while some have gained, many more have fallen behind. Despite the large number of countries, in all parts of the world, that have been forced to embrace globalization, not all have been successful in increasing their share of world trade.

The problem is that many countries have globalized, i.e. liberalized their economies, and yet have not been able to increase their share of participation in the global economy or even to hold steady. This is a serious failure, because if the expectation was that by liberalizing, countries will attract foreign capital and investments, that is not necessarily what has happened. Capital flow to developing countries is largely concentrated in a few countries in East Asia and India.

Only two regions have improved their trade share in the world but according to David Dollar and Aart Kray, they have also increased their growth rates. They write that globalizers had a growth rate of 2.9 percent a year in the 1970s but 5 percent in the 1990s and those that did not globalize, had a growth rate of 3.3 percent in the 1970s but only 1.4 percent in the 1990s. The incomes of the least globalized countries during this same period, including Iran, Pakistan and North Korea, dropped or remained static. The suggestion is that the difference between a fast and slow growing developing country is its openness to trade.

In principle, Stiglitz says that globalization is neither good nor bad and that it has the power to be beneficial to developing countries. He also argues that countries that embrace it on their own terms and at their own pace do better than countries that are forced to embrace it without proper institutional foundations. This means that globalization must not precede the development of adequate institutional structures. For example, before capital market liberalization, a country should first develop a viable and strong banking sector. However, when Indonesia liberalized its banking sector in the 1990s, it had 130 domestic banks and most of them were small and weak institutions, and liberalization added to the economic and financial strains that led to the financial crisis of 1997.

For many developing countries, globalization and liberalization have allowed many firms to relocate to developing countries where environmental and safety standards are either very weak or simply non-existent. This has led to exacerbation of pollution and health crises. Hazardous products, toxic materials are being pushed on developing countries. It is estimated that 40,000 people in developing countries die of pesticide poisoning every year. Moreover, by linking into the global economy they became suppliers of raw materials to developed countries and this worsened the problem of deforestation in Latin America and Asia. Moreover, if we assume that globalization is good because it produces better growth, we also find that along with growth, there also came, greater income inequality. In China the benefit of economic globalization has been restricted to a few geographical areas along the coast and income gaps have widened. China's Gini coefficient, a measure of income inequality (0 being perfect equality and 100 being perfect inequality) rose from 28.8 in 1981 at the start of liberalization to 38.8 in 1985.[27]

Critics of globalization in developing countries argue that its practice has been selective and that there is little globalization in areas of particular interest to them like, agriculture, labor intensive manufacturing and labor mobility. For example, while capital is highly globalized, labor mobility is severely restricted. There are restrictions on labour moving across borders and critics argue that just as capital mobility benefits the developed countries which are well endowed with capital resources, labor mobility should also be increased so that globalization might benefit these poorer countries. The issue has been on international negotian agenda for a number of years but little progress has been made so far, especially because of the paranoia generated by the September 11 terrorist attacks in the United States. But to the extent that many developed countries have guest worker visa provisions for other developed countries, there is no reason why similar schemes should not be made available to all countries. Developing countries probably need such provisions even more than backpackers from developed countries.

Apart from labor mobility, developing countries have also been denied all the benefits of globalization because of the embedded practice of selective liberalization, where many of the products of interest to developing countries, such as agriculture, continue to attract high levels of protection in developed countries, particularly the United States and European Union (EU).

Chapter Two

INTERNATIONAL TRADE:
FROM GATT TO THE WTO

A s a source of dynamism and development, international trade was a solvent of feudalism and a catalyst for industrial revolution in Europe. Today, it is the key to understanding economic globalization. While the benefits of trade, in terms of employment, growth, and prosperity, are well recognized in economic theory, alternatives, such as mercantilism, protectionism, and economic nationalism, have always obstructed the flow of goods and services across borders. States have never sanctioned complete free trade and, instead, the best that has been achieved are periods of liberal, or freer, trade.

Mercantilist theories dominated and informed trade practices for several hundred years until the 1800s. For mercantilists, economic growth and welfare were contingent on expanding the domestic supply base of monetary metals, like gold and silver, to fuel a concomitant increase in money supply. Contraction in the availability of monetary metals was, on the other hand, associated with reduced money supply and downward pressure on prices, lower growth, lower incomes, and reduce welfare. Mercantilists viewed international trade as a zero-sum activity and, consequently, emphasized the importance of trade controls to benefit the national economy. According to Kristof Glamann, under mercantilist principles, how to "acquire the largest share of what was commonly seen as a more or less fixed volume of international trade, and how so to manage the national share as to produce a favorable balance of trade and a net import of bullion and precious metals, were the twin tasks to which governments of the day addressed themselves".[1] This meant limiting imports and generating exports to accumulate precious metals.

Adam Smith (1723–1790) provided the earliest liberal critique of mercantilism in his book *An Inquiry into the Wealth of Nations*. He defended free trade and criticized mercantilists for confusing national wealth with national treasure. For Smith, wealth and welfare were functions of living standards and consumption possibilities, which could be maximized if a country specialized in the production of some goods and exchanged its surplus production for the surplus production of other countries producing different commodities. Liberal economic theory defends free trade from narrow considerations of national interest but in the conviction that free trade is in the national interest of all countries. At an empirical level, this may be demonstrated by looking at how nations fared in the age of mercantilism, given that different countries pursued it with more or less vigor. According to Fellner, "Even during the era of mercantilism there was much less regulation and control in England than in some of the Continental countries. At the end, the more rigorously 'mercantilistic' nations [such as France] fared worse".[2] France had a larger population and was better endowed with natural resources, but it was England that emerged as the leading industrial power in the 19th century. Fellner acknowledged that while it may be impossible to assert, with confidence, that French mercantilism caused it to lag behind Britain, the possibility that it did cannot be ruled out either.

However, despite the compelling logic of free trade, policy makers have never embraced anything more than freer trade.[a] That was first achieved in the 19th century under British leadership but the early 20th century saw a resurgence of protectionism. Liberal trade was revived under American leadership after the Second World War. There are a number of similarities between these two periods, such as leadership by a single dominant political power, but there are important dissimilarities as well. Nineteenth century liberal trade was a unilateral decision by Britain whereas 20th century and contemporary liberal trade are premised on the

---

[a] The sake of simplicity, however, I will use the term free trade to mean freer or liberal trade.

principle of reciprocity. Moreover, as we shall see below, 19th century liberal trade included trade in agriculture but its later manifestation specifically excluded agriculture, which continued to benefit from high levels of protectionism. This practice of selective liberalization has been particularly damaging to developing countries, which are essentially primary and farm producing countries.

Free Trade in Practice

In Britain, free trade made slow headway following the industrial revolution which began around 1780. The industrial revolution was characterized by a shift away from the dominance of mercantile capital to fixed industrial capital, and away from labor intensive to capital intensive manufacturing.[3] It was not a single cataclysmic event that changed the shape of British society and economy but rather a process that, between 1780 and 1860, gradually transformed Britain from an agricultural to an industrial economy. The reasons for the industrial revolution cannot be ascertained with any certainty but population growth and increased availability of productive tools were important factors.[4] Together they increased the level of domestic demand and the economic capacity to respond to higher demand.

The growth in manufacturing opened up new trade possibilities given that consumption of manufactured goods had high income elasticity.[b] However, in the early period of industrialization, Britain actually introduced higher tariffs to protect its declining agricultural sector. This was done through price supports, and restrictions on agricultural imports until domestic prices had exceeded certain threshold levels. These became generally known as the Corn Laws. Fielden writes that the "British tariff of 1815 was harsher than the eighteenth century's. In that year, too, the final great Corn Law excluded foreign wheat until home prices reached 80 shillings per quarter".[5] This meant that farm products could not be imported into Britain unless there was a famine or some other extenuating circumstance.

---

[b] Income elasticity refers to the ratio of the percentage increase in the demand for goods or services (in our case, manufactured goods) to an increase in income.

There were also export controls and the British government restricted the export of machinery and technology to preserve its own manufacturing advantages. Despite the prohibition, however, machinery continued to be smuggled out of the country and there was a constant flow of foreigners entering Britain to learn and master the latest technology, especially after 1815. The French, German and American industrialization started around this time and they made rapid progress as they could implement quickly what had Britain achieved over a longer period of time.

Britain heralded the movement to free trade by ending import restrictions and export controls in the mid-1840s. Industry groups, particularly the textile industry, lobbied for this and played a leading role in the Anti-Corn Law League. It helped that the textile industry was highly organized, which Cheryl Schonhardt-Bailey explained was due to the concentration of the industry in Manchester.[6] Being geographically concentrated meant that the costs of organizing for lobbying activities were small relative to the benefits of free trade, expected to be substantial, and which would also concentrate in the same geographic area.

As a result of the activities of the League, the prohibition on export of machineries was lifted in 1843; and in 1846 the Corn Laws were repealed. The attraction of free trade policies can be explained in terms of the potential gains from trade and, no doubt, there was also an awareness that Britain's trading partners required export opportunities, in agriculture, if they were to import British manufactured goods. For the export oriented textile industry in Britain, the transition toward free trade was a logical product of their international competitiveness. The lifting of the ban on export of machineries, however, also contributed to the spread of industrialization to more remote parts, such as Russia, where the process of industrialization had not yet begun.[7]

Initially, the foreign reaction to British free trade policy was that it was a conspiratorial and clever move designed to preserve Britain's position as the premier industrialized country. Nineteenth century critics of free trade, in Europe and America, argued that it would establish a system of unequal development, since a country specializing in manufacturing, a dynamic sector, could expect to grow faster than another country specializing in primary production. The American economist Henry Carey (1793–1879) and the German economist Friedrich List (1789–1846), denounced British free trade as a ploy to "...keeping the rest of the world occupied in subordinate pursuits — mere hewers of wood and drawers of water for an industrial England".[8]

However, the "inevitable" failed to eventuate. Instead, by the early 20th century, Britain was a country in economic decline. There are numerous explanations for this unexpected turn of events including, for instance, wage differentials between Britain and the new colonies which spurred investments in labor saving technologies in the United States and elsewhere while Britain lagged behind in technological innovation because of the absence of a wages pressure. Britain's economic decline instigated a general retreat from free trade practices during the First World War and fuelled rampant protectionism during the inter-war period. Disruptions to normal trade during the First World War encouraged many countries to embark on domestic industrial production in order to satisfy unmet import demand. After the war, these new industries, threatened by resumption of imports and loss of market share, lobbied for, and obtained protection from foreign competition.

In 1922, the United States introduced the Fordney–McCumber tariffs which raised average tariff levels on dutiable imports from 27 percent to 39 percent. Despite the increase in tariff levels, the Fordney–McCumber Act introduced a single tariff rate applicable to all countries. The US government, with some justification, could claim that this new system was, at least, non-discriminatory and accorded each trading partner "most favored nation" treatment.[c] The United States also used it to extract similar MFN treatment from other countries. For example, France was pressured into granting the United States the same preferential tariff rate that it extended to Germany under the Franco-German treaty of 1927. According to Conybeare, "The Fordney–McCumber tariff from 1922 to 1929 may be regarded as a successful example of hegemonic predation that probably raised the national income of the United States by obtaining tariff concessions from the rest of the world...".[9]

---

[c] Most favored nation (MFN) treatment refers to a practice of nondiscriminatory trade and constitutes a central pillar, also, of the postwar GATT regime. The difference is that whereas the Fordney–McCumber tariffs introduced MFN treatment at higher levels of tariffs, the GATT system is based on MFN treatment at progressively lower levels of trade restrictions.

These gains were more than reversed when the United States introduced the infamous Smoot–Hawley Tariff Act in 1930 and increased tariff levels to 53 percent. This quickly provoked widespread retaliation against American exports. As access to the American market became more restrictive, other countries introduced retaliatory tariffs. The net result was a spiralling of tariff levels and average tariff in major countries increased to around 50 percent. Some examples of post-Smoot–Hawley retaliation are listed below:

- In April 1930 Australia increased tariff levels beyond an earlier increase in June 1929.
- In July 1930 Spain, concerned with Smoot–Hawley tariffs on grapes, oranges, cork and onions, passed new prohibitive legislation.
- In June 1930 Italy increased tariffs on American and French automobiles in retaliation for higher tariffs on olive oils, hats, etc.
- In September 1930 and in 1932 Canada introduced new tariffs in retaliation of American restrictions on timber and agricultural products.
- Switzerland introduced a boycott on American exports in response to American tariff on watches, shoes, etc.

Due, largely, to the tariff war, total world trade, between 1929 and 1933, shrank from about US\$3 billion to US\$1 billion,[10] and the world was plunged into the Great Depression. This, arguably, also contributed to the onset of the Second World War, because trade contraction, declining production and rising unemployment were important factors that led states to switch idle industrial capacity to military production and to draft the army of unemployed into national armed forces. This fuelled an arms race that sent the world down the slippery slope of hostility and war. Another factor in the inexorable drift towards war was the punitive peace that had been imposed on Germany as part of the Versailles Agreement that ended the First World War. The terms of the peace agreement inflamed German discontent, which the nationalist forces exploited to their advantage. German disinterest in preserving international stability was an important factor in the escalating crisis of the period.

Even as the world hurtled towards the precipice of war, the view that free trade was beneficial for national economic welfare and for world peace was becoming part of the accepted logic. The American Secretary of State, Cordell Hull, was a leading advocate of free trade. He stated that, "...enduring peace and the welfare of nations [were] indissolubly connected with friendliness, fairness, equality and the maximum practicable degree of freedom in international trade".[11]

Still, national governments found it difficult to extricate themselves, in time, from their folly. Only after the devastation of the Second World War was there a concerted attempt, on the part of British and American leaders, to create a lasting structure for a postwar liberal trading regime. The US commitment to liberal trade was significant in the context of isolationism after the First World War. It was also not surprising in the context of interwar experiences. Moreover, the government and business leaders in the United States recognized that free trade was in their own interest. This was, because American industry had survived war-time destruction and could be expected to dominate world trade. National interest proved a powerful incentive for the United States to assume leadership in creating a liberal trade structure. Other countries, too, had a stake in liberal trade as they hoped to rebuild their economies, and benefit by exporting to a relatively open American market.

Liberal Trade After the Second World War

In planning for the postwar period, supporters of free trade viewed it also as essential to world peace and prosperity.[12,d,e] The move toward free trade began before the end of the Second World War. In the Atlantic Charter, signed in August 1941, the Allied Powers committed themselves to "...endeavor...to further the enjoyment of all States, great or small,

---

[d] The view that free trade and economic interdependence is a force for peace is a reasonable assumption but it cannot be proved that deep economic interdependence is necessarily able to control the more capricious aspect of human nature, ethnic and national conflict. While founders of the postwar liberal trade regime were driven by this fundamental belief, it should be noted that less than 50 years earlier, growing interdependence had failed to avert the First World War. Barbara Tuchman, in her brilliant account of the onset of the First World War, states that, "...the interlocking of finance, commerce, and other economic factors — which had been expected to make war impossible failed to function when the time came. Nationhood, like a wild gust of wind, arose and swept them aside."

[e] The degenerative impact of ethnic conflict remains relevant in the 1990s.

victor or vanquished, of access on equal terms to trade and raw materials of the world which are needed for their economic prosperity".[13]

Multilateral negotiations on promoting liberal trade began in 1946 and at the final negotiating conference in Havana in 1948, 56 countries were represented and agreed to the Havana Charter. The Charter emphasized 'balanced growth' of the world economy and a revival of the world economy based on market forces. The signatories agreed to establish an International Trade Organization (ITO) that would supplement the International Monetary Fund and the International Bank for Reconstruction and Development (the World Bank). The ITO was to be rule-oriented institution to oversee the transition to free trade by 1952. Deviant members could be expelled and subject to sanctions but the consensus view was that the threat of sanctions would be enough to secure compliance with the established trade rules. It was agreed that voting within the ITO would be based on "one state, one vote", despite American demands for weighted voting that would ensure its dominance over the ITO. This was rejected by a majority of countries (35) present at the Havana Conference.

Almost immediately, the ITO came under intense criticism within the United States. Business groups objected that ITO would regulate private business practices. Others argued that ITO rules would not apply equally to developing countries, which could introduce and maintain protectionist policies in order to promote development. Much weightier was the criticism that the ITO was a supranational organization that would compromise US sovereignty and independence by making American trade policy subject to an international organization not controlled by the United States. The US Congress indicated disapproval of the ITO and this effectively scuttled its establishment, because Congress, not the president, had jurisdiction over international trade policy. The US government did not even bother to submit the Havana Charter for ratification by the Congress. According to Jeffrey Schott, the Havana Charter was subject to criticism "both from the 'perfectionists' who thought its provisions flawed, and from the 'protectionists' who increasingly clamored for safeguards for national trading interests".[14] Instead of the ITO, the General Agreement on Tariffs and

Trade (GATT) became the main vehicle for liberalization of international trade after the war.

The General Agreement on Tariffs and Trade

The GATT was signed in October 1947 by eight countries and its primary function was to record ITO agreements. Unlike a formal organization where states might join as members, it was simply a treaty with contracting parties. Over time, however, the GATT acquired a small secretariat and became both a multilateral agreement and an "international organization".[f] The function of the GATT Secretariat was to provide support facilities for the various negotiating rounds to reduce trade barriers. Accession to GATT was open to countries that embraced the dual principles of open markets and decentralized decision making. Since it was only intended as a temporary mechanism until the ITO had become a reality, it inevitably was a less complete document.

The GATT system was based on two main rules. The first rule was that of *most favored nation* (MFN) treatment (Article 1), which prescribed bilateral deals in favor of multilateral agreements that did not discriminate against any contracting party of the GATT. To promote multilateralism and non-discrimination, the MFN clause required that where negotiations between two or more countries lowered tariffs the lower tariff should be available to all exporters of that product. This was to prevent trade benefits from being granted on a preferential basis to only a few countries because that would only lead to trade diversion rather than trade creation — the goal of liberal trade. MFN ensured, what Kenneth Dam called, the "spillover effect", whereby all contracting parties of GATT benefited when one country lowered its tariffs as a result of negotiations with another country. The same principle, of course, also applied when one country decided to increase existing

---

[f] The GATT secretariat is staffed by a relatively small staff. In the mid-1960s the GATT Secretariat had only 179 full-time employees compared to the 773 staff members of the IMF. In 1984, the IMF Secretariat had 1750 employees, the World Bank had 5700 employees and GATT only 283. In 1986, the GATT Secretariat was staffed by about 400 employees.

tariff levels. Provision for increasing tariff levels was contained in Article 19 of the Agreement, known as the safeguard clause.[g] The MFN clause had the following three exceptions:

- Pre-existing preferential trading arrangements were excluded from MFN clause. Thus Britain was allowed to maintain preferences granted to former colonies under the British imperial preferences. Later, GATT also allowed preferential treatment for developing countries.
- Customs unions and free trade areas were also exempted from MFN conditions. Under this exclusion, free trade agreements within the EU, for example, need not be extended to non-EU countries but the assumption was that free trade areas would gradually expand membership and become increasingly global in scope.
- A new contracting party to GATT could also be denied MFN privileges by existing members. Indeed, when Japan joined GATT in 1955, 14 member countries denied MFN privileges on grounds of undesirable low wage competition.

The second GATT rule was that of *national treatment* (Article 3), which prohibited states from discriminating against imports once these had cleared all border measures and entered the domestic market. Of course, GATT rules applied only to government and there was nothing it could do to prevent private citizens from conducting "buy local" programs. Moreover, even governments failed to adhere to the spirit of GATT rules.

In devising a system for adjusting trade imbalances, Lord Keynes, the British negotiator, argued that the burden of adjustment should fall on

---

[g] Some countries have devised ingenious ways of circumventing the non-discriminatory principle of the GATT. Japanese imports of plywood used to be classified under the two categories of "hardwood plywood" and "softwood plywood". The lower tariffs for softwood plywood effectively discriminated against the developing countries because softwood plywood, made from pine, came essentially from the developed countries of the United States and Canada. Under criticism that this was discriminatory, Japan abolished this categorization but instead introduced differential tariffs depending on the thickness of plywood, with lower tariff levels for thick plywood. This is as discriminatory as before because softwood plywood tends to be thicker than hardwood plywood. In general, developing countries criticize the developed countries for discriminating against their exports.

both surplus and deficit countries. Under his proposal a country in deficit would be required to lower consumption, and import demand, while a country enjoying trade surplus would be compelled to use monetary and fiscal policies to increase consumption demand and imports. The United States, expecting to remain a surplus country for a considerable period after the war, rejected this suggestion. Instead, it shifted the burden of adjustment entirely on deficit countries. The United States was thus spared, at least for the time being, the pain of adjustment policies for reasons of international trade. Interestingly, however, when the US trade balance moved into deficit after the 1970s, rather than implement adjustment policies to correct the payments imbalance, the US government attempted to shift the burden back on its trading partners, arguing that US deficits were a result of closed foreign markets rather than uncompetitive American products.

Like the abortive ITO before it, GATT had a 'one state, one vote' principle and decisions required a majority vote. In practice, however, trade negotiations and agreements were based on the principle of consensus. Amendments to the GATT required a two-third majority of the contracting parties except in the case of the MFN clause; the escape clause (Article 19), and the amendments clause (Article 30), all of which required unanimity. Despite the absence of weighted voting, GATT was more palatable to the United States because it contained clear assurances that western interests would dominate. It did not contain provisions favored by developing countries but which had been included in the Havana Charter, such as the provisions on economic development, commodity agreements and business practices considered unfavorable by the developing countries.[15] In 1965, however, an amendment and addition to GATT, Part 4 of the Agreement, did provide for special consideration to be given developing countries in, for example, stabilizing commodity prices and improving access to markets in developed countries for their processed and manufactured exports.

One of the principal objectives of GATT was to replace the more pernicious quota restrictions with tariffs, which were less restrictive of international trade. Thus, as Bhagwati stated, GATT was based on a "fix-rule" rather than "fix-quantity" principle. Two exceptions, however, permitted states to introduce quota restrictions. The first was agriculture and this sector of economic activity was carefully excised from the liberalizing discipline of GATT. Many countries, like Japan, maintained quota restrictions on some agricultural products into the 1990s. The second was quota restrictions for balance of payments reasons on the reasoning the quotas were more effective in reducing imports and, therefore, in achieving payments balance. The United States had, originally insisted that all quotas be abolished, which, if accepted, would have been advantageous to the United States since it was the largest exporter, also, of primary products. Other countries, however, rejected this for balance of payments reasons. The result was a compromise in which all states agreed to end quota restrictions eventually but such restrictions were permitted as long as these could be justified on grounds of payments imbalance.[16]

Apart from the exceptions, an "escape clause" (Article 19) permitted a country to re-introduce higher tariffs, albeit on a non-discriminatory basis, if that country could demonstrate that an earlier tariff concession had resulted in serious injury to domestic industry. It was intended as a temporary relief although most tariff increases under Article 19 were, in fact, never rescinded. Article 19 also provided that if negotiations were unsuccessful, the country seeking to invoke Article 19 could unilaterally suspend tariff concessions. In this case, however, the affected party also had the right to suspend concessions of approximate equal value. To invoke Article 19, a country had to demonstrate causation between a tariff concession and injury to domestic industry. The burden of proof was

Table 2.1: GATT negotiating rounds.

Round	Year	Countries	Trade covered
Geneva (Switzerland)	1947	23	US$10b
Annecy (France)	1949	33	Na
Torquay	1950–1951	34	Na
Geneva	1955–1956	22	US$2.5b
Dillon (Geneva)	1961	45	US$4.9b
Kennedy	1962–1967	48	US$40.0b
Tokyo	1973–1979	99	US$155.0b
Uruguay	1986–1993	107	[1]

Note: [1] It was estimated that, over a 10-year period, the Uruguay Round would lead to annual global GNP expansion of US$230 billion and merchandise trade expansion of US$745 billion.

difficult to establish and, consequently, led to unilateral or bilateral measures, outside of GATT, to restrict trade, as in the case of the US–Japan
auto-dispute of the early 1980s, which resulted in a Japanese decision to
exercise voluntary export restraint (VER).

The GATT and its successor institution, the World Trade Organization,
have operated much like a club for the rich with only marginal benefits for
developing countries. In the early years of GATT, developing countries,
consequently, relied on the UN Conference for Trade and Development
(UNCTAD) to achieve improved trade opportunities. Their demand was
for special and differential treatment (SDT), a form of positive discrimination to promote development and industrialization. But against these
arguments for *proportionality* of commitments, developed countries
insisted on full and complete *reciprocity* between developed and developing countries. Ultimately, however, GATT members agreed to introduce a
Generalized System of Preference (GSP) which allowed developing countries to export some of the commodities to developed countries at below
MFN tariff rates. The GSP scheme was introduced largely in the 1970s but
by the time of the Doha Round (2001–), its privileges had become
insignificant as a result of the progressive decline in MFN tariffs.

Trade Liberalizing Achievements of the GATT

GATT's liberal achievements came from eight multilateral tariff negotiating rounds. As a measure of these negotiations, average tariff on manufactured goods was reduced from 47 percent in 1947 to below 5 percent
in 1990s.

The Kennedy Round was the first comprehensive attempt to liberalize world trade. It began with an across the board tariff cut of 50 percent
followed by negotiations to adjust tariff levels. The end result was that
30 percent of dutiable imports of the major participants were left untouched
by tariff reductions and approximately a third of the reductions on the
remaining imports were of less than 50 percent.

The US government pushed for the Kennedy Round in the belief
that lower tariffs globally would help domestic exporters and restore
confidence in the US Dollar. It also persuaded the Congress to accept a
"fast track authority" (renamed trade promotion authority in 2002) to

ensure Congressional vote to accept or reject the resulting trade agreement without amendments. This made Congressional ratification of any agreement more of a formality and reassured other negotiating countries that difficult negotiations, once completed, would not be reopened for negotiations by Congressional insistence on amendments.

The Kennedy Round was followed by the Tokyo Round, which began in 1973 and was scheduled for completion in 1975. The Round took much longer to conclude because of the difficult nature of issues and because of global economic turbulence, such as the two oil crises, currency devaluation and general stagflationary (a combination of stagnation an inflation) conditions. Moreover, because of persistent American trade deficits, the domestic support base that had been instrumental in the success of earlier rounds had weakened and there was little political will to pursue liberalization. Between 1967 and 1975, the American Congress refused to give the president the authority to press ahead with a trade deal and, consequently, trade negotiations made little headway during this period.[17] Only later when fast track was approved did negotiations begin in earnest.

The primary negotiating agenda in the Tokyo Round was non-tariff barriers (NTBs). Although tariff cuts were significant in percentage terms, tariff levels were generally low to begin with. Tariff rates for all industrial products for the United States, European Community and Japan were between 5.5 percent and 6.6 percent, and tariff cuts for industrial goods was about 33 percent to be phased in over an 8-year period.

The Tokyo Round also resulted in a number of agreements and understanding among selected group of countries on issues of specific interest to them. For example, the Agreement on Trade in Civil Aircraft involved only 39 countries. Some of the other Agreements were on technical barriers to trade (66 countries), government procurement (56 countries), and import licensing procedures (66 countries). Seven of the agreements contained precise obligations on countries that had agreed to ratify them and these are referred to as "codes".

The government procurement code detailed the rules/procedures for competitive bidding for government contracts with a view to give foreign contractors national treatment. However, not all areas of government procurement were covered by these codes, the main exception being in the areas of national security and defense. The target country for liberalization of government procurement was Japan which had a long history of denying foreign companies equal treatment to domestic suppliers. At one time, the Chairman of Nippon Telephone and Telegraph (NTT), the domestic telecommunications giant had arrogantly brushed aside criticisms, and American pressure, to buy US telecommunication products by saying that all the US had to offer were "mops and buckets". After the Tokyo Round agreements, NTT foreign procurement was gradually opened up.

The issue of rolling back state subsidy was important in order to create a level field for exporters from all countries. Government subsidies enhanced the competitiveness of a firm or industry by socializing some of the costs and gave exporters of subsidized products the ability to undercut competitors without subsidies. The problem was that most countries provided some form of subsidy to specific domestic producers.

The subsidies code agreed in the Tokyo Round distinguished between export subsidies and subsidies "for the promotion of social and economic policy objectives".[18] Whereas, the existing GATT subsidy clause stipulated that no new subsidies were to be allowed for non-primary products; the new code prohibited export subsidies for non-agricultural products. This modestly strengthened GATT because it was still difficult to distinguish between the two types; and subsidies, in various forms, continued to be offered. For instance, in the five-year periods to 1982, EU provided US$30 billion in subsidies to the steel industry; and Japan, in 1982, announced a US$750 million plan to subsidize development of the next generation computer.

Uruguay Round

The period from the late 1970s through till the end of the 1980s was marked by a resurgence of protectionist sentiment in some western countries, most prominently the United States. Protectionism in the United States stemmed from a persistent trade deficit and a perception that trading partners were exploiting relative open markets in the United States while denying American exporters equal access to their own markets.

Sections of the business community, displaced workers, and legislators chafed at the 'unfairness' of international trade and demanded a level playing field that protected American manufacturers and jobs. These groups insisted that the US government, for instance, abandon its commitment to liberal trade in favor of strict reciprocity and protection for domestic sectors, adversely affected by imports.

While Congress was more easily swayed by these protectionist sentiments, the US administration remained committed to liberal trade principles. In this period, there were some deviations from the established rules of liberal trade but no wholesale questioning of the trade regime. The US government recognized that any reversal of the hard fought gains would be detrimental to long term prospects both in the United States and globally.

To stem the tide of protectionism, trade ministers from 90 countries met at Punta del Este, Uruguay, in September 1986, and issued a declaration launching the Uruguay Round (UR) of trade negotiations. They also agreed to 'standstill and rollback' existing levels of trade protectionism. The objective was to restore confidence in GATT and contains the crisis of protectionism that threatened to erode past achievements. A significant aspect of UR was the decision to incorporate into GATT system those sectors that had previously been excluded from GATT purview, like agriculture and textile, and formulate rules to deal with a more complex and globalized trading world.

To highlight the commitment on standstill and rollback, a Surveillance Body was set up to maintain a moratorium (standstill) on trade restrictions and facilitate the dismantling (rollback) of protectionist measures. The agreement, however, was only partially respected. Between September 1986 and November 1990, 25 possible violations of the standstill commitment were brought to the attention of the Surveillance but only six were successfully resolved. The process of GATT initiated rollback of protectionism, produced even fewer results.[19] Even if less than salutary, standstill and rollback were worthy principles in focusing the attention of the world community and as a moral deterrent to flagrant violations.

To address the broader negotiating agenda, the Punta del Este Declaration set up three specialized committees:

- A Trade Negotiations Committee (TNC) with overall responsibility for the Round.

- A Group of Negotiations on Goods (GNG) to oversee 14 negotiating committees established in January 1987 to lower trade restrictions on goods trade. It reported to the TNC.
- A Group of Negotiations on Services (GNS) to promote liberalization of services trade. This group also reported to the TNC.

The negotiating agenda was an ambitious attempt to broaden the scope of the GATT and to include international trade in services and agricultural commodities. The expansive negotiating agenda, however, complicated the work of trade negotiators and even though the Round was scheduled for completion in 1990, agreement was delayed until 1993. Apart from the negotiating agenda itself, another reason for the delay might be the large membership base of GATT and the attendant difficulty of reaching consensus. At the time of the Kennedy Round, GATT members numbered 53 countries but the Uruguay Round negotiations involved around 100 countries. However, although the expanded membership base complicated the task of negotiators, agreement in the Uruguay Round was held up not by the majority of the members but by a few of the large and influential trade actors.

Once agreement had been reached, GATT estimated that if all the provisions were faithfully implemented by signatory countries, the deal would add US$230 billion to world GNP and lead to a merchandise trade expansion of US$745 billion over a 10-year period.[20]

For developing countries, the UR can be singled out as the first round that promised relief from existing inequities. The GATT had operated like a rich man's club because while it offered some concessions, such as the Generalized System of Preferences (GSP),[h] it failed to promote liberalization in areas of greatest interest to developing countries. Agriculture had been excluded from GATT purview and trade in textile was regulated by a highly restrictive Multi Fibre Agreement (MFA) that allocated export quotas to each developing country with a textile exporting capacity. As a result of these exclusions, GATT was very different to 19th century free

---

[h] Under the GSP program, developed countries unilaterally offered to permit duty free imports of selected commodities from developing countries. Over time, as overall tariff structures in developed countries came down to insignificant levels, duty-free status for developing countries lost most of the potential advantages.

trade. In the 19th century Britain introduced free trade by repealing protection on agriculture but 20th century free trade excised agriculture and labor-intensive textiles from the liberalizing disciplines of GATT. It may not have been designed with particular malice towards developing countries but the result of selective liberalization was detrimental to their developmental goals.

The Uruguay Round provided the first opportunity to redress the imbalance. This was important in the context of liberalization that had been encouraged in developing countries following the Latin American debt crisis and IMF structural adjustment programs. Developing countries used the UR to secure a better trade deal and given that both textile and agriculture were included in the negotiating agenda, participated in negotiations more keenly than in earlier trade negotiating rounds. The agreement on textile committed developed countries to phase out MFA over a 10-year period. At the end of the phase-out period, on January 1, 2005, MFA quotas were lifted and replaced with tariffs, albeit at relatively high levels.

Liberalization of Agricultural Trade

At the time of UR negotiations, agricultural products constituted only about 13 percent of world merchandise trade. However, with the incorporation of agriculture into the GATT framework, agriculture trade was expected to grow significantly and it is not surprisingly that much of the anticipated welfare gains of the Uruguay Round liberalization was expected to be the result of liberalization of agriculture trade, especially given high tariffs on agricultural products compared to manufactured goods.

Previous exclusion of agriculture from GATT negotiations was necessitated by domestic political sensitivities in the European Union (EU),[i] the United States, and Japan. The Japanese government, for example, insisted on protecting domestic rice production on grounds of food

---

[i] In the Uruguay Round, the EC, not the individual European countries, has the negotiating authority. This is in keeping with the decision to establish a Common Market that would maintain a common external policy.

security — a critical component of comprehensive national security. The European Union also was highly protectionist and provided generous subsidies to farmers under the Common Agriculture Policy (CAP). The CAP helped maintain high domestic prices through state purchase of agricultural outputs and through other subsidies, which encouraged farmers to produce in excess of domestic demand. The resulting surplus production was, in turn, disposed in third country markets with the help of export subsidies.

Subsidized European exports were a source of irritation for American farm producers who found their traditional export markets undercut by aggressive European policies. In retaliation, the US government increased subsidy payments to its farmers and with the help of these subsidies, American exporters, in turn, encroached into traditional export markets of Australian, Canadian and other agricultural exporters. Unable to match the European Union or the United States in subsidies, these smaller countries, in 1986, formed the Cairns Group of Fair Traders[j] to campaign for subsidy-free liberal trade in agriculture. The Cairns Group was composed of both developed and developing countries and in the UR negotiations played an active role in focusing attention on farm liberalization. It was supported by the United States because the subsidy war with the European Union was becoming increasingly costly for taxpayers. According to OECD calculations, agriculture support policies, in 1989, cost consumers and tax payers in OECD countries roughly US$251 billion.[21] However, in negotiations neither the US nor the EU could muster the political will to step back from existing farm support policies. In December 1990, the deadline for completing the UR expired with a wide chasm separating the United States and European Union. Intermittent negotiations continued even after the deadline had expired but produced no real breakthrough. The American government, supported by the Cairns Group, insisted on a 75 percent cut in internal support and border protection and 90 percent cut in export subsidies whereas the European Union was willing to concede

---

[j] The Cairns Group includes Australia, Argentina, Brazil. Canada, Chile, Colombia, Fiji, Hungary, Indonesia, Malaysia, New Zealand. the Philippines, Thailand, and Uruguay.

no more than a 30 percent reduction. The two sides were also locked in disagreement on the appropriate base years for these reductions.[22]

European resistance was spearheaded by France, the world's second largest exporter of agricultural products. For employment reasons, the French government felt compelled to defend and protect its farming community from more efficient agricultural producers. Agriculture was also an important source of employment for several other EU countries and not easy to liberalize, given existing high levels of unemployment. The importance of agriculture as a source of employment is shown in Table 2.2.

Frustrated by lack of progress, the American Congress imposed a new deadline of December 15, 1993 for fast-track approval of any agreement. Without fast track authority Congress could veto specific aspects of the final agreement and force their re-negotiation. This threat prompted a fresh impetus for further negotiations to resolve differences between the European Union and the United States over agriculture. In the shadow of a Congressional "ultimatum", it was, ironically, an American concession that made agreement possible. Negotiations were concluded by the December deadline and the final agreement was signed by GATT member countries in April 1994, in Morocco.

Table 2.2:   Agriculture in the European Union countries.

Country	Percent of population in agriculture in 1986	Share of agriculture in national output in 1986
France	7.3	4.0
West Germany	5.3	2.0
United Kingdom	2.6	2.0
Netherlands	4.8	4.0
Portugal	21.9	10.0
Spain	16.1	6.0
Italy	10.9	5.0
Ireland	15.8	14.0
Greece	28.5	17.0
Denmark	6.2	6.0
Belgium	2.9	2.0
Luxemborg	4.0	—

Source: El-Agraa (1990).

The UR accord stipulated that non-tariff barriers to agriculture trade be replaced by tariffs and that all tariffs, including existing tariffs, be reduced by an average of 36 percent, over six years, in the case of developed countries and 24 percent, over 10 years, in the case of developing countries. The developed countries also agreed to reduce budgetary outlays on export subsidies to a level 36 percent below the 1986–1990 base period over six years and to reduce volume of subsidized exports by 21 percent over six years.[23] Developing countries had to reduce export subsidies by 24 percent and subsidized exports by 14 percent over the same period. However impressive the agreement looked on paper, the reality was that it effectively postponed the task of farm liberalization. It was a major setback for developing countries and for the Cairns Group.

On new issues, the UR extended GATT's reach to include services trade, foreign investments (TRIMs, or Trade Related Investment Measures), and intellectual property rights (TRIPs, or Trade Related Aspects of Intellectual Property Rights). These were issues of particular concern to developed OECD countries, which generated 84 percent of all services exports and 90 percent of all investment flows. Developing countries, on the other hand, opposed the inclusion of these sectors, first, because of a fear that their inefficient domestic services sector, such as banking, insurance and telecommunications, would be swamped by western multinationals, and second, because they considered investment controls and other TRIMs as essential to their developmental objectives. The TRIMs agreement required developed countries to remove all non-conforming TRIMs within two years, the developing countries within five years, and the least developed countries within seven years.[24]

The importance of services trade had increased progressively through the postwar period and in 1990, global services trade was worth US$820 billion, or 23 percent of total merchandise trade. Moreover, for individual developed countries, the services component of economic output and exports had increased substantially to alter the structure of their economy. In 1993, for example, services generated 74 percent of American gross domestic product, and produced a balance-of-trade surplus of US$55.7 billion against a deficit of US$132.4 billion for goods trade.[25] For developed countries, a more liberal regime of services trade was essential to enhance GATT, not only because services were an important trading category, but also because services and goods trade had become inter-linked, with services accounting for a sizeable component of the value of all goods.

On services, the UR produced a *quid pro quo* agreement giving developing countries more liberal rules on textiles trade in exchange for agreement to include services, and foreign investment, within GATT/WTO. The General Agreement on Trade in Services (GATS) emphasized the dual principles of transparency of trade regulations and most favored nation treatment. At the same time, countries were permitted to exempt certain services from MFN treatment, provided that exemptions were reviewed at the end of five years and limited to no more than 10 years. The agreement on services was modest compared to initial expectations but significant in, progressively, realizing a more complete trade regime. Separate negotiations later produced a Basic Telecoms Agreement and an Information Technology Agreement.

The protection of intellectual property rights had been a running sore in relations between developed and developing countries because of allegation that developing countries failed to respect property rights, such as trade marks and copyright, resulting in loss of incomes for owners of such rights. Treaties guaranteeing such rights have existed since the 1960s[k] but enforcement has always been a problem. In the UR Agreement on the TRIPs, countries agreed to make wilful trade mark counterfeiting and infringement of commercial copyright, a criminal offence. The Agreement covered a range of intellectual properties such as copyright, computer programs, trade marks, designs, patents and layout of integrated circuits and also geographical indications (to identify area of origin, especially for wines).

GATT Reform and the WTO

A final significant outcome of the UR was the decision to establish a World Trade Organization (WTO). The necessity of institutional overhaul

---

[k] The specific treaties include the International Convention for the Protection of Performers, Producers of Phonograms and Broadcasting Organizations (Rome, 1961); the Paris Convention for the Protection of Industrial Property (Paris, 1967); and Treaty on Intellectual Property in Respect of Integrated Circuits (Washington, 1989).

can be traced to a number of factors. According to Lutz, reform was an important step toward minimizing the "de-liberalization of international trade".[26] The rise of protectionism and retreat from liberal achievements was a strong incentive to reinvigorate free trade principles by strengthening institutional structures. A new organization and stricter rules may not be the complete solution to protectionism but as The Economist observed, "...a purposeful and influential [WTO] can put up more of a fight than one that is badly run and lacking in confidence".[27]

Others argued that while GATT had progressively acquired a semi-institutional status, it was still not the ideal mechanism for globalized economic relations. A more formal institutional arrangement was considered appropriate to the new realities. Blackhurst argued that with globalization, "...multilateral organizations which provide the institutional and legal frameworks for these cross-border commercial activities need to evolve in ways that allow them to continue to keep pace with the changing conditions".[28] Bringing GATT into the global age was, therefore, an important reason for changing the structure of liberal trade.

The European Community and Canada proposed the establishment of a WTO. The UR agreement approved its establishment and the WTO began operations in January 1995, replacing the GATT. To facilitate its operations, many of the existing rules were revised to encourage the contracting parties to rely on formally sanctioned dispute resolution procedures rather than on unilateral measures, as had become the norm during the GATT period.

One of the main weaknesses of GATT was its dispute resolution mechanism, which, in keeping with the original distaste for legalism, relied on negotiations and conciliation rather than on legal adjudication. According to Edward McGovern, "In the first decades of its existence, particularly under the tutelage of its Director-General, Eric Wyndham-White, there was a deliberate attempt to avoid anything smacking of legalism, an approach illustrated by the complete absence until recent years of any post of legal advisor in the GATT secretariat".[29] This system may have suited the early GATT, when it was a small institution composed largely of western countries, with similar cultural, social, political and economic backgrounds, but the increase in membership and compositional diversity enhanced the need for a more rule-based adjudication procedure.

The GATT dispute settlement mechanism was contained in Articles XXII and XXIII of the General Agreement. Until the end of 1986, Article XXII dispute settlement procedures had been used only on about 10 occasions whereas 100 complaints had been filed under Article XXIII.[30] Under Article XXIII, a dispute arose when one country alleged another to be guilty of nullification or impairment of a GATT benefit or an impediment to realization of a GATT benefit. In the initial stages of a dispute, Article XXIII provided for bilateral consultations but if the dispute persisted, a special panel could be set up to examine the complaint. The panel report was submitted to the GATT Council for formal adoption if the panel failed to convince the disputants to accept its ruling. The panel report had to be unanimous and the adoption of the report by the GATT Council also required unanimity. This meant that the 'losing' party could easily prevent adoption of the report by the Council. However, in so far as success of the dispute settlement procedures was concerned, of the 100 cases referred to a panel, only two eluded successful resolution.

Nevertheless, dissatisfaction remained that procedures were time consuming and cumbersome and that by the time a report had been prepared, the affected industry could suffer irreparable injury. This explains the growing reliance on dispute settlement outside of GATT, such as bilaterally negotiated voluntary export restraint agreements and other neo-protectionist measures. Another source of problem was the proliferation of dispute settlement procedures, which led to confusion. As part of the Tokyo Round agreements, various countries agreed on Codes governing specific areas and many of these Codes had their dispute settlement procedures that varied from those specified in the GATT.

The WTO streamlined dispute resolution by establishing the Dispute Settlement Body (DSB) to hear disputes between members. To expedite resolution of disputes, it also imposed time limits between the establishment of a panel to hear a dispute and the adoption of the panel report by the DSB. Most importantly, the WTO abandoned the unanimity principle for adoption of panel findings and instead established a new rule of "reverse consensus" to ensure that a panel finding would be automatically adopted unless there was unanimity against its adoption by the General

Council, a reality that was unlikely to eventuate unless even the "winner" agreed to set aside a panel finding and block its adoption by the General Council. The "loser" had access to an appeal mechanism but the entire dispute resolution process was designed to ensure that disputes were resolved in a timely manner, even if there was an appeal. The DSB established the following time lines for dispute resolution:

60 days	Consultations, mediations
45 days	Panel set up and panellists appointed
180 days	Panel report to parties
21 days	Panel report to WTO members
60 days	Panel report adopted by DSB

The entire process, from initiation to resolution, was to take only one year but an appeal could add another three months before a decision became binding on disputants. The WTO, of course, still had no enforcement powers but the agreement provided for retaliation if a member country failed to comply with rulings within a specified time limit.[31] In 1995, the DSB was asked to rule on 20 trade disputes, a number that was far greater than what GATT ever had to deal with in one year.[32] On average, the GATT dealt with six disputes a year but the WTO, in its first two years, dealt with 40 disputes per year. By October 2004, the WTO had adjudicated in about 317 trade disputes, a clear testimony to the effectiveness of the new dispute resolution processes.

The establishment of WTO had been partly instigated by the rise of protectionism in the 1980s but it would be naive to assume that institutional reform alone can contain the appeal of protectionism. The Director General of GATT, Peter Sutherland, hailed the establishment of WTO as a victory for liberal trade but acknowledged that we have not heard the last of "managed trade", an idea which is the antithesis of an open multilateral system.

The appeal of protectionism is inevitable under adverse economic conditions. The founders of GATT recognized that protectionism could not be entirely avoided and allowed for temporary protectionist measures under Article 19. However, they attached strict conditions which rendered Article 19, the so-called "safeguard clause", relatively unattractive to member states. The UR attempted to rectify some of the ambiguities in Article 19 and to make it more readily available to members confronting "serious injury" as a consequence of an import surge. The UR agreement clarified that "serious injury" or the "threat of serious injury" meant significant or clearly imminent "overall impairment in the position of a domestic industry", which had to be based on facts and not on allegations, conjecture or remote possibility. On the process of determining injury, it was decided that the criteria had to be clearly defined and made public, and that all interested parties had to be given the opportunity to give evidence before the relevant national authority charged with determining the applicability of safeguard action. The agreement suspended the automatic right to retaliate for the first three years of a safeguards measure, "...providing an incentive for countries to use established safeguard rules when import-related, serious injury problems occur".[33]

Anti-dumping provisions of GATT were also strengthened. The main users of anti-dumping measures, such as countervailing duties, were the United States, the European Union, Canada, and Australia, which together accounted for more than 90 percent of anti-dumping measures in the 1980s.[34] The new anti-dumping codes are more stringent and designed to ensure that anti-dumping proceedings were conducted in an 'unbiased and objective' way. It required national authorities to affirmatively ascertain the degree of support for a petition to begin anti-dumping investigation. Anti-dumping investigation could only begin if at least a quarter of the affected industry supported such a move. It also provided for a fairer method for constructing values for anti-dumping purposes.[1] In the past, the United States, for example, assumed an eight percent profit margin in constructing the value of a product, which was high even by domestic standards and disadvantaged foreign manufacturers that

---

[1] In the absence of available data on the cost structure of a commodity, which firms guard as a trade secret, national governments would resort to "constructed values" based on approximations in order to determine whether a country was guilty of dumping. Given the laxity of regulations, constructed values could easily be manipulated to produce a positive finding of dumping which could then justify the introduction of anti-dumping measures.

operated on lower profit margins. The anti-dumping code also stipulated that anti-dumping measures could be introduced only if the dumping margin was greater than two percent of the export price.[35,m] The standard American practice had been to determine dumping if the margin exceeded 0.5 percent.

Although the WTO acquired many additional responsibilities and functions, its administrative support structure was deliberately kept small and its funding was not increased commensurate to its additional tasks. Richard Blackhurst noted two main reasons why the larger member countries were unwilling to empower the WTO with a larger secretariat. First, a larger secretariat would require an increase in their financial contribution, based on shares of world trade, and second, the benefit of a larger and more active WTO would accrue mainly to the smaller countries, which, in the absence of an activist WTO to champion all the diverse interest, were more pliant and susceptible to western influence.[36]

Moreover, the United States, because of budgetary constraints and domestic political reasons, such as Congressional hostility to funding large multilateral institutions, refused to countenance any increase in funding for the WTO. Funding for WTO was frozen in 1995 at 118 million Swiss Francs, which the United States insisted should continue into the next century. In 2004, the total administrative and appellate budget for the WTO had increased to about 162 million Swiss Franc, or about US$143 million. In terms of absolute and relative funding, WTO is dwarfed by both the International Monetary Fund (IMF) and the World Bank. The WTO, in the late 1990s, had an administrative budget of US$140,000 per employee compared with US$280,000 for the World Bank and $230,000 for the IMF.[37]

The Doha Round

The WTO launched the Doha Round (DR) trade negotiations in 2001. Developing countries were not keen launching a new round even before all the UR agreements had been fully implemented (the agreement on

---

[m] The dumping margin is defined as the percentage by which export price is below the constructed value calculated by national authorities.

textiles, for example, was not fully implemented until January 2005) but they were won over by a promise that the new round would deliver pro-development outcomes. The DR was, accordingly, headlined as the Development Round that would address issues of importance to developing countries, such as pharmaceuticals, agriculture, and special and differential treatment (SDT). Developing countries welcomed this "window of opportunity" to achieve a more equitable multilateral trading system.

The issue of special and differential treatment for developing countries is a long-standing claim for positive discrimination to facilitate industrialization and growth. It seeks to exempt developing countries from full reciprocity and, in particular developing countries have argued that their special circumstance required easier access to western markets even as they maintained protection at home to nurture infant industries. This was begrudgingly accepted by the West, in the 1960s, and resulted, for instance, in the introduction of Generalized System of Preferences (GSP), whereby developing country exports were granted access to developed country markets at below MFN tariffs. Over time, however, the margin between MFN and GSP tariffs had shrunk as MFN tariffs were negotiated down and this had eroded the principle of SDT. According to Ha Joon Chang, SDT under WTO was a pale shadow of what it used to be under GATT and that while some exceptions were made for developing countries, "...especially the poorest ones, many of these exceptions were in the form of a slightly longer 'transition period' before they reach[ed] the same final goal as the rich countries, rather than the offer of permanent asymmetrical arrangements".[38] In the DR, developing countries sought to restore the principle of SDT and argued for less onerous liberalization commitments against western demands for balanced and strict reciprocity.

On pharmaceuticals, developing countries argued for access to cheap pharmaceuticals produced by countries like India and Brazil to combat tropical diseases and health epidemics, like Acquired Immunodeficiency Syndrome (AIDS). In principle, any country had the right to manufacture pharmaceuticals developed by major drug companies under compulsory licensing provisions but few developing countries had a domestic manufacturing capacity to benefit from compulsory licensing. India and Brazil, on the other hand, have relatively sophisticated manufacturing capabilities and produce generic medications, under license from western pharmaceutical companies, for a range of health problems confronting developing countries, including anti-retroviral medicines to address a growing AIDS problem in Asia and Africa. Compulsory licensing provisions, however, prevented producers of generic medicines from exporting to other countries. This limitation was detrimental to sub-Saharan African countries in particular because of their large AIDS infected population and an incapacity to provide AIDS patients with expensive branded anti-retroviral medicines purchased from the West. The inclusion of pharmaceuticals on the DR agenda was to ensure that developing countries had access to cheap medicines for their health crises. Negotiations, however, became deadlocked when developing countries demanded access to generics for all health crises but the United States was prepared to accept it for only a few specific health epidemics, like TB, malaria and AIDS. An internal WTO deadline of December 2002 for a preliminary pharmaceuticals deal passed without any agreement. In the end, just before a WTO ministerial meeting in Cancun in September 2003, the US relented and accepted the majority position that developing countries should have access to generic medicines for all established health crises.

The other main issue for developing countries in the DR was agriculture but they encountered stiff resistance from developed countries that could not convince domestic interest groups to accept freer trade in agriculture. The main issues, as in the UR, were tariff protection and subsidies. In 2003, the OECD countries provided US$257 billion in various subsidies to their farmers, grossly distorting global production and trade, particularly of rice, sugar and milk. It is interesting to note that in that same year the total Official Development Assistance (ODA) to developing countries by the Development Assistance Committee (DAC) of the OECD was only about US$70 billion. In principle, developing countries could forego development assistance if developed countries scaled back farm protection and permitted imports from developing countries.

Tariff levels on agricultural products in developed countries were also high, with tariffs on keys products exceeding 100 percent. For Iceland and Norway, such mega-tariffs exceeded 70 percent of all agricultural tariffs, while for Japan it was 40 percent and for the European Union and the United States, 30 percent and 12 percent, respectively.[39] To press for a liberalization of agriculture trade, a number of developing countries formed the Group of Twenty (G20) just before a WTO mid-term review of the DR in September 2003.

Developed countries were constrained, domestically, from making any significant changes to existing levels of protection and subsidy but developing countries, led by the G20 refused to accept anything that did not deliver on the spirit of the Doha Declaration that had launched the DR. Developing countries had a right to feel aggrieved by outcomes on agricultural negotiations in the UR and were determined to prevent a similar result in the DR. The UR agreement on agriculture looked impressive on paper but agreements can be made to look good even when they fail to create a more liberal trade environment. This is because negotiations are generally based on 'bound tariffs' and 'permissible subsidies', rather than applied tariffs and actual subsidies. Bound tariffs are higher than applied tariffs and permissible subsidies are again much higher than actual subsidies. In practice, therefore it is possible for the United States, for example, to cut permissible upper ceiling on subsidies without having to reduce actual subsidy payments to farmers.

The Doha ministerial meeting of the WTO had established deadlines for preliminary agreement on the various agenda items but none of these deadlines had been met when a ministerial meeting of the WTO convened in September 2003, in Cancun, to review progress in the DR. Apart from a last minute agreement on pharmaceuticals, the series of missed deadlines inspired no optimism for the Cancun meeting but negotiations quickly degenerated into a farce when they pushed to have the so-called Singapore Issues, such as trade facilitation and government procurement policies, added to the negotiating agenda. Developing countries, led by the G20, refused to broaden the agenda without prior agreement on agricultural liberalization. Their determined stance at Cancun led to a collapse of the Cancun ministerial meeting.

Negotiations resumed after a one year hiatus but differences between the developed and developing countries, especially on agriculture, could not be reconciled. The DR was to have been concluded in 2005 but that did not happen and negotiations continued until the WTO formally suspended negotiations in July 2006. In early 2007, there was a series of four party talks on agriculture involving the United States, the European Union, India and Brazil, but these too failed to bridge the divide. In the end, Crawford Falconer, the Chair of the Agriculture Negotiating Committee of the WTO was forced to concede that farm liberalization may have to await a "better generation" than ours.[40]

Conclusion

The WTO marked a new beginning for global liberal trade. There is now a better structure in place but its success will obviously depend on voluntary compliance, by the key trading countries, of the existing rules and regulations. In the absence of enforcement powers for the WTO, the future of liberal trade depends on political commitment and readiness to eschew deviant and arbitrary practices. Still, by making trade liberalization a permanent feature of international political economy, the WTO may help restrain protectionism. In the past, in between trade negotiating rounds, the GATT was inactive, and this, according to GATT Director-General Peter Sutherland, effectively vacated the policy space to protectionists who were able to berate liberal trade principles. The WTO is, consequently, a better check against deviant tendencies.[41]

In the UR, global corporations emerged as advocates of global liberalism in order to create a uniform operating environment across national borders. In the process leading to American ratification of the UR agreement, global corporations played an important role, against antagonists who tried to create an impression that the agreement infringed American sovereignty by denying the United States the right to resolve trade disputes according to its trade laws. For global corporations the advantage of the UR agreement and GATT was partly the tariff reductions, but more so the protection it promised against a fragmentation of the trade regime. The failure to successfully conclude the GATT round would have added to their transaction costs as a result of having to cope with segmented international regulatory regimes. Global corporations recognized the advantages of standardized regulatory policies in ensuring easier market access and argued forcefully for successful completion of the UR negotiations.

The GATT successfully completed eight trade negotiating rounds but the WTO, despite success in the dispute resolution area, is finding it extremely difficult to complete its first trade liberalization round. This is largely because of the difficult nature of issues under negotiations, issues that had either been excluded from, or glossed over by the GATT. Failure to complete the DR will no doubt have some detrimental impact on the WTO but even so this failure alone is unlikely to raise questions about its future viability or legitimacy.

Chapter Three

International Monetary Relations: Bretton-Woods and Beyond

As discussed in Chap. 2, planners of the postwar international order were convinced that future peace and prosperity required a framework for progressive trade liberalization. But, protectionism was not the only demon to be exorcised. Trade disruptions before the war had resulted also from restrictions on currency convertibility, cycles of competitive devaluation, and general volatility of exchange rates. The period between the two world wars witnessed three separate exchange rate regimes: floating exchange rates between 1922 and 1926; fixed exchange rates between 1927 and 1931; and managed floating exchange rates between 1932 and 1936. Nominal exchange rates were four times as volatile under floating rate system as under the managed float, and rates under managed float were four times as volatile as under the fixed rate system. Real exchange rates were similarly volatile.[1] This had detrimental economic consequences because when exchange rates fluctuate wildly, prices lose their reference point, markets cease to function efficiently, and resource allocation and trade consequently become similarly distorted.[2,a]

---

[a] We do not intend, however, to prejudge a system of flexible exchange rates and advocates of exchange rate flexibility insist that, other things being equal, markets will settle on a stable equilibrium exchange rate.

The problem in the interwar period was that the gold standard, which stabilized monetary relations in the 19th century had disintegrated by the First World War. Great Britain had adopted the gold standard in 1821 but gold did not become the international standard until the 1870s. Under the gold standard, individual governments agreed to abide by the following three rules:

- define national currency units in terms of weight of gold;
- where notes were issued in addition to gold coins, the notes had to be freely convertible into gold; and
- allow free import and export of gold.[3]

The advantage of the gold standard, in its pure form, as pointed out by David Hume in the 18th century, was that it produced automatic adjustments to trading imbalances. In a deficit country, the surplus of imports over exports had to be financed out of available gold stock and the resulting decline in reserves automatically reduced money supply, consumption and imports. Simultaneously, lower prices of domestic products added to export competitiveness and the combined effect was to increase exports and reduce imports, leading to balanced trade. The reverse would happen in the surplus country where the inflow of gold would increase the supply of money and domestic prices which would consequently reduce export competitiveness while higher domestic income would boost imports, reducing the level of surplus.

Another advantage of the gold standard was its anti-inflationary bias since money supply could not increase without a concomitant increase in gold reserves. By the same logic, trade growth, under the gold standard, was theoretically limited by growth in international liquidity. Fortuitously, in the 19th century, world gold stocks kept pace with demand for liquidity, mainly due to new discoveries of gold in the United States, Russia, Australia and South Africa. Otherwise, shortage of gold supply might have impeded economic growth and the growth of world trade.

The drawback of the gold standard was that international monetary stability was achieved at the expense of domestic economic stability because national policy makers could not insulate their economy from shocks and deflationary pressures resulting from movements in gold reserves. As a result, governments tried to avoid the discipline of market forces and, according to Ian Drummond, "the rules of the game were frequently ignored, and ... most though not all central banks had no intention of playing the gold-standard game by any particular rules".[4]

In the early 20th century, Britain consistently avoided adjusting to trade deficits, relying instead on other countries' willingness to hold Sterling as a reserve currency. The Sterling had, indeed, become an acceptable reserve apart from gold.[b] The final blow to the gold standard was dealt by the First World War. Most governments, with the exception of Britain, suspended the gold standard in order to protect their domestic economy. However, Britain's adherence to the gold standard was merely a legal formality as the policies of the British government had begun to deviate from the essential rules of the gold standard even before the outbreak of the War in 1914. Moreover, although the British government introduced no formal barriers to the export of gold, it discouraged this through moral suasion, appeals to patriotism, cumbersome procedures at the Bank of England and various other measures.[5]

During the war, Britain's position as the premier economic power was irrevocably lost due to its concentration on the war effort. With disruptions to British exports, other countries turned to alternative sources or began import substitution industrialization. The war was a boon to the United States as the alternative source of supply and also led to nascent industrialization in Latin America, Canada and several other former markets for British exports. Britain failed to regain these markets after the war and domestic economic problems and structural adjustment delayed its return to the gold standards until 1925. In 1931, however, Britain was forced to abandon the gold standard altogether after sustained gold losses.

Although the United States was ideally placed to replace Britain after the First World War, American policies did not reflect its international standing. Worse still, the US government insisted that Britain and France repay their war debts to the United States because domestic opinion in the United States would not countenance any loan cancellation. Both France and Britain, in turn, insisted that Germany pay war reparations. For a

---

[b] As we shall see below, the United States, in the postwar period, also avoided policies to overcome its balance of payments deficits because other countries were willing to accumulate Dollar reserves.

while the resulting pressure on the international monetary system was kept in check by large flow of funds from the United States to Germany, which enabled it to continue payment of reparations. Unfortunately many of the investment loans made by financial institutions in New York, the new international financial center, turned out to be speculative and without sound commercial viability. Consequently, when the stock market crashed in 1929 and flow of funds from New York dried up, Germany's problems were further compounded as it "...still had heavy reparations obligations along with sizeable debts to U.S. bondholders".[6] Repayment of debt by Germany, Britain and France was made more difficult by American trade policy and creeping protectionism which denied these countries' an opportunity to export manufactured goods to the United States, earn dollars and repay their debts. The decade of the 1930s was marked by fluctuating exchange rates and competitive devaluations as countries jostled with each other for trade advantages.[7]

To prevent future recurrence of destructive competition, a number of countries led by Britain and the United States initiated discussions to create international financial stability. This led to the Bretton-Woods agreement, which was signed by 44 countries in 1944. It became the basis for a postwar monetary order structured around stable exchange rates and liberalized capital transactions. The object, again, was to facilitate trade expansion. This system lasted until 1973, when fixed exchange rates were abandoned in favor of floating exchange rates. In the new system, exchange rates were to be determined by market forces but, in reality, governments intervened persistently to protect exchange rates they considered desirable and appropriate. Because of the pervasiveness of political intervention, the floating rate system was better known as "dirty" or "managed" float. In the mid-1980s, western governments experimented with coordinated intervention in order to achieve specific outcomes, such as a devaluation of the dollar from the high levels it had reached in the early 1980s. This restored some stability without completely sacrificing flexibility.

In this chapter, I will consider the main features of the three postwar monetary regimes: (i) the reasons for the collapse of fixed exchange rate system; (ii) the promise and performance of flexible exchange rates; and finally (iii) the institutionalization of periodic, but imperfect, exchange rate cooperation and macroeconomic management.

The Bretton-Woods Regime

A monetary regime, according to Richard Cooper, is a set of rules or conventions governing monetary and financial relations between countries...A monetary regime specifies which instruments of policy may be used and which targets of policy are regarded as legitimate, including of course the limiting cases in which there are no restrictions on either.[8,c]

Initial negotiations between the United States and the United Kingdom to create a monetary regime began in the early 1940s. The key negotiators were Lord Keynes for United Kingdom and Harry Dexter White for the United States. Each side prepared a draft plan for a financial regime centered around an International Clearing Union (ICU) and a Stabilization Fund,[9] respectively. The two plans reflected their narrow national interests.

International Clearing Union

The ICU was intended as an international central bank with powers to issue its own currency, the Bancor, that would be traded among national central banks. Each member country was to be allowed to borrow Bancor, up to a specified limit, as and when required by balance of payments considerations. Bancor could be used to repay international debt. The advantage of such an adjustment mechanism was that it obviated the need for contractionary economic policies and, instead, allowed for continuous expansion in world trade. The reflected lessons learned from earlier experiences were trade adjustment had inevitably resulted in domestic economic deflation and hardships for the general population. The British government also proposed that responsibility for trade adjustment be shared by the surplus country, which would be levied a charge on surpluses as an incentive to correct balance of payments surpluses.

---

[c] This is a very broad definition that includes rule-based, interventionist regimes, such as fixed exchange rate regimes and market based, non-interventionist regimes, such as flexible exchange rate regimes.

The Stabilization Fund

The United States rejected the British proposal for two reasons. First it argued that the ICU, by issuing its own currency would undermine American sovereignty and be politically unacceptable. Second, that the proposal minimized the imperative of domestic economic adjustment and was excessively biased toward financing, which would inevitably be provided by the United States as the only country with sufficient credit resources. The United States objected to the near automaticity of borrowing from ICU and insisted that funding be both limited and conditioned on specific corrective measures. White, instead, proposed a Stabilization Fund. Under this plan, member countries could obtain limited credit for temporary balance of payments deficits but would be required to undertake economic adjustment for structural or chronic deficits. The American plan was more conservative than the British proposal. It was dictated by political considerations, primarily the belief that Congress would not sanction a blank check for deficit countries.

Other differences between the British and American positions ranged from the seemingly trivial to the serious. At one end there was disagreement whether to name the proposed monetary institution the International Monetary Union (the British suggestion) or the Stabilization Fund (the American proposal). Ultimately they agreed on the International Monetary Fund. The issue may seem trivial but for White the term 'union' was politically unacceptable.[10]

A more significant disagreement was whether trade adjustment should be primarily a responsibility of the deficit or the surplus country. The British proposal was that the burden of adjustment be shared jointly by deficit and surplus countries. This was rejected by White, who insisted that adjustment was a responsibility of the deficit country. Each position reflected their respective national interests. Since America expected to be a surplus country after the war, it chose to shift the onus of adjustment on deficit countries whereas Britain, expecting trade deficits for the foreseeable future wished to shift some of the pain of adjustment upon surplus countries. The British government wanted to avoid having to tailor its reconstruction program to balance of payments considerations and the Americans, for their part, did not wish to bankroll deficit countries indefinitely. The final agreement, given the financial and political power of the United States, was closer to the American proposals.

les prêts . sont officiel.

The International Monetary Fund

The bilaterally negotiated agreement on monetary rules was then presented to, and accepted by 44 countries at the Bretton-Woods Conference in July 1944 and led to the establishment of two separate institutions. The International Bank for Reconstruction and Development (IBRD or the World Bank) was designed to provide long-term financing for economic development and reconstruction projects. Complementing that, the International Monetary Fund (IMF or simply the Fund) was set up to provide trade adjustment financing for deficit countries to allow them to overcome temporary balance of payments difficulties. The IMF began operations in March 1946. It is led by a Managing Director nominated by the European countries.

The mechanism and amount that member countries were entitled to borrow from the IMF depended on their quota assessment, that is, their deposits with the IMF (Table 3.1). Of the total assessed quota, 25 percent had to be paid in gold (after the late 1970s, in SDRs or any other useable currency) and the rest in their own currency. IMF quotas, like membership dues, are assessed every five years and the last assessment was done in 1999 which forms the basis of current quotas. It was reviewed in 2003 but did not result in any change. Total quotas in 2006 amounted to US$308 billion, some of which was paid in gold.

Quotas are largely based on national GDP and determine voting rights within the IMF. Every country is allocated 250 basic votes plus one vote for every SDR 100,000 in quota (1SDR = US$1.49). Contemporary quota

Table 3.1:   IMF quota allocation.

Country	Quotas (%)	Votes (%)
United States	17.40	17.08
Japan	6.24	6.13
Germany	6.02	5.99
United Kingdom	5.02	4.95
China	2.98	2.95
Australia	1.52	1.50
Palau	0.001	0.01

Table 3.2:   GDP and voting rights.

Country/Region	2002 GDP (trill)	2002 voting rights (%)
US	US$9.3	17.1
EU (15)	US$8.5	29.9
Japan	US$4.5	06.1

allocations have resulted in considerable disparity between actual economic weight and voting rights within the IMF, as shown in Table 3.2.

There is a large imbalance between the economic weight of the EU, as measured by its combined GDP, and its allocated voting rights within the IMF, relative to economic weight and voting rights of Japan and the United States. But any attempt to redistribute voting rights inevitably draw resistance from the likely losers. The United States, for its part, has not pushed for any major reassessment of quota and voting rights, comfortable in the knowledge that its current allocated voting rights give it a veto within the IMF, as all decisions require a 85 percent voting majority.

When a member experiences balance of payments difficulties, it is entitled to borrow from either its "gold tranche" or "credit tranche". The original lending arrangements were as follows:

- *Gold tranche*: members can borrow the equivalent of 25 percent of their total quota, or the amount of gold held with the IMF. Borrowing against the gold tranche is a members' right and not subject to any conditions.
- *Credit tranche*: members can borrow in four equal tranche of 25 percent of their quota each time. However, borrowing is subject to conditions determined by the IMF and, in general, more stricter the conditions are, the greater the level of borrowing. Conditions include policy measures that a borrower has to implement in order to restore trade balance. *Conditionality* forms the heart of IMF financial assistance.

Under the original agreement, any country could borrow up to 125 percent of their IMF quota but this was subsequently increased in the 1970s when other credit facilities were introduced to supplement the gold and the credit tranche. By 1979, a deficit country could borrow up to 467.5 percent of the quota.[11] Countries borrow from the IMF not only for balance of payments' reasons but also to assist with economic restructuring programs. In 1997, 58 countries had borrowed US$23 billion from the IMF to support macroeconomic and structural reforms. The amount borrowed was three times that which had been borrowed in 1996 but slightly below the figure lent out by IMF in 1995.

Members of the Bretton-Woods regime agreed to maintain a system defined by fixed exchange rates; currency convertibility to gold; and removal of exchange restrictions and controls for current account transactions. The agreement to maintain fixed exchange rate allowed for small movement within a narrow band of one percent on either side of the par value. To prevent exchange rates breaking out of the acceptable range, central banks were expected to intervene in currency markets to stabilize rates against market pressures. The process of currency realignment had to be initiated by the concerned country but with the approval of the IMF. If currencies were devalued against the advice of the IMF, the errant country could potentially be expelled from the world body or lose its borrowing privileges from the Fund, *unless* decided otherwise by the Fund. In 1948, when the French Franc was devalued despite objections from IMF, France was denied access to resources of the Fund.[12]

Membership in the Fund implied a willingness to abide by the rules on exchange rate stability and unitary exchange rates. However, meaningful rule compliance was not achieved until about a decade after the establishment of the Fund. Even then, there were some exceptions. Many countries, especially Latin America, maintained a system of multiple exchange rates, as revenue collection devices or as protectionist mechanisms. Multiple exchange rates were used by cash-strapped developing countries to restrict the import of non-essential or non-preferred imports. The Fund opposed multiple exchange rates because of the potential for discrimination against certain products or products from certain region but tolerated it as unavoidable. The practice was phased out gradually but countries, like Egypt, continued with more than one exchange rate into the 1990s.

The Bretton-Woods agreement required currency convertibility and removal of exchange restrictions but allowed for a transition period of five years, until February 1952, by which time all countries were expected to allow full currency convertibility. The actual transition, however, was much longer. The priority for European countries and for Japan was economic reconstruction, which necessitated exchange controls to allow for the prioritization of capital goods imports. They were also protective of their relatively small foreign exchange reserves that could be further reduced if full convertibility was introduced at the end of the transitional period. The Fund promised to underwrite the transition to convertibility with its own resources, the paid up subscription of members. However, as W.M. Scammell wrote, "The promise that the Fund would meet part of the cost of convertibility was cold comfort to a nation like Britain which had experienced the gold drain and crisis attendant upon a premature experiment made under duress in the summer of 1947. The rest of the larger members had observed and learnt the lesson of that experiment and they listened politely to the Fund's homily but shook their heads".[13] The European countries accepted convertibility in the late 1950s, and Japan in the 1960s.

When the Bretton-Woods regime was established, there were concerns that a shortage of international liquidity might jeopardize the reconstruction of the European countries and also induce severe deflation in the United States. These concerns were compounded by the communist threat. The West European countries confronted the danger that if growth and reconstruction faltered, a bleak economic environment would provide fertile grounds for the spread of communism. In this context of political and economic uncertainty, the United States played the crucial role as a source of international liquidity in the postwar period. The United States provided international liquidity primarily through its preparedness to run balance of payments' deficits. As Eichengreen pointed out, "...it is difficult to envisage an alternative scenario in which the U.S. balance of payments was zero but the world was not starved of liquidity".[14] Another source of international liquidity was the European Recovery Program, commonly known as the Marshall Plan, which provided European countries with economic assistance, either as grant (92 percent of the total Marshall Aid in 1946 was in the form of outright grant), or as long-term low interest loans.[15]

The Marshall Plan was critical to the stability of the new monetary order. Indeed, the US government tried to link Marshall Aid to compliance with the fixed exchange rate rules of the IMF. Ultimately, however, this had to be dropped in the face of stiff European opposition.[16] The Marshall Plan helped maintain high foreign demand for American products and hastened the process of European economic reconstruction and adoption of free and convertible currencies for current account purposes. In Asia, the outbreak of the Korean War in 1950 and the American special procurements program had a similar effect. Japan was the primary beneficiary of the special procurement plans of the US armed forces and this aided the process of Japanese recovery.

As a result of the Marshall Plan and special procurements, the dreaded liquidity crisis failed to materialize. Indeed, in the period 1950–1956 the United States ran a modest balance of payments deficit of about US$1.5 billion per year. In the end, however, the weakness in the monetary regime was not potential liquidity shortage but surplus liquidity, especially after President Johnson initiated the Great Society program and escalated the Vietnam War. Excess liquidity and global inflation became the main sources of international financial instability.

In the 1960s, before the Great Society programs and the Vietnam war had produced excess international liquidity, the need for maintaining adequate liquidity was a major consideration. Existing reserve assets were gold and increasingly the American dollar. Although most countries agreed on the need for additional reserve instruments there was disagreement on the nature of that instrument. On the one hand, France and West Germany, argued for a reserve asset that was more like credit and which would eventually have to be repaid, with gold retained as the 'heart' of the international monetary system. On the other hand, the United States and the United Kingdom preferred the creation of a genuine reserve asset that could be freely used in place of gold.[17] Both the United Kingdom and the United States were experiencing balance of payments' deficits and advocated the creation of a new reserve asset that would eliminate the need for domestic economic adjustment, made all the more difficult by the demands of the welfare state. The Special Drawing Rights (SDRs) that was agreed to was a compromise solution and came into existence in

August 1969, six years after the idea had first been mooted. Subsequently, to give the SDR a larger profile and importance, the IMF adopted it as its accounting unit but the role of SDRs in national reserves has remained small.

The Collapse of the Bretton-Woods Regime

Until the end of the 1950s, the Bretton-Woods system, according to Scammell, remained in abeyance, as many countries continued practices that violated the established rules.[18] It became a constraining regime only in the 1960s and by the late 1960s, there were enough pressure points to force its collapse. The backdrop to the eventual collapse of the Bretton-Woods system was the US balance of payments deficit through much of the 1950s and 1960s. In the 1950s, the deficit was functional in that it provided international liquidity and sustained trade expansion. In the 1960s, however, deficits generated excess international liquidity and the concern now was that surplus dollars would erode confidence in dollar as reserve currency, if foreign dollar holdings exceeded US gold stocks, as pointed out by Robert Triffen.

By 1965, foreign dollar holding exceeded gold reserves in the United States and by the early 1970s, US liabilities exceeded gold stocks by 300 percent. Surplus dollars in foreign central banks, the so-called dollar overhang, fuelled speculation that the US government would be forced to devalue the dollar to reduce the prospect that foreign countries might cause a run on the dollar and deplete US gold holdings. Confidence in the American economy was shaken also when the US trade balance recorded its first deficit in 1968. The deterioration in American trading position can be attributed to a decline in relative international competitiveness. Whereas investment in new and modern factories and plants in Europe and Japan gave their industries a competitive edge, capital investment in the US failed to keep pace. The normal American practice of setting up overseas factories to consolidate and increase market share did not help either because the "decision to sell to a foreign market through branch plants rather than through exports often meant that capital was diverted from the expansion and modernization of domestic facilities".[19]

However, despite fears to the contrary, foreign central banks did not initiate a run on US gold reserves and were content to hold on to dollar as the reserve currency. Private holders of dollars were, however, less confident about the dollar especially after the devaluation of the Sterling in November 1967. The British government devalued the Sterling by 14 percent after chronic balance of payment deficits; this only heightened speculation that a dollar devaluation, too, was inevitable. After devaluation of the Pound, gold purchases in London shot up. Gold had been supplied to the London market by seven central banks (Gold Pool) since 1966 and in the fourth quarter of 1967 alone, the United States lost US$953 million worth of gold deposits to the private markets.[20] Although the pressure eased after that, there remained a sense of uncertainty about the future of the dollar. Apart from the loss of gold from US reserves, the process was adding to inflationary pressures in other countries by increasing their levels of gold and dollar reserves. During 1970–1972 and the first three months of 1973, for example, official foreign holdings of US dollar claims increased by 346 percent.[21] Moreover, as private holders of dollars switched to other forms of assets, central banks in these countries were obliged to purchase the surplus dollars to support the value of the dollar but in the process only added to domestic liquidity and to inflation.

Another source of instability in the international financial system was the speculative flow of capital across borders. The architects of the Bretton-Woods system had intended convertibility to apply to transactions on trade accounts but not on capital accounts, because freedom to import or export capital was incompatible with the fact that countries were required to periodically contract or expand their domestic economies to maintain fixed exchange rates. For example, efforts to contract the domestic economy through higher interest rates could be easily undermined unless capital imports were restricted. However, capital flowed freely and rapidly across countries aided by advances in international communications and which were quick to respond to real interest rate changes, in the expectation of easy speculative gains.

Removal of controls and restrictions on capital accounts transactions allowed currency speculation to exacerbate pressures on a given currency. Corporations and speculators recognized the potential for easy profits by shifting capital from one country to another in anticipation of exchange rate changes. This flow of international capital undermined national economic management and allowed for the rapid dissemination of inflationary pressures throughout the system. From a purely national point of view, fixed exchange rates coupled with capital movements were becoming increasingly undesirable. A system of freely floating exchange rates seemed more promising since it would reduce speculative capital movements because exchange rates would adjust rapidly without there ever being a perceived fundamental disequilibrium.

A final factor in the collapse of the Bretton-Woods system was an apparent reluctance of major countries to deal with their payment imbalances. According to Margaret Garritsen de Vries, the IMF historian, the primary cause of the collapse of fixed exchange rate system was "without doubt...the failure of the adjustment process".[22] That failure might be attributed to the ambiguity in the definition of "fundamental disequilibrium" in IMF Articles of Agreement. This concept was left vague and there were no real pressures on surplus countries to make exchange rate adjustments.

The burden of adjustment was on the United States and there were two possible adjustment strategies: deflation and devaluation. Deflation and forced economic contraction were politically unacceptable because of the resulting hardship on individuals. Similarly, while devaluation of the dollar, by changing the price of gold that had been fixed at US$35 per ounce, would have effectively reduced American obligations arising out of the balance of payment deficits. It was ruled out as risky given the position of the dollar as an international reserve currency. Any devaluation would have undermined confidence in the dollar. The nature of the monetary system, where US dollar was the key currency and all exchange rates were pegged to the dollar, made it difficult for the United States to devalue the dollar. Devaluation was ruled out also because of its inflationary consequences.

The international monetary system demanded that the United States government assume a passive position with regard to exchange rates and rely on speedy rate adjustments by other countries. Other countries, however, avoided this and the United States smarted at its own inability to act and the refusal of others, especially Japan and West Germany, to revalue their currencies. Just as the United States had decided that it was impossible or impractical to devalue the dollar, the European countries, too, were reluctant to accept currency revaluation. During the 1960s, a consensus was formed that fixed rates could not be tampered with. The reason was that such a step would be unpopular with exporters and have negative political fallout. For example, a five percent appreciation of the deutsche mark in March 1962 had sent shock waves through the export industry and created within German industry a determination that it should not be repeated.[23]

The IMF agreement allowed for adjustments to par values but this happened only on a handful of occasions. The result of delays was to promote capital flows as speculators chased profits by moving currencies out of weak and into strong currencies. This added to adjustment pressures but, as Kenneth Dam writes, national authorities responded to this by "new forms of capital controls, and, in some cases, by new controls on trade flows to attempt to stave off devaluation".[24] The net result of this was that where the monetary system had been intended to lubricate and facilitate trade expansion, trade was being sacrificed to stabilize a particular set of par values of currencies.

One reason why the United States could not devalue its currency, in the 1960s, was because its overall trade balance was actually in surplus until 1968. Devaluation, under these circumstances, would have had the undesirable consequence, from European and Japanese points of view, of further increasing the American trade surplus. This might have prompted retaliatory devaluation. According to Block, "had a U.S. devaluation in the early 1960s improved the U.S. international trade position, it is likely that other countries would have devalued correspondingly to regain their earlier competitive position and to reverse any improvement in the U.S. trade balance".[25] In 1971, however, the US current account registered a deficit for the first time in the postwar period and, on August 15, 1971, the United States ended convertibility of the dollar. The American government also imposed a 10 percent surcharge on imports to force other countries to revalue their currencies. Later that year, the Smithsonian agreement did bring about a 8–9 percent depreciation of the dollar against other currencies and, consequently, the surcharge was removed. The Smithsonian agreement also widened the band within which currencies could fluctuate from one percent to two and a half percent on either side of the par rates. This revised monetary arrangement lasted until 1973 when a fully floating exchange rate system was adopted.

The Floating Exchange Rate System

By 1968, according to Gottfried Haberler and Thomas Willett, "the great majority of academic economists [were] in favor of flexibility of exchange rates".[26] A leading advocate of flexible exchange rates, Harry Johnson, argued that the price of a currency, like all other prices, ought to be decided by market forces rather than by governmental fiat. The presumed advantages of exchange rate flexibility include automatic adjustment to balance payment imbalances, through the exchange rate mechanism which, like a sentinel on guard at a country's border, neutralized all external disturbances before they could impact on the domestic economy. Under fixed rate system, on the other hand, domestic economic activity, where necessary, had to be varied to defend the exchange rate. In principle, flexible exchange rates have a number of advantages.[27]

Under a regime of flexible exchange rates, monetary policy becomes a viable policy instrument for domestic economic objectives. Under fixed exchange rates, the sole function of monetary policy was to maintain par rates. Stable exchange rates were maintained by varying the level of money supply within a economy (a key element of monetary policy) depending on whether or not the exchange rate required defending or by altering interest rates to make the local currency more or less attractive to foreign investors and depending on whether the local currency required external support to sustain the par rates. As such, monetary policy under fixed exchange rates is available only as an instrument in securing external policy objectives but not very useful in securing domestic policy objectives. According to Milton Friedman, a system of flexible exchange rates, by contrast, would allow monetary policy to be used for domestic policy objective, such as controlling the level of inflation,[28] since exchange rates would no longer a responsibility of national governments. In the 1960s, the German government, despite strong domestic anti-inflationary policies, could not avoid inflationary pressures imported from the United States, which was following opposite macroeconomic policies of promoting employment even at the risk of inflation. Consequently, in the 1970s, when the opportunity presented itself, the German government was supportive of flexible rates, which, as Cooper observed, "...insulated West Germany from imported inflation...".[29]

Another advantage of exchange rate flexibility is automatic trade adjustments and the sharing of the burden by both the deficit and the surplus country. Also because of quick adjustment, it was possible, at least theoretically, to avoid sustained misalignment and overvaluation of currencies, with the attended risk of protectionism. According to Bergsten and Cline, the three periods of high protectionism in the United States were also periods of an overvalued US dollar.

- *Late 1960s–1971*: this was just before the collapse of Bretton-Woods, when the dollar was overvalued by about 20 percent. Many protectionist bills, like the Mills Bill were introduced in the Congress in 1971 and this was also the period of the textiles dispute between Japan and the United States, which resulted in restrictions on Japanese textile exports.
- *1975–1976*: the dollar was overvalued around 15 percent and this was also the period when the United States introduced import restrictions on Japanese steel, through the trigger price mechanism.
- *1981–1985*: the dollar was overvalued by around 35 percent and this was the period when protectionism in the United States reached its peak. Currency revaluation was finally achieved after the Plaza Accord of September 1985.[30]

The examples cited above show also that currency misalignment is possible even under flexible exchange rates. This might be attributed to a tendency for exchange rates to overshoot equilibrium rates, and to government intervention in currency markets. Overshooting, both under and overvaluation, is problematic. When currencies remain undervalued over a long period, there is a danger of competitive devaluation as other countries try to regain lost competitive advantage. On the other hand, sustained overvaluation of a currency is likely to worsen a country's trade balance by discouraging exports and promoting imports. This, in turn, may generate protectionist pressures. As pointed out above, it was coincidence that the two periods of heightened protectionism in the United States, the mid-1970s, and the early to mid-1980s, were also periods of both a significant overvaluation of the dollar and deterioration of the balance of trade. In each of these two periods, the American response was to engineer a coordinated depreciation of the dollar to reduce trade deficits and lower domestic protectionist sentiments. The results, however, were not as effective as anticipated and tended to support the view that exchange rate changes, by themselves, could not restore trade balances.

In dealing with trade deficits against Japan, the United States relied on exchange rate changes to reduce its trade deficit but without much success, perhaps because of American unwillingness, until the newly elected Clinton administration announced budget cutbacks in early 1993, to reduce fiscal imbalance. An adviser to President Clinton, Robert Shapiro, vice president of the Progressive Policy Institute, admitted that the ability of currency realignments to restore trade balance was "much less than many economists once thought".[31,32]

The period of floating exchange rate also witnessed considerable, and erratic, fluctuation in rates. It had been anticipated that rates would reach equilibrium points quickly and maintain a level of stability but this proved not to be the case and exchange rates remained highly volatile. The volatility and uncertainty correlates with a deterioration of economic performance in the 1970s (Table 3.3). For example, in 1994, the Bretton-Woods Commission, composed of former bankers and experts, estimated that exchange rate instability had contributed to halving the long-term economic growth rate of industrialized countries to about 2.5 percent, compared to the period when exchange rates were fixed.[33] Similar conclusions were reached by others.

It would be simplistic, however, to blame flexible exchange rates for a slowdown in economic and trade growth. There were a number of reasons for the slowdown in GNP growth, including a quadrupling of oil prices in 1973. According to Blackhurst and Tumlir, the slowdown in

Table 3.3: Macroeconomic performance of the United States, Japan and Germany.

	Unemployment rate	Inflation rate	GNP growth rate
Fixed exchange rates 1961–1971			
US	4.8	2.8	3.6
Germany	0.8	2.8	4.2
Japan	1.2	5.6	10.4
Flexible exchange rates 1973–1979			
US	6.6	8.6	2.3
Germany	3.8	4.6	2.3
Japan	1.9	9.8	3.5
Flexible exchange rates 1980–1987			
US	7.7	5.3	2.4
Germany	7.8	2.9	1.5
Japan	2.5	2.5	3.9

Source: Shinkai (1990).

world trade was also a reflection of domestic economic dislocation, such as inflation. The average rate of inflation in the seven major OECD countries in 1960–1965 was 2 percent but in the period 1970–1975 it was 7.9 percent. Inflation, they argued, affected national economic growth because it ultimately necessitated restrictive monetary and fiscal policies, leading to a recession.[34]

Moreover, the flexible exchange rate system was not untainted by government intervention. Most major governments were reticent about allowing market forces alone to determine exchange rates and, instead, intervened actively in foreign exchange markets to support 'desirable' rates. According to Kenneth Dam, "...the level of intervention since the commencement of generalized floating in 1973 has been as great and perhaps greater than during the par value period prior to 1971".[35] At the same time, Richard Cooper argued that there were legitimate reasons for state intervention in managing exchange rates. According to him "For most countries, the exchange rate is the most important single price...it is inconceivable that a government held responsible for managing its economy could keep its hands off this particular price".[36] Others, like Franco

Modigliani suggested a reconsideration of fixed exchange rates saying that, "...I think that, in the long run, we ought to aim for a gradual return to a system of fixed exchanges like Bretton-Woods, but one purged of the major faults...".[37,38] Although a return to fixed exchange rates is fanciful, it is obvious also that states are unlikely to let capital markets freely determine exchange rates. At the same time, constrained by foreign exchange reserves at their disposal, states recognize also the desirability of orderly and coordinated intervention in capital markets rather than unilateral actions.

Policy Cooperation and Monetary Stability

Currency instability and exchange rate pressures are largely the result of speculative capital flows which have increased exponentially, as a result of capital market deregulation and globalization of communication systems. The financial revolution and pervasive misalignment of currency values led to new initiatives to preserve regional and global monetary stability. At a regional level, the European Monetary System, established in 1979, was fairly successful in preventing excessive volatility of European currencies through coordinated capital market interventions. For instance, in January 1993, when speculators launched an onslaught on the French franc, the French and the German central banks intervened with about US\$50 billion to prop up the French franc.[39] The system depended on the German mark as the key currency and proved viable as long as Germany itself emphasized monetary stability. However, confronted with the huge costs of reunification, Germany abandoned its commitment to EMS and exchange rate stability in August 1993.[40]

At a global level, the annual meeting of central bankers and finance ministers of the seven leading industrialized countries (G7), and the annual summit meeting of heads of the five leading economies (G5, later G7) assumed primary responsibility for policy coordination to ensure monetary and exchange rate stability. The G7 mechanism was institutionalized at the Tokyo summit of 1986 and meetings have been held three to four times each year. At the G5 summit meeting in Rambouillet (1975) it was agreed that "monetary authorities will act to counter disorderly market conditions or erratic fluctuations in exchange rates".[41]

Policy coordination, however, was relatively ineffective in preventing misalignment of exchange rates in the early years and only began to have a discernible impact in the mid-1980s.

The Plaza Accord of 1985 was a significant new beginning in policy coordination. The Accord was the result of a summit meeting among the G5 countries (the United States, Japan, Germany, England and France) in September 1985 in the Plaza Hotel, New York. Prior to 1985, the United States was less interested in correcting exchange rate disequilibrium because of the paramount interest in reducing domestic inflation. It was feared that a devaluation of the dollar against other currencies would only exacerbate inflation in the United States by making imports more costly. Thus, despite support for currency revaluation elsewhere, the United States failed to go along with this. In the mid-1980s, however, US trade position had deteriorated drastically,[42,d] and amid mounting protectionist pressures, the government was forced to try and seek currency readjustment as a way of reducing trade deficits. The depreciation of the dollar that was achieved under the Plaza accord was also desirable because it, at one stroke, reduced foreign claims on the United States by reducing the value of their dollar holdings. The Plaza Accord committed the United States, Japan and Germany to intervene, in a coordinated manner, in foreign exchange markets to produce an appreciation of the Yen and the Deutsche Mark. This was an example of successful policy coordination to counter rising protectionism in the United States, resulting from a loss of American competitiveness caused by the appreciation of the dollar in the early 1980s.

The Plaza Accord was followed by the Louvre Accord, signed in February 1987 at Louvre, France. This committed the G7 countries (G5 plus Canada and Italy) to achieving monetary stability around target zones. The argument for target zones had been put forward by several scholars, such as by Williamson, Miller, McKinnon, and Kenen, for exchange rate stability through target zones and monetary policy coordination. John Williamson and Marcus Miller developed a specific proposal

---

[d] Until 1984, US current account was either in surplus or almost balanced but in 1984, the US current account deficit was 1.5 percent of GNP. This increased to 2.0 percent of GNP in 1985, to 2.5 percent in 1986 and to 2.7 percent in 1987.

for international economic cooperation that extended beyond the targeting of exchange rates alone. They argued that policy coordination should include, apart from exchange rate coordination, macroeconomic policy coordination to achieve low inflation, high employment, rapid growth, and appropriate balance of payment outcomes.[43]

At the time of the Louvre Accord, the target zones, reportedly, were set at between 1.77 and 1.87 marks and between 137 and 147 yen to the US dollar. Two years later, the target zones were believed to have been readjusted at between 1.6 and 1.9 marks and at between 120 and 140 yen to the dollar.[44] The establishment of target zones, however, did not sanction intervention whenever rates reached the margins. The only obligation was to consult rather than to intervene in a prescribed manner. A practical difficulty in exchange rate management is securing agreement on appropriate exchange rates. There is no consensus as to how to determine target rates and, in the past, analysts have come up with different equilibrium exchange rates.[45]

Critics of policy coordination argued that this was a misdirected focus on exchange rates to the neglect of broader macroeconomic policies. Milton Friedman, for example, argued that exchange rate volatility was simply the result of underlying macroeconomic imbalances, and eliminating those imbalances will lead to a more stable exchange rate structure. Supporting government non-intervention in exchange rates and floating system, he argued, "Instability of exchange rates is a symptom of instability in the underlying economic structure. Elimination of this symptom by administrative pegging of exchange rates cures none of the underlying difficulties and only makes adjustment to them more painful".[46] Similarly, according to Funabashi, the Louvre Accord was a quick-fix solution to the balance of payments problem of the United States rather than a determined attempt to tackle the real issue.[47] The argument is that exchange rates are simply a reflection of fundamental imbalances in macroeconomic policies and focusing on exchange rates, as such, merely concentrates attention on the symptoms rather than the basic problem. However, underlying macroeconomic imbalances have not been entirely neglected but, it is true, they have not received enough coordinated attention. Under the Louvre Accord the United States agreed to reduce its fiscal 1988 budget deficit to 2.3 percent of GNP compared to the estimated 3.9 percent in fiscal 1987. Large American budget deficits meant high domestic inter-est rates, capital inflows, strong dollar and, consequently, poor export prospects and ballooning imports. Despite a commitment to reduce deficit spending, there was little serious attempt to cut the deficit by lowering spending or increasing tax revenue.

In recent years, central bank intervention in currency markets has been largely to iron out excessive volatility in floating exchange rates, or to keep inflationary pressures under control. This followed years of infla-tionary pressures that ultimately led to a growing consensus that only independent central banks could deal effectively with inflationary pres-sures. The Reserve Bank of New Zealand was an early trailblazer in estab-lishing the principle of central bank independence but in Europe as well, a key element of the European Monetary Union was formation of an inde-pendent supranational central bank.[48] This of course meant that policy makers could not use central banks to fuel inflation, whether to secure bet-ter employment outcomes or other policy objectives. Central banks were guaranteed freedom from governmental interference so that they could concentrate on achieving a low inflation environment. The principle of central bank independence was progressively accepted by many of the transitional economies. Independent central banks have focused on domestic price stability rather competitive and stable exchange rates and their task is made easier by the new orthodoxy that exchange rate stabil-ity depends on stable domestic macroeconomic policies.

IMF in the Post-Bretton Woods Period

The abolition of fixed exchange rates initiated a period of crisis for the IMF because it had lost its primary function in the international mone-tary system. The Bretton Woods agreement had given it the responsibil-ity of maintaining fixed exchange rates but the changed circumstances inevitably raised questions about its future relevance. The future of the IMF was debated both in academic and policy circles but uncertainty was short-lived. In 1982, the Latin American debt crisis gave the IMF a new lease of life as crisis manager and lender of last resort to countries in crisis. The Latin American debt crisis was followed by a series of debt and financial crises in developing and transitional countries (the former

East European and socialist countries) and the IMF quickly consolidated its position in guiding crises economies through structural adjustment programs intended to restore economic growth and confidence.

Yet, given its increasingly close involvement with developing countries, it appeared to have lost a distinctive identity. It was seen as behaving like the World Bank because, as noted by Jacques Polak, both institutions were providing similar types of credit on similar terms to the same group of countries.[49] The IMF had found a role to play but it still had no distinctive identity. It was perceived more as an "aid" agency rather than a "monetary" institution. However, even if IMF looked like an "aid" agency to most observers, Michel Camdessus, the former Managing Director of the Fund defiantly protested that, "We shall not get out of the aid business because we are not in it".[50] Starting in the late 1980s, the IMF also positioned itself at the forefront of western efforts to assist the former communist economies make a transition to market-based economic systems.

Countries in crises turned to IMF for bailout assistance but IMF financial assistance came with strings attached. Bailout packages were linked to structural adjustment programs which were often extremely intrusive and onerous. For example, in one instance, the IMF ventured so far as to stipulate the appropriate urban property taxes for the borrowing country.[51] IMF packages also tended to be formulaic and insensitive to specific conditions of affected countries and, at times, created more problems than solutions, as happened in Indonesia following the Asian financial crisis. The IMF was criticized also for neglecting the poor in the developing countries and for pursuing economic rationalism with total disregard for the bigger picture.

As crisis manager, IMF played a largely reactive role but the succession of crises, from 1980s onwards, created interest in developing a more robust international financial system. To understand the interest in systemic reform, it is useful to review the basic foundation of the Bretton-Woods system. The founders of the Bretton-Woods regime did not anticipate that national financial deregulation, mandated as desirable in the interest of financial openness, would contribute to the scale of international financial flows that it ultimately did, to the extent that international capital transactions vastly exceed total world trade. The enormity of foreign exchange transactions, only a small portion of which was necessary for trade and investment purposes,[52,e] was facilitated by advanced communications technology which made it possible to shift capital, almost instantaneously, from one country to another to maximize returns. Markets had become sensitive to external events even in the absence of logical connections. For example, in the early 1995, when the Mexican debt crisis resurfaced and the peso slumped, it affected currencies and stock markets in countries that, unlike Mexico, were in sound financial condition. Investors pulled money out of Brazil despite Brazilian reserves of US$43 billion, and East Asian currencies and stock markets were similarly affected despite the unparalleled success of East Asian economies.

Suggestions for controlling speculative capital included a transactions tax, proposed by James Tobin in 1982. He argued that a relatively small transaction tax (small enough not to impact on trade transactions) would be sufficient to deter short-term speculative capital flows and eliminate the major source of exchange rate volatility.[53] Similarly, Will Hutton proposed a concerted approach by the United States, Japan and Germany to create a "…new Bretton Woods system of bracketed but flexible exchange rates, protected against excessive speculative currency flows by some form of turnover tax on financial transactions".[54] However, an effective transaction tax required agreement of all countries, without which any such measure would only lead to the emergence of tax havens. And a global consensus on tax, and remains, was unlikely today.

In 1994, a report by the Bretton-Woods Commission, suggested that a new global monetary regime could be based on policy coordination between the United States, Japan and Germany. It also proposed that IMF exercise general surveillance globally as well as keep exchange rates within a target band to eradicate excessive volatility. Policy coordination, however, is cumbersome and slow, and limited also by the fact that the United States, as noted by Peter Kenen, does not have large foreign currency reserves with which to intervene in currency markets.[55] While systemic policy coordination remains an unfinished project,

---

[e] It is estimated that more than 80 percent of foreign exchange transactions in New York, Tokyo, and London are for speculative gains.

there is support for an expanded surveillance function for the IMF, especially in light of recurring global crises. The Managing Director of the IMF, Michel Camdessus also emphasized the importance of surveillance.[56]

The first task is to ensure transparency of national and international banking regulations and to collect and disseminate relevant data and information to ensure that market decisions are informed and considered. This is necessary to sustain confidence in smooth and effective functioning of capital markets. The Latin American debt crisis was an important source of financial instability and although it led to a more active IMF role in debt management, the repeat of the Mexican crisis in 1995 and the East Asian crisis in 1997, revealed areas where IMF could significantly improve its surveillance function and perform an early warning function. The events underscored the importance of establishing a code of conduct to ensure that member governments adhered to standards of transparency. IMF surveillance can be an important step in international financial stability. According to Manuel Guitian of the IMF, surveillance "...must pinpoint the sources of instability and assign policy responsibilities for their correction to member countries. It is now necessary for all countries to keep their economies on an even keel for not just balances to obtain in each of them, but also to avoid the spillover of disruptions to other countries".[57]

Had the Mexican government been obliged to publish details of its reserve movements and short-term liabilities, financial markets and commercial banks would have been better informed about their exposure in Mexico. The Mexican government, too, might have been forced to take remedial action much earlier. One reason the debt crisis flared up again in 1995 was because there were no established mechanisms to study, identify, and prescribe correctives to potential problems. With better reporting and regulatory transparency, the free-fall of the Mexican Peso against the US dollar might have been averted. Instead, the problem was hidden from view until it assumed crisis proportions. According to Mark Siegel of Putnam Investments, "The reason the marketplace was blindsided in Mexico has everything to do with...an absence of information about day-to-day and week-to-week short-term changes in current account and reserve levels".[58]

The 1995 Mexican crisis indicated that the lessons of earlier debt crises had gone largely unheeded by lending institutions. In the 1970s, commercial lenders to developing countries had failed to assess the net debt exposure of borrowing countries and their capacity to repay. Lack of due diligence encouraged some countries to borrow and spend imprudently which led them to repayment difficulties. The IMF, as a leading lending institution in the 1980s, should have exercised greater surveillance on borrowing countries, including Mexico, and acted sooner to prevent a recurrence of the Mexican debt crisis. If the Mexican crisis of 1995 revealed the inadequacies of global surveillance system, the East Asian debt crisis in 1997 was the evidence of a need to devise crisis prevention strategies, not simply to empower the IMF to manage crises and act as a lender of last resort.

The IMF could also be given additional responsibility for exchange rate stability within target zones. However, for the IMF to participate in capital market interventions to defend exchange rates, it will have to receive a significant boost in funds through increase in members' quota but the ninth quota review, completed in 1990 following lengthy negotiations, provided an increase in quota that was much less than what had been requested by the Fund. In the end the IMF Board of Governors adopted a resolution of increasing members' quota by 50 percent to US$190 billion.[59] This quota increase was related primarily to IMF lending requirements to the East European countries and to the indebted developing countries. For the IMF to undertake the role of defending exchange rates, it will require a greater infusion of funds from the members. In late 1994, the IMF pushed member governments to approve a US$50 billion increase to international reserves through the Special Drawing Rights but this was rejected by the United States, Germany and the United Kingdom as part of an empire-building campaign by Mr. Camdessus and the IMF.

There remain other political impediments to a larger IMF role. It would diminish the lustre of the G7 summits and diminish, also, the authority and responsibility of the respective central banks, especially at a time when central banks themselves have expanded their autonomy and influence. Indeed, the leaders of the G7 countries reacted with hostility to the remarks of the Chairman of the Bretton-Woods Commission.

Following the G7 meeting in Naples in 1994, the joint communique in an obvious reference to the IMF hinted that "some supranational bodies might have outgrown their usefulness — and that it was time to start thinking about building new ones".[60] The IMF can hardly be termed a supranational institution and even the proposed changes would not transform it into a supranational institution, as long as the G7 countries, themselves, remained the arbiter of appropriate exchange rates. The June 1995 G7 summit meeting in Halifax, Canada, included discussions on international monetary reform and the future role of the IMF but, interesting enough, the leaders of the seven countries refused to invite the head of the IMF to their meeting.[61]

The difficulty for the IMF is that it is composed of the member nations and lacks autonomy. It has little capacity to dictate policies to members, unless when countries require IMF assistance for balance of payment reasons. For the IMF to be an effective world central bank, it has to have autonomy and independence but it may take a while before the member states are prepared to contemplate this possibility. Should the IMF move toward becoming an international central banker, it will be a small step away from the possibility of issuing an international currency. Richard Cooper advocated the adoption of a common currency since the "...most effective way to eradicate exchange rate uncertainty is to eradicate exchange rates...".[62] The idea of an international currency, obviating even the need for exchange rates, can only be a long term proposition but the European Union, with its agreement on a common European currency, has shown that it is not unthinkable.

Conclusion

The postwar Bretton-Woods agreement had produced a system of relatively rigid and fixed exchange rates. Its collapse in the early 1970s led to a flexible exchange rate structure, but one which was also volatile. To control volatility, the advanced industrial countries agreed upon policy coordination and intervention to stabilize exchange rates. The new arrangement, unlike the Bretton-Woods regime, promised a combination of flexibility and stability based on periodic policy coordination. To these changes in monetary relations, it is necessary now to add the impact of financial globalization.

The international flow of capital and emergence of a 'borderless economy' have, undoubtedly, complicated the task of economic management. Capital moves freely and quickly between states and industrial production also is organized on a global scale that weakens the extent of national control. Participation in the global economy is certainly advantageous to countries but demands also a sound institutional base and regulatory transparency in order to ensure confidence in national markets. When the IMF was established, it was meant largely to ensure compliance with the fixed exchange rate structure but new conditions demand that IMF become more active in other areas as well. Since the collapse of the Bretton Woods system, IMF has carved out a niche for itself in debt management and the stabilization of international financial relations.

Since the early 1980s, IMF has been intimately involved in providing financial assistance to countries in financial crisis but this aid had strings attached. IMF supported structural adjustment programs were not easy for countries to implement, whether politically, economically, or socially but they had little choice but to submit to conditions that demanded economic liberalization, fiscal balance, privatization, and integration into the global economy. Even if the recipient countries had to endure hardship, IMF had found a reprieve for itself.

However, as the first decade of the new millennium wound to a close, IMF confronted a new challenge to its role in crisis management. Many countries in Latin America and Asia, including three of the four largest borrowers from IMF Argentina, Brazil and Indonesia, fed up with IMF imposed conditionality, have either paid off or are in the process of discharging their debt to IMF and "liberating" themselves from IMF control. With fewer clients borrowing from the IMF, it will be forced to seek out a new alternative role for itself or once again be subject to questions about its relevance in the global political economy.

Chapter Four

INTERNATIONAL DEBT CRISES

S ince the early 1980s, stability of the international banking and financial system has been rocked by a number of international debt crises affecting developing countries, In each of these crises, the IMF played a pivotal role in providing financial assistance for debt repayment in return for structural adjustment measures to stabilize these economies. As a result of its involvement, the IMF successfully carved out a niche for itself in the international financial system following the collapse of the Bretton-Woods system. The flexible exchange rate system contained no role for the IMF and the IMF also was not given any positive function in the system of coordinated market intervention and policy coordination. That task was assumed by the G7 (Group of Seven) meeting of industrialized countries. The IMF had seemingly outlived its mandate but the first debt crisis, in Latin America, gave it a new lease of life.

The consequences of the Latin American crisis set back the developmental objectives of many countries and the 1980s is frequently described as a decade lost to development. Growth in developed OECD countries was also affected where, according to William Cline, the first debt crisis reduced exports by US$14 billion between 1981 and 1982, equivalent to the loss of approximately 350,000 jobs.[1] The immediate response of the international community, and of the IMF to the Latin American debt focused on preserving the western banking system and the stability of international monetary relations. The associated structural adjustment programs were designed to restore long term growth prospects in the crisis affected countries but the IMF did not offer any immediate debt relief to these countries. In this chapter, I will discuss the series of debt crises in terms of the specific causes and international management strategies.

The Latin American Debt Crisis

The Latin American debt crisis began on Friday, August 13, 1982. On that inauspicious day, the Mexican Finance Minister Jesus Silva-Herzog met with Paul Volcker of the US Federal Reserve Bank and bluntly admitted Mexico's inability to meet scheduled debt repayments. The crisis spread to other developing countries, in Latin America, Africa and elsewhere, but not, however, to the developing economies in East Asia. The contagion effect was a feature of other crises that followed. The difficulty in debt servicing (interest payments on accumulated debt) in Latin America was brought on by several factors, including higher interest rates, collapse of commodity prices, poor policy choices by debtor countries, and failings within the international banking community.

The potential for widespread debt default threatened the viability of the international banking community that had, through the 1970s, increased its exposure in the developing countries. More than 80 percent of total third world debt was owed to about 200 western banks, but about half the debt was owed to only 20 banks, seven from the United States, four from the United Kingdom, three from Germany, three from France, two from Japan, and one from Canada. The vulnerability of the major western financial institutions and the attendant potential for serious economic disruption was the key to western strategies designed to prevent debt default.

The debt, referred to as "sovereign debt" because it was incurred by sovereign countries, had been contracted with private bank which were simply recycling surplus dollars accumulated by the Organization of Petroleum Exporting Countries (OPEC) and deposited in western financial institutions. OPEC's surplus liquidity, known as petrodollars, had been boosted by a quadrupling of oil prices following the Arab-Israeli war of 1973.

Prior to the easy availability of petrodollars from commercial banks, assistance to developing countries was given either directly by Western governments or by the two Bretton-Woods institutions. The IMF provided funds, known as program aid, to countries experiencing balance of payment difficulties while the World Bank provided funding for large projects, such as infrastructural developments in the developing countries. IMF loans were conditional loans and borrowing countries were required to implement economic policies that would ensure their ability to meet debt service obligations. Typically this meant restructuring the economy toward export markets rather than domestic consumption, and an emphasis on macroeconomic stability through spending cutbacks and budgetary restrictions. The immediate outcome usually was higher unemployment and inflation, and a general economic crisis, involving labor unrest and militancy. In the Philippines such a crisis had led to the collapse of democracy and imposition of martial law by President Marcos in September 1972. Not surprisingly, IMF loans were not looked upon with much favor by developing countries.

Escape from IMF conditionality came in the 1970s when private sector capital flows to developing countries dwarfed IMF and other official aid programs. Western commercial banks became agents for recycling 'petrodollars'. They targeted developing countries partly because growth in developed countries had slowed and there was insufficient demand to absorb the available liquidity. On the other hand, growth prospects in the middle-income developing countries looked promising. Banks did not regard such loans as risky because of the perceived negligible risk of loan default. For instance, Walter B. Wriston, Chairman of Citicorp, was fond of repeating that "Sovereign nations don't go broke".[2]

Commercial banks were reassured also by the knowledge that international loan losses were only a small proportion of their total nonperforming loans. For the 10 largest American banks, international net loan losses were only 0.10 percent of average international loans in 1980 and constituted only 15 percent of total losses incurred by these banks. Consequently, foreign lending was not considered very risky. Moreover, as Wiarda suggests, if bankers did, in fact, recognize the riskiness of loans, they were also convinced that the US government would be obliged to bail them out and not risk a collapse of the banking sector, much as it had bailed out saving and loan banks in the early 1980s. Still, they were selective in their lending programs. Banks lent mainly to the rich Latin American and Asian countries rather than to the poorer African and South

Asian countries, which were a riskier proposition. The primary risk, nonetheless, was defined in political terms as unwillingness to repay, rather than inability to repay. The debt crisis, however, demonstrated that countries, like firms and individuals, could also become insolvent.

With relatively easy lending available to them, developing countries accumulated debt at a rapid rate through the 1970s. They were encouraged to borrow in a regime of high inflation and low interest rates, which meant that the real cost of borrowing and interest payments were small and negligible. For some countries, the real cost of borrowing was negative because developed countries were reflating their way out of the global recession. For the period 1977–1982, the real interest rate in Bolivia was −10.1 percent and that for Ghana was −32.8 percent, which meant that borrowing, instead of incurring interest costs was actually profitable.[a] Low interest payment on sovereign loans probably encouraged the developing countries to borrow more than they would have if the cost of borrowing had been higher. Total LDC debt increased from US$167 billion in 1977 to US$248 billion in 1979 and to about US$400 billion in the critical year of 1982. Some of the largest debtor countries in 1982 were Brazil (US$93 billion), Mexico (US$86 billion), Argentina (US$44 billion), Venezuela (US$32 billion) and the Philippines (US$25 billion). Total accumulated debt would not have become a problem if borrowing had been directed to project development and other productive purposes. But borrowing, instead, sustained a conspicuous consumption and import pattern. In Mexico, for example, the import bill increased from US$6 billion in 1977 to US$23 billion in 1981. Moreover, the lending institutions had little information of how the loans were being employed and were unaware, even, of the total debt burden of each debtor country. East Asian countries, like South Korea, also increased their debt liabilities through the 1970s but avoided the Latin American contagion by investing in productive activities to generate export revenue. This enabled them to keep debt servicing to manageable proportions.

---

[a] The average real interest rate on sovereign loans during the period 1974–1978 was only half a percent per year and this increased to more than 7 percent in 1981 and 1982. Real interest rate is defined as the London Interbank Offer Rate (LIBOR) on three month US Dollar deposits less the rate of change of the GNP deflator in the United States.

Table 4.1:   Debt indicators of 15 heavily indebted countries.

	1970–1979	1980	1981	1982	1983
Total debt (US$b)	97.5	271.1	332.4	380.1	395.9
Debt service (% of exports)	26.0	29.4	38.9	49.8	39.9

Source: *World Economic Outlook* (October 1988, p. 40).

Debt servicing involves payment of interest on loans, in foreign currency, and requires a debtor country to generate sufficient export revenue to finance both its import requirements and interest payment on loans. It is commonly assumed that a safe level of external debt means a debt servicing ratio of no more than 25 percent of export revenue. Table 4.1 is indicative of the magnitude of the debt problem for the fifteen heavily indebted countries.

Causes of the Latin American Debt Crisis

Causes of the debt crisis might be separately classified as those originating within developing countries and those beyond their control, such as the rapid increase in real interest rates, which increased their debt servicing burdens. As far as conditions within the developing countries were concerned, a main factor was misuse of funds and government policies that encouraged a pattern of conspicuous domestic consumption rather than productive investment. In turn, the crisis reinforced perceptions that developing countries were steeped in structural impediments to growth and development and that restoration of financial solvency and economic growth required structural reform and adjustment.

Externally, in the late 1970s, several factors combined to end the relatively comfortable position of indebted developing countries. These included the second oil crisis of 1979, fall of the Shah in Iran, and renewed attempts to control inflation in the West.

The Iranian revolution and the second oil crisis were an indication that market stability was fragile. Uncertainty made lenders more cautious and while loans were still available, loan terms were shortened. Consequently for developing countries, loan repayments became bunched together and this affected their ability to meet payment obligations.

The low cost of borrowing was possible only as long as inflation remained high. In 1979, however, the Federal Reserve Bank in the United States tightened monetary policy to bring inflationary pressures under control. Great Britain introduced a similarly restrictive monetary policy. These measures were successful but in the process the cost of borrowing went up. An upward drift in American prime lending rate and the London Interbank Offer Rate (LIBOR)[b] directly affected the cost of debt servicing. Problems for developing countries were compounded by the fact that loans had been contracted at floating interest rates. For example, Brazil, Argentina, and Mexico, had floating rate debt that was in excess of 75 percent of their total debt. This meant interest rates at market prices and as the US tightened monetary policies, market interest rates went up. Some countries, however, ignored the risks of high interest rates. Mexico, for example, confident that its oil wealth would enable it to make timely repayments, continued to borrow into the early 1980s. In 1981 alone, it added US$21 billion to its total debt. Moreover, the high interest rate policy in the United States and elsewhere, encouraged business to run down inventory levels because it was more costly to hold inventories when interest rates were high. The reduction of inventory levels initiated a collapse of commodity prices. In turn, this had an adverse effect on export revenue of developing countries and worsened their capacity to service existing debts.

Progressively through the 1970s, the ability of developing countries to service their debt was undermined also by increasing protectionism in developed countries that made it harder to maintain the same export and revenue profile.

Finally, the Falklands War, which began in April 1992 when Argentina invaded the Falkland Islands to wrest control from Britain also contributed to the debt crisis as other Latin American countries, like Venezuela, in a show of support for Argentina, switched deposits out of

---

[b] LIBOR is the rate used between the banks when they provide loans in Eurocurrencies to each other. Lending to developing countries is usually at rates that are 2–3 percentage points higher than the LIBOR rates. It has been estimated that, given total accumulated debt, a one percent increase in LIBOR directly translated to an additional US$850 million in interest payment for Brazil and US$790 million for Mexico.

bank in London. In retaliation, the British government urged banks to reassess risks across the continent which, given that most Latin American countries already had a poor liquidity position and high accumulated debt levels, resulted in a general downgrading of their credit ratings.[c] As credit ratings fell, applicable interest rates went up and this affected Mexico the hardest because, in the interest of securing lower interest rates, it had opted for shorter maturity periods. Mexico had relied on its ability to roll over existing loans but when credit rating was downgraded, it became harder to refinance existing loans on equally favourable terms.

In August 1982, Mexico was forced to seek international help in meeting its debt repayment obligations. This resulted in a two-fold crisis, one for developing countries and another for lending financial institutions. Most analysts agreed that the debt crisis had the potential to seriously undermine international financial stability if it led to large-scale collapse of major western banks. To stave off global financial meltdown, it was necessary to ensure that developing countries continued to service their debt. Debt write-off was unacceptable because of the precedent it would establish and also because banks did not have sufficient loan loss provisions to undertake debt forgiveness. For developing countries, the only real solution was debt relief and debt forgiveness but this did not happen until much later. The IMF, as manager of the Latin American debt crisis and others that followed, was seemingly more intent on averting global financial collapse and instability and less concerned with consequences for individual crisis countries. Its programs were onerous for developing countries but commercial banks were spared the consequence of their own poor lending decisions.

Given the policy objective of protecting lending institutions and global financial stability, the strategies employed by the IMF and western governments sought primarily to restore debtor countries to acceptable levels of solvency. The fact that this was also a crisis of development was a secondary concern. It mattered even less that the involvement of western governments highlighted a policy contradiction. These governments intervened in capital markets in violation of market principles to save institutions that 'deserved' to go bankrupt while insisting that debtor

---

[c] Credit rating is important in securing new loans or to roll over existing loans.

countries transition to a more market-oriented economic structure as the best remedy to revive growth and ease debt servicing problems.

Debt Management Strategies

To deal with the Latin American crisis, western governments adopted, sequentially, three separate debt management strategies. These were the Mexican Model; the Baker Plan; and the Brady Plan. Apart from management strategies at the official level, commercial banks also introduced various measures, like debt swaps and debt discounting, to deal with the crisis and these will be considered further below. The distinction between official and private sector responses is somewhat arbitrary since many of the official initiatives also included specific steps to be taken by commercial banks.

The Mexican Model

The Mexican model was a case-by-case approach to debt management, beginning with Mexico and later applied to other debtor countries. Within two days of the Mexican notification that it was unable to keep up interest payment, the United States arranged an emergency assistance package of US$4 billion, with US$3 billion coming from the United States, of which US$2 billion was advance payment for purchase of oil from Mexico and the balance comprised of bridging loans from a group of central bankers. This was a short term package to ensure that Mexico kept up interest payment but the United States also forced Mexico to negotiate with the IMF for long term credit arrangement. On November 10 of that year, agreement was reached between the Mexican government and the IMF for a credit line of US$3.84 billion for the period 1983–1985, in return for strict austerity measures. The IMF conditions included:

- *Fiscal discipline*: reduction of public expenditure from the 1982 figure of 16.5 percent of GDP to 8.5 percent of GDP in 1983 to 5.9 percent in 1984 and down to 3.5 percent in 1985.
- *Liberalization of the economy*: Mexico had maintained a protectionist import substitution industrialization strategy which undermined its

export potential by keeping import prices and prices of intermediate imported inputs high. Liberalization, it was believed, would enhance export competitiveness and increase export revenue, much as had happened in the East Asian economies.

*   *Elimination of new state investment plans*: including an increase the prices of goods and services in the public sector. The government also had to negotiate with commercial banks for debt rescheduling, i.e. arrangements to stretch out interest repayment and extend maturity of loans to lessen the repayment burden.

The bailout package negotiated for Mexico established a central role for IMF in future debt management. Although the debt was owed to commercial banks, these banks refused to reschedule debts without prior agreement between the debtor countries and the IMF on domestic economic restructuring, which would presumably enhance their capacity to repay. The role of IMF was central because commercial banks, themselves, could not presume to impose conditions on sovereign countries. In 1982–1983, 39 countries negotiated structural adjustment agreements with the IMF. Table 4.2 gives the number of such agreements concluded on a yearly basis between 1983 and 1989.

The decline in IMF involvement was not necessarily an indication of a general improvement in the debt position of developing countries but rather a reflection of difficulties debtor countries faced in complying with IMF conditions. Even Mexico was unable to meet its obligations and

Table 4.2:   Debt rescheduling agreements.

Year	Number of countries
1983	20
1984	17
1985	16
1986	12
1987	17
1988	10
1989	9

Source: International Capital Markets (1990).

withdrew in 1985. The austerity conditions demanded by the IMF seriously strained domestic political legitimacy of governments that had bought popular support through profligate spending. Usually they found ways around the austerity conditions. For example, in 1985 under the watchful eyes of visiting IMF delegates, the Mexican government retrenched 50,000 public sector employees, but then rehired 35,000 of them in the next few weeks when it thought no one was looking, and by the end of the year had found ways to put the rest — and more patronage persons besides — back on the public payroll.[3] Miles Kahler correctly summed it up by stating that "Latin American elites were restorationists not reformers".[4]

It was ironic that strict fiscal austerity induced economic deflation and low growth at a time when the debtor countries required high growth rates to repay their debts. Structural adjustment, however, was considered essential to restore viable long-term growth even at the risk of short-term difficulties. Fiscal austerity also resulted in higher unemployment and lower wage levels. For example, between 1982 and 1987, real wages in Mexico declined by 51 percent. The weakness of IMF conditionality was that it left the overall debt burden of debtor countries unchanged and, moreover, threatened to unleash domestic political instability.

There was no provision for debt reduction or forgiveness, nor was there any, even temporary, debt relief. Western governments and lending institutions enforced loan conditions to avert a crisis of confidence in the international financial structure. For them, the debt crisis would *become* a crisis only if the developing countries either repudiated or were granted a reprieve from their contractual obligations. Developing countries remonstrated for relief but failed to convince their creditors. In June 1984, the Cartegna Declaration, issued by 11 Latin American countries following a meeting in Cartegna, Colombia urged a fair resolution of the crisis, including deferral of interest payment without penalty to the debtor countries. This was a modest proposal for relief until their economic situation had improved to enable full repayment of debt. However, debt relief did not become a part of the western strategies until the late 1980s.

The Baker Plan

The Baker plan was announced by US Treasury Secretary James Baker at a joint IMF–World Bank meeting in Seoul in October 1985. The plan was not markedly different from the Mexican model. It, too, relied on a case-by-case approach but give the World Bank a greater role in helping the poorest debtor countries of Africa. It also acknowledged US governmental responsibility in managing the debt crisis and while the plan did not include significant financial outlays, was an important transitional stage to a more comprehensive approach, the Brady Plan. The Plan, at least acknowledged that austerity and slowdown of economic growth were not the answers to the difficulties in debt servicing and, instead, emphasis shifted to measures promoting growth. The three main principles of the Baker plan required:

- Debtor countries to implement macroeconomic and structural policies to promote growth, reduce inflation, and become more export competitive.
- The IMF to remain the central player but financial aid to be provided by other development banks as well.
- Increased lending by commercial banks.

As before the Baker plan rejected debt reduction because it would undermine the return to credit worthiness of the debtor countries. Instead, stretching out repayment was believed sufficient to restore prosperity. Debt forgiveness also was not considered seriously because it would make private lending institutions wary of loans to sovereign countries, at a time when there was high demand for such funds in Eastern Europe and Russia and which the Western governments wanted to encourage. The Baker plan ran for three years and called for additional new bank loans of US$20 billion. A total of 15 debtor countries participated in the Baker plan scheme and had to introduce drastic domestic structural adjustment.

The Brady Plan

The Brady plan was announced by new US Treasury Secretary, Nicholas Brady, in March 1989. The main architect of the plan was David Mulford, under Secretary of the Treasury who, earlier, as Assistant Secretary of the Treasury had also helped draft the Baker plan. Mulford embraced the idea of debt relief, which he had previously dismissed as "bonehead".[5]

The plan reflected a belated acceptance by the United States that the debt problem could not be approached simply at the technical level of ensuring short-term debt servicing by the developing countries and required hard political decisions to reduce overall debt levels in order to create conditions for economic growth. It had become obvious that existing arrangements were not producing the desired result. The plan also mirrored concern for the future of fledgling democracies in Latin America. The year 1989 not only began a new administration in the United States but also witnessed the installation of new governments in Mexico and Venezuela, and democratic elections in Argentina, Brazil, Chile and Uruguay. Debt reduction, in this context, was one way of strengthening incipient democracies in Latin America. These countries, in turn, used their democratic transition as a bargaining chip to obtain more advantageous debt management strategies. As emerging democracies, they felt that insistence on strict austerity and repayment of debt in full would alienate a newly empowered electorate and jeopardise the survival of democratic regimes. President Garcia, in September 1985, stated very bluntly that, "We are faced with a dramatic choice: it is either debt or democracy".[6]

Until 1988, commercial loans contracted by developing countries were being fully serviced but financed by the IMF and other multilateral development banks. This was at a time when the commercial banks had shown, by their actions, a readiness to accept losses on their loans by increasing loan loss reserves. On May 19, 1987 Citicorp led other commercial banks in announcing an addition of US$3 billion to its loan-loss reserve fund to cover possible losses on its sovereign debt of US$14 billion. This signalled the banking community's willingness to write down assets (loans) and it, also, enhanced their capacity to resist arm-twisting by the Treasury or the Federal Reserve to provide new loans.

Rather than simply continue to provide new loans, the banks, enabled by their own loan-loss provisions, added debt-discounting to their debt-conversion strategies. Prior to this, the more common practice was to exchange debt in the form of a straight asset swap, with no discount on the face value. The two were no longer mutually exclusive and combined debt-conversion and debt-reduction strategies included debt-for-equity swaps, debt-for-nature swaps, and debt-for development swaps. By engaging in debt discounting, the banks demonstrated a readiness to accept losses by selling their loans to other institutions at discounts of, as much as, 20 cents to the dollar. The benefit of this type of debt-discounting, however, did not always flow back to the developing countries, because they could still be required to service their debts as before.

The Brady Plan emphasized debt reduction and relief for the developing countries was to reduce both the outstanding debt and the interest payable. More specifically, it was expected that commercial banks would cut about US$70 billion of the US$340 billion owed to them by 39 developing countries and that the banks would also reduce by US$20 billion the total interest that they would be owed over the next three years. It was anticipated that only those countries that had initiated structural adjustment to improve economic efficiency would qualify for consideration under the Brady Plan. Actual debt reduction ranged from 23 percent of present value to about 35 percent. For Peter Kenen, however, even the higher estimate was insufficient debt relief and he advocated approximately 50 percent as the desirable rate for debt reduction.[7] Robert Wesson went a step further and argued for totally abolishing all debt. He wrote that "If as acknowledged by the Brady Plan, it would be a good idea to cut it [debt] by 20%, it is a better idea to cut it more. *Any capital transfer from the Third World is undesirable. That is, the debt should be abolished*".[8]

By 1992 debt reduction packages had been completed for six countries — Mexico, Costa Rica, Nigeria, the Philippines, Uruguay and Venezuela; and their debt was reduced by about two-fifths of the total, or US$38 billion in present value terms.[9] Overall, the plan brought only modest improvement to the debt financing difficulties of the debtor countries.

In the meantime, commercial banks, reluctant to submit to regulation by national authorities, developed innovative measures to deal with the debt problem through market mechanisms. One such innovation was debt-for-development swap which involved discounted sale or donation of debt to charitable institutions which, in turn, could swap it with the debtor country for payment in local currency. Such swaps were established in

1987 and examples include the Bank of America (BOA) announcement that it would donate up to US$6 million, over a three year period, to Conservation International and the *World Wildlife Fund*, to fund debt-for-development swaps in Latin America. The BOA gift was specifically earmarked for rain forest conservation and required the environmental organizations to swap the debt with governments at 100 percent of the face value, but in local currency.[10]

Critics of the Brady plan inveighed against the fact that it contained no enforcement mechanism. Indeed, commercial banks were not compelled to participate. The creditor institutions could simply endorse it without taking concrete actions and as already mentioned, banks were not favorably disposed to the objective of debt reduction. More seriously, it left open the possibility of some banks "free riding" on the efforts of other financial institutions. The free rider problem presented itself because debt reduction was voluntary and banks that held out could improve their net position after other banks had entered into debt buyback schemes. The objective of the Brady plan was to reduce total debt so as to ensure that the remaining debt was at least repayable. To the extent that the remaining debt was repayable, debtor countries also improved their credit rating and credit worthiness. Credit worthiness can be conceptualized as a public good that would benefit all credit agencies regardless of whether or not the costs had been socialized. As such, if, however, some creditor institutions chose to hold out and not participate in buyback schemes, they could potentially be in a better position than before, even though they had not borne any of the costs of the buyback mechanism. Apart from the free rider problem, another flaw of the debt buyback scheme was that it was not universally advantageous to the debtor country, especially if the debt buyback was only partial and did not include total outstanding debt. This and the free rider problem can be illustrated through the Bolivian debt buyback scheme.

Total Bolivian debt in early 1988 were US$670 million and in March of that year the Bolivian government used US$34 million of its own resources plus donated resources from Spain, the Netherlands and Brazil to buy back $308 million of total debt at a discount of 11 cents to the dollar. Total remaining debt was reduced to $362 million but as Rogoff explains, the entire scheme was of dubious merit, as far as Bolivia was concerned Table 4.3.

Table 4.3: The 1988 Bolivian debt buyback.

	Before buyback	After buyback
Secondary market price times	0.06 cents	0.11 cents
Debt outstanding equals	$670 million	$362 million
Total market value	$40.2 million	$39.8 million
Total benefit to Bolivia	=$40.2–$39.8	=$0.4 million

Source: Rogoff (1992).

The net result of the buyback deal was that Bolivia had used 34 million dollars to secure debt relief of only 400 thousand dollars. Bolivia, Rogoff argued, would have been unambiguously better off if it could have bought back all of its $670 million debt for $40.2 million ($670 million × 0.06 cents = $40.2 million). The partial debt buyback offered no significant real debt relief to Bolivia. The above example also illustrated the free rider problem where creditors, before the buyback, could only expect to receive six cents to the dollar but, after the buyback, could expect to receive 11 cents because Bolivia was now assumed to have improved its credit worthiness, regardless of whether or not they participated in the buyback scheme.

Apart from the practical inefficiencies of the system, debt reduction and bailout were criticized also for benefiting mainly the Highly Indebted Countries which, in 1987, had an average per capital annual income of US$1430 and, therefore, undeserving of the limited pool of international capital for development purposes. Critics argued that it was morally indefensible to bankroll the relatively rich at the expense of the deserving needy, and to allow aid decisions to be straight jacketed by decisions of commercial banks in 1970s. Under the Brady Plan, about US$30–40 billion was pledged by the West and multilateral institutions for debt buyback purposes when the poorer countries of Asia and Africa were in much greater need of these funds.

The Latin American debt crisis festered for a decade during which time many of the countries made little or no headway in promoting development or overcoming national poverty. Indeed, the decade of 1980s is usually considered as a decade lost to development. The debtor countries bore the brunt of western debt management strategies while the creditor institutions were protected from the fallout of their poor lending decisions.

The 1994 Mexican Debt Crisis

In late 1994, Mexico reignited the fuse of another debt crisis when a sharp collapse of the Mexican currency spread fears default of debt. Several factors contributed to the crisis, including the rapid appreciation of the Peso. Between 1990 and 1994, the real value of the Peso had appreciated approximately 20 percent and eroded the country's international export position. The crisis was also a result of political instability. In January 1994, the Zapatista rebels launched an uprising in the state of Chiapas and in March the presidential candidate of the ruling party was assassinated at a political rally. These were indicators of social problems and inequalities, and contributed to a climate of uncertainty for international investors.

In the period before the crisis, fooled by deceptive information and data released by the Mexican government that painted a rosier picture of the economy than warranted, foreign capital flows into Mexico had increased sharply.[11] Mexico was touted as Latin America's miracle economy but, according to Sebastian Edwards, this was an 'invented' miracle.[12] Capital inflows reached 10 percent of the GDP in 1993 and fuelled expansionary credit, excessive consumption and increasing current account deficits. On December 20, the Mexican government announced plans for a controlled devaluation of the Peso by 13 percent. Markets, however, were not convinced that such a devaluation, after years of determined resistance to currency realignment, could be executed.

The problem was that by the time of the announcement, the Mexican government had already depleted its foreign reserves and had little fighting fund to manage a controlled devaluation. An overvalued Peso together with political uncertainties within Mexico encouraged domestic capital flight and eroded the international reserve base of the central bank. Instead of a controlled devaluation, the currency collapsed from 3.45 to 5.57 Peso Dollar in early January 1995, a devaluation of more than 60 percent. The devaluation was a positive development for exporters in Mexico but added to their debt servicing difficulties. This was compounded by the fact that approximately US$17 billion of the debt was to mature within the next six months.[13]

As in the earlier crisis, the US government quickly announced plans to extend large-scale loan guarantees to the Mexican government. However, with uncertainty over whether the US Congress would approve the plan to provide US$40 billion in loan guarantees, President Clinton by-passed the Congress and promised US$20 billion from the US currency stabilization fund and also committed the Bank of International Settlement and the IMF for additional loan guarantees of nearly US$30 billion. The European leaders were displeased at the lack of adequate prior consultation but, nonetheless, agreed that decisive action was necessary to avert a repeat of the debt crisis.

Mexico recovered quick and was assisted also by easy access to the US market as a result of the North American Free Trade Agreement (NAFTA) which came into effect in 1994 and liberalized trade between US, Canada and Mexico. According to Nora Lustig, one indicator of NAFTA's role Mexican recovery was that the "average rate of growth of Mexican exports to the United States was more than 10 percentage points higher after 1994 than in the period 1991–1993".[14]

The East Asian Currency Crisis of 1997

At the time of the Latin American debt crisis, the contrast with East Asia was striking. Many of these countries, too, had high debt levels but still managed to keep debt service ratios to within manageable limits by pursuing export oriented growth strategies to generate adequate foreign exchange revenues. Very simply, the debt crisis of 1982 was seen as a vindication of export oriented industrialization (the East Asian model) and a castigation of import substitution industrialization (the Latin American model). Bolstered by economic success through the 1980s, these countries continued to benefit from readily available investment capital from overseas to sustain and boost economic growth. This private sector capital inflow continued unabated through the mid-1990s. Unlike the Latin American sovereign debt, East Asian debt was owed mainly by the private sector.

Foreign capital supplemented domestic savings that was high by international standards, but insufficient to meet domestic investment needs. A significant portion of this capital inflow was short term which, in Thailand, accounted to as much as five percent of GDP during 1994–1996.[15] The attraction of short-term lending was that it carried less risk for creditors and lower interest rates for borrowers. The danger, of course, was that any loss of investor confidence would reverse capital inflow and make it difficult to either rollover existing debt or to meet debt service obligations.

In the lead-up to the debt crisis, most accounts presented a glowing picture of development and industrialization in East Asia. A World Bank report, prepared a few years earlier, referred to these as 'miracle economies' because of their sustained and equitable economic growth. The World Bank attributed this miracle to good macroeconomic policies and selective state intervention in the economy to channel investment to growth industries or to compensate for periodic market failures. That state intervention had been beneficial was an important and controversial acknowledgment, especially in the context of dominant economic theories and the principles that underpinned World Bank and IMF structural adjustment programs. However, World Bank did add the note of caution that state intervention in Southeast Asia was often less constructive than in Northeast Asia.[16]

A somewhat less glorious explanation was provided by Paul Krugman, who argued that there had been no miracle because the East Asian growth cycle was premised simply on factor input growth rather than productivity growth. Denying that the East Asian had achieved a miracle, he argued that once, "one accounts for the role of rapidly growing inputs in these countries' growth, one finds little left to explain".[17] The conclusions reached by Krugman generated considerable controversy but it needs to be reiterated that the East Asian miracle was not simply in achieving high growth but rather growth with equity. Despite the controversy sparked by Krugman, the mood of optimism about East Asian growth remained strong.

Few detected any signs of serious troubles on the horizon. In a report released in 1997, but before the Asian currency crisis could be factored in, the World Bank sounded a positive note on the East Asian lending situation. It pointed out that, unlike Mexico, countries like Indonesia, the Philippines, and Thailand had been able to avert a banking crisis because of their sound macroeconomic fundamentals.[18]

The rapidity with which the economic miracle was reduced to a meltdown also raised questions about the role of governments in achieving economic growth. The crisis, blamed partly on political mismanagement, undermined the credibility of arguments supportive of state intervention in the market. But rather than dismiss government intervention as always detrimental, it may be sufficient to caution about periodic government failure.

The East Asian crisis was triggered by a dramatic loss of investor confidence. This reversed capital flows and resulted in sharp currency devaluation. The countries most severely affected were Malaysia, Thailand, Indonesia and South Korea. The collapse of Korea was spectacular because it, together with Taiwan, Hong Kong and Singapore, was one of the original newly industrializing country and widely recognized as an East Asian success story. Interestingly, while South Korea was gripped in currency turmoil, Taiwan remained relatively unaffected by the conflagration raging around it. In 1997, the decline in the value of the Taiwan currency was modest and its stock exchange was the only major Asian market to post a gain for the year.[19] Consistent with what we would expect from a capital surplus countries, the private sector in Taiwan had low exposure to foreign debt and this fact, by itself, ensured that Taiwan would escape the worst of the debt crisis. Another advantage for Taiwan was that its industrial structure was dominated by small firms which had less access to foreign capital than the large *chaebols* in South Korea. With limited access to 'easy' foreign capital, investment decisions tended to be more prudent and this may have enabled the private sector to avert the trap of fanciful investments indulged in by some of the other East Asian countries. Taiwan also had an efficient capital market to channel savings to potential investors and, importantly, large foreign exchange reserves to resist speculative pressures on the local currency.

In hindsight, we can say that profligate spending and a bubble economy with inflated asset prices could not continue indefinitely but a climate of economic optimism had inured East Asian governments and foreign investors to the potential dangers. They had become accustomed to high economic growth and could not imagine the possibility of a drastic slowdown or reversal. Foreign investors continued to pour additional liquidity into these countries. And, as in the earlier Latin American debt

crisis, foreign debt in East Asia was being used increasingly for speculative investment in real estate, show-piece developments, and luxury and
conspicuous consumption. Instead of market discipline, countries, like
Indonesia, descended into crony capitalism, where political cronies and
family members of President Suharto were permitted lucrative monopo-
lies. This did not bode well for future debt servicing requirements and
they could not, of course, factor in the Chinese currency devaluation in
1994. The large devaluation of the Yuan boosted China's export competitiveness relative to other East Asian countries. It led to an export boom
and substantial increases in Chinese trade surpluses, US$40 billion in
1997, and a concomitant deterioration of the trade position of other East
Asian economies. Moreover, with local currencies tied to the US Dollar,
East Asian economic prospects were affected by an appreciation of the US
Dollar that undermined their export competitiveness. Trade surpluses
turned into deficits. In 1993, for example, South Korea had a modest current account surplus of US$385 million but the surplus turned into a
deficit of $453 million in 1994 and a deficit of $23,716 million in 1996.
At the same time, its external debt increased from $78.4 billion in 1995 to
$104.7 billion in 1996.[20] In 1996, Thailand's current account deficit was
eight percent of GDP, that of Malaysia was 5.5 percent and Indonesia had
a deficit of more than four percent. Nonetheless, while external factors,
such as appreciation of the US Dollar, devaluation of the Chinese Yuan,
and increase in global interest rates, contributed to the crisis, the role of
domestic political corruption and cronyism, and economic mismanagement should not be underestimated. In the backdrop of misspent debt
and worsening trade outlook, news that Japan was about to raise interest
rates helped trigger the crisis by exacerbating serviceability concerns. This
induced capital flight from the region. Capital flight from the five worst-
affected Asian economies (South Korea, Indonesia, Thailand, Malaysia
and the Philippines) amounted to US$12 billion in 1997 compared to an
inflow of $97 billion in 1996.[21] This capital shift of $105 billion represented 11 percent of their collective GDP and was a strong vote of no-
confidence in the affected regional economies.

     As capital flight set in, speculators added to pressure on local curren-
cies. It is estimated that speculative investors and hedge funds, had, at the

time, approximately US$100 billion at their disposal and that this could be leveraged by several multiples to launch speculative attacks on currencies.[22] Speculative capital and hedge fund managers saw an opportunity to profit from the gathering dark clouds but the Prime Minister of Malaysia added a conspirational motive to speculative capitalists. He singled out George Soros as leading this band of capitalists and intent on punishing non-democratic East Asian regimes by undermining economic growth and political stability. This conspiracy theory was fanciful but steps taken by the Malaysian government to embargo capital flight out of the country helped stabilize the situation in Malaysia sooner than other regional countries which went through a tortured process of structural adjustment reforms under the guidance of the IMF.

The first country to experience speculative pressures on its currency was Thailand. Prior to the onset of capital flight, Thailand had been gripped in a strong bubble economy fuelled by speculative real estate and equity investments. Several years earlier, the Thai government had set up an off-shore banking facility, the Bangkok Interbank Facility (BIBF) to provide investment capital to countries of Indo-China since they could not access such capital in their own capacity. However, as Indo-Chinese countries normalized relations with the United States, their reliance on Thailand as a conduit of investment capital declined and the off-shore banking facility that has been structured as an in–out facility (bringing *in* foreign capital and lending it *out* to Indo-China) became an in–in facility to fuel speculative investments within Thailand. But once market sentiment had turned sour, investors withdrew. The Thai Baht came under pressure in early May 1997 and this was followed by similar pressure on other regional currencies. As currencies tumbled, East Asian governments intervened extensively in capital market in defense of pegged exchange rates. The Central Bank of Thailand lost US$30 billion in foreign reserves in a failed attempt to shore up the value of the Baht and having depleted its reserves, the government of Thailand abandoned its defense of a pegged exchange rate in early July 1997. As a result the Thai Baht devalued sharply.

The crisis in Thailand spread to surrounding countries, of Indonesia, Malaysia, and the Philippines. As the contagion spread, currencies tumbled.

For example, the Indonesian Rupiah declined from a pre-crisis rate of around 2,500 to 17,000 against the US dollar in January 1998. This had a severe impact on the capacity of borrowers to service their debt or to finance the import of intermediate goods necessary for their export industries.

The East Asian currency meltdown again resulted in an extensive bailout operation led by the IMF. The IMF had assisted Mexico in its 1994 crisis, in what is widely acclaimed as a success since Mexico was able to repay its debt to the IMF ahead of schedule. In East Asia, IMF stepped into the breach with extensive aid packages for South Korea, Thailand, and Indonesia totalling US$109 billion. In return, each of these countries were forced to accept strict austerity measures, cut subsidies on key commodities, and pursue greater economic deregulation and liberalization. IMF conditions came under some criticism on grounds that the directives went beyond what was required to manage a currency crisis. It was certainly understandable that IMF should require greater openness and transparency in financial regulations and greater liberalization of the banking sector but it was not plainly obvious how, for instance, the demand for tariff reduction in auto industry or the abolition of the Clove Marketing Board in Indonesia might help stablilze the Indonesian currency. As far as critics were concerned, the IMF was simply exploiting an opportunity to bring about massive changes in the economic structure of affected countries. In defence of IMF conditionality, it might be said that if liberalization did result in more reasonable investment policy decisions and abandonment of investments in for example a national car industry that had more to do with prestige than economic rationality, then it was a step in the right direction toward sustainable economic growth. Indeed, the IMF was prepared to admit that its reform conditions in this debt crisis were markedly different from IMF conditions in the 1980s, which had relied extensively on austerity measures. In East Asia, the objectives of reforms were to change domestic business practices, corporate culture and government behavior. The IMF justified its reform agenda as necessarily harsher and more far-reaching in order to restore market confidence and return these economies to viability.[23]

The Korean government also negotiated extensions on $24 billion of short-term loans with 13 creditor banks in order to ease its debt service burden. More importantly, the new loan conditions were not harsh.

Initially, the creditor institutions insisted on an interest rate of at least 12 percent per annum for new loans while the Korean government argued that the interest rates should be less than 8.6 percent. In the end, the two sides agreed on new loans at around 8.4 percent. The low interest rate meant considerable savings for Korea since a difference of just one percent on debt of around $25 billion implied savings of around $250 million annually.[24]

The IMF reform and austerity conditions imposed considerable hardship on the people because the effect of reforms was to significantly lower the levels of economic activity. From example, before the crisis, in May 1997, the IMF had predicted a 1997 GDP growth rate of 7.4 percent and 7.0 percent for Indonesia and Thailand, respectively, but soon afterwards growth forecasts for 1997 were lowered to 2.0 percent and zero for these two countries. The IMF, however, forecast a higher growth rate of 6.0 percent for South Korea, up from 5.6 percent, despite the financial crisis. This was perhaps because the South Korean crisis was managed very quickly and effectively by restructuring the country's debt.

The crisis was expected to have major long-term consequences for the affected countries, though perhaps not as severe as that confronted by the Latin American countries in the 1980s. The ambitious developmental objectives were the first obvious victims of the crisis and it became quickly obvious that Malaysia was unlikely to achieve the status of a developed economy by the year 2020, as envisioned in "Vision 2020".

In Indonesia, with the burden of adjustment falling heavily on the most disadvantaged groups in society, there was considerable domestic violence and unrest. People vented their frustration and anger against the long established dictatorial regime of President Suharto. Here, economic crisis became a political crisis and opposition forces rallied the people to demand change and an end to the system of political patronage and corruption that had allowed family members and close associates to obtain lucrative economic deals from the state. IMF conditionality in Indonesia threatened the welfare of political cronies and family members of Suharto because the IMF demanded economic reforms, transparency of regulations, and policies to end anti-competitive practices within the Indonesian economy. The dilemma for President Suharto was that it was impossible to safeguard family interests while advancing the national interest. The Indonesian government resisted scaling back several of the mega-projects in order to protect financial interests of the ruling and business elite, even though it was now obvious that these projects were not viable.

As the government dragged its feet on reforms, it further undermined international market confidence and renewed speculative pressures on the Indonesian currency. The Rupiah continued to free-fall and this only added to domestic inflationary pressures and economic hardship, as well as exacerbating debt servicing difficulties. The government toyed with the idea of re-pegging the currency at a much more favorable exchange rate and announced, in mid-February 1998, a plan to establish a Currency Stabilization Board. The intention was to provide relief to local debtors and to political cronies but was immediately dismissed by IMF and the international community, because any attempt to re-peg exchange rates would invite the same currency speculation that had triggered the crisis in the first place, especially if the peg was deemed to be at an inappropriate levels.

When Indonesia defaulted on promised reforms, the IMF withdrew its monetary support. This exacerbated the economic uncertainty and chaos. Confronted by a possibility of large-scale social dislocations, some western governments advocated a more measured pace of IMF reform. The reasoning was that political instability would impede a resolution of the economic crisis and that social and political instability in a large and populous country like Indonesia could also undermine overall regional stability. The Australian government was particularly concerned that social collapse would re-create a refugee problem in the region.

Finally, in April 1998, the Indonesian government and the IMF agreed to a new package of reform conditions, which Indonesia promised to implement faithfully and expeditiously. The new package permitted Indonesia to continue subsidies on some basic commodities in order to minimize popular backlash against the government, but price rises in oil and some other commodities still unleashed a massive wave of social unrest and violence. A few months earlier, President Suharto had, arrogantly, brushed aside growing societal demand for political change and secured a fifth term as President. The price rises that followed inflamed simmering popular resentment and led to rioting in Jakarta and elsewhere. The target of the protest movement was the Suharto administration but its immediate victims were members of the Chinese community, who seemingly had benefited from policies of the Suharto government to amass large fortunes. The Chinese became the scapegoats in the power-play but ultimately the protesters secured their objective and Suharto was forced to resign in May 1998. This ended more than 30 years of the 'New Order' government.

The fall of Suharto led to hesitant and uncertain steps towards democracy. A decade later Indonesian democracy was still in the process of being consolidated but at least the military had renounced its claim to a legitimate role in domestic politics.

The Japanese response to the crisis was interesting. Japan was a major source of financial assistance to the crisis countries but the Japanese government also took the unusual step of proposing the establishment of an Asian Monetary Fund (AMF), with a US$100 billion contribution of its own, to stave off future currency attacks against regional currencies by enabling crisis countries to access liquidity at short notice and without preconditions. The proposal had considerable merit and, indeed, if Thailand had access to funds from such an AMF, it could arguably have fought off currency speculators and prevented the subsequent contagion. But the proposal was quickly rejected by the United States which argued that unconditional lending was financially irresponsible and that a new multilateral institution would be in competition with the IMF and unnecessary. The Japanese government, in the face of US hostility, backed away from what, in hindsight, was an eminently sound proposal.

The Asian financial and economic crisis came amid an on-going economic crisis in Japan, which meant that the Japanese economy, despite regional expectations, was not well positioned to act as the engine of regional growth. Nonetheless, addressing the World Economic Forum, the Thai Prime Minister Chuan Leekpai bluntly stated that the Japanese economy had to be stimulated to act as "an engine for recovery in the region...".[25] Unfortunately, the Japanese government had failed, since the early 1990s, to find a way out of its own economic crisis and, during the Asian crisis, it had no capacity to respond to regional expectations. Consequently, the US Trade Representative depicted Japan's response as 'woefully inadequate' while Malaysian Deputy Prime

Minister Anwar Ibrahim criticized Japan for being slow to respond to the crisis.[26] These criticisms, however, were simplistic in assuming that there was an easy exit strategy out of Japan's long economic crisis and, in any event, Japan's proposal for an AMF was clear evidence that the government was not oblivious to its role and responsibilities.

For China the crisis was an opportunity to repair its relationship with regional countries after the damage it had done to itself in the missile crisis of 1996. To demonstrate its goodwill, the Chinese government also promised to refrain from any further currency devaluation that might exacerbate the situation in Southeast Asia.

The Asian crisis was a liquidity crisis and in its aftermath, regional countries, led by Japan and the ASEAN (Association of Southeast Asian Nations), put together an elaborate currency swap arrangement, known as the Chiang-Mai Initiative. The objective was to ensure that regional central banks could borrow additional liquidity to fight off currency speculators. At the same time, regional countries also built up their own foreign exchange reserves, which in early 2007, stood at US$3.1 trillion, a third of which had been accumulated by China alone. As a result, East Asia had 'proofed' itself from any recurrence of the 1997 currency crisis. But any future crisis, if it happens, will probably be different in nature and, indeed, crises are by definition unforeseen events to which there is no perfect prophylactic.

Argentinean Crisis, 2001

In the early postwar period, Argentina, at a commensurate level of economic development as Canada and Australia and with comparable resource and human capital endowments, was expected to follow a similar growth trajectory. Instead, Argentina fell steadily behind. Between 1970 and 1995, average annual growth rate of per capita GNP in Argentina was marginally negative, and reasonably good growth performance in the 1990s could not compensate for the failures of the 1970s and 1980s. In the late 1980s, inflation in Argentina was 200 percent a month; and between March 1989 and March 1990, inflation peaked at over 20,000 percent. Gross domestic product fell more than six percent and imports fell 21 percent that year.

In 1991, the government of Carlos Menem, responding to popular demands for price stability, adopted the Convertibility Plan, with an exchange rate peg to the US Dollar (a Currency Board), macroeconomic policies consistent with the peg, and sweeping structural reforms. The Currency Board successfully scaled back the growth of money supply and brought inflation under control. In 1995, inflation was down to 1.6 percent and through till 1997 economic growth averaged six percent a year. In the 1990s, foreign capital returned to developing countries and Argentina. But fixed exchange rates also have the problem of combining with residual inflation to undermine competitiveness of an economy, unless there is downward adjustment of wages and prices, which is politically difficult and dangerous. Not only that but Argentina's export competitiveness was also affected by a progressive appreciation of the US Dollar between 1995 and 1999, given the 1:1 peg of the Peso to the Dollar. Finally, with 30 percent trade dependence on Brazil, Argentinean trade deficits worsened when Brazil devalued its currency in 1999. The fall in export revenue was a dangerous development because it worsened the country's debt service ratio. By the late 1990s debt service was absorbing about three-quarters of export earnings. The Asian crisis of 1997 in the meantime, triggered a flight of capital from all developing countries and Argentina's foreign exchange reserves dwindled rapidly. In May 2000, the government cut $1 billion from its budget hoping that this show of fiscal responsibility would restore investor confidence in the Argentinean economy but this has little effect. Argentina's foreign exchange reserves decline to less than $2 billion and in December the government imposed a withdrawal limit of US$1000 a month on all savings accounts. After the currency peg, savings had been dollar denominated to give confidence to Argentineans that their savings will be protected. The decision to limit withdrawals and an 18 percent reduction in government spending shortly before Christmas led to rioting and union strikes. Unemployment reached a high of 18 percent as the economy continued to nosedive and shrank by five percent in 2000–2001.

The Currency Board had been introduced to combat inflation but the problem now was unemployment. In January 2002, the currency peg was ended and when foreign exchange markets resumed trading the Peso was devalued by about 70 percent. It had a negative impact on domestic savings but provided a huge boost to Argentinean exports.

The Argentinean crisis began as a financial crisis, became a social crisis with large scale looting of supermarkets and about 30 deaths and then became a political crisis with five presidential appointments in the short space of two weeks in late 2001 and early 2002. In the end, De La Rua, having resigned in December 2001, was reappointed in January 2002 as interim president until the next election in 2003.

The role of the IMF in managing the Argentinean crisis again attracted considerable criticism. In December 2001, the Argentinean government requested the IMF to release the disbursement of $1.3 billion dollars, but it refused saying that the government had failed to meet the mutually agreed target of zero fiscal deficit. In reality, Argentina's fiscal spending was not excessive with only very small overall deficits. But IMF insisted on budget surplus in order to prepare for an economic downturn and when that did not happen, it withheld the disbursement of funds. With no capital injection, Argentina defaulted on its debt repayment obligations. This was the largest debt default in history but the government was able to restructure its debt liability and exchanged about 80 percent of its outstanding debt for a lower nominal value, at longer terms.

In presidential elections in 2003, Kirchner triumphed over Menem and immediately set about large scale administrative and judicial reforms. His economic reform package also was effective in lowering unemployment and restoring economic growth. Between 2003 and 2006, economic growth averaged about 9 percent a year and unemployment was brought down to single digit levels. More significantly, Argentina, in January 2006, was able to pay off its debt to IMF in a single payment, rather than in instalment over several years. Although this momentous decision cancelled less than 10 percent of outstanding debt, it resulted in substantial saving of interest payments. And it ended Argentina long and unhappy association with the IMF. Kirchner's actions stemmed from a belief that IMF policies were ultimately responsible for the social unrest and violence in 2001 but his actions also were reflective of the times. His decision to pay off the IMF came on the heels of a similar decision by President Lula of Brazil to repay all its outstanding loans to the IMF two years ahead of schedule and marked a general turn around in the economic position of Latin American countries.

Structural Adjustment and Change in Developing Countries

The structural adjustment programs introduced by the IMF following the onset of the Latin American debt crisis became a medium for rapid change in the developing countries, even change that was not warranted by the crisis. Consequently, in the decade of the 1980s, apart from the former communist countries in Russia and Eastern Europe, a similar transition toward openness and liberalisation swept through the developing world.

Debt crisis provided a rationale for drastic economic restructuring in the developing countries, from import substitution industrialization (ISI) to export oriented industrialization (EOI), and from economic regulation to market orientation. The primary focus of structural adjustment and reform was to enhance economic performance and export competitiveness in the developing countries. It was assumed that such reforms would boost economic growth and enhance their export earnings, which would lead to improvements in balance of payments position and enable them to finance their foreign debt. Structural adjustment programs promised a virtuous cycle of higher growth and higher exports through a deeper commitment to liberal economic principles, as envisaged by the founders of, for example, the GATT. By the early 1990s, about 70 countries had embarked upon structural adjustment.[27]

The thrust of structural adjustment was to force developing countries to adopt export oriented and open economic structures in place of earlier policies that promoted import substitution behind protectionist trade barriers. It was, as mentioned above, a key component of the Baker and the Brady plan and was successfully implemented in many Latin American countries as part of IMF conditionality. The importance of openness has been strongly asserted by one recent study by Jeffrey Sachs and Andrew Warner in which the authors conclude that openness, along with private property, is a sufficient condition for growth in developing countries.[28]

Structural adjustment was not confined to the Highly Indebted Countries of Latin America but was imposed, with greater vigor, in the poorer countries of Africa and Asia. The former group of relatively rich developing countries turned to the multilateral agencies only after the debt crisis had blocked their capacity to borrow from commercial banks. The latter group of countries were considered a bigger risk and did not venture extensively into the commercial sector. Their borrowing was limited, to a large extent, to the multilateral agencies. For example, whereas more than 70 percent of the debt owed by poorer countries of Asia and Africa was either multilateral or bilateral debt, 70 percent of the Latin American debt was owed to private lending institutions.[29] For the poorer countries, structural adjustment was, from the beginning, a condition of multilateral financing.

The IMF and the World Bank were at the forefront of structural adjustment programs, providing not only financial assistance but also policy advice. The ideas informing structural adjustment were articulated in, for example, various World Bank reports. For example, in a 1981 report on economic stagnation in Sub-Saharan Africa, the World Bank observed that "Three major policy actions are central to any growth-oriented program: (1) more suitable trade and exchange-rate policies; (2) increased efficiency of resource use in the public sector; and (3) improvement in agricultural policies".

Structural adjustment programs were intricately linked with policies of trade liberalization and export promotion,[d] which created a bias in favor of export sales over domestic sales. Behind the push for economic rationality and export promotion, was the view that countries that permitted a greater play of market forces and encouraged exports (Taiwan, South Korea, Hong Kong and Singapore) achieved superior economic results than countries that regulated their economies and pursued import substitution industrialization. The incorporation of export oriented policies into structural adjustment programs reflected the belief that the East Asian model was not historically unique and could be replicated in other developing countries.

---

[d] In general, developing countries have the option of choosing export oriented or import substitution policies to promote development and industrialization. Although the two sets of policies are not mutually exclusive, developing countries have emphasized one or the other as the most suitable to their particular condition. In the postwar period, the Latin American countries pursued import substitution policies whereas the East Asian countries opted for export oriented policies. However, the adoption of export oriented industrialization strategies by the East Asian economies in the 1960s did not immediately lead to general renunciation of import substitution or to a general withdrawal of protection given to domestic industries.

Economic liberalization was necessary to enhance export competitiveness through lower prices for imported inputs and, together with export promotion, was essential to correct domestic price distortions. Given the practical difficulty of determining real market prices for any given economy, the IMF and the World Bank used world market prices as indicators. It was consequently necessary to liberalize trade regimes to ensure that domestic prices reflected world prices. In general, the reform program can be discussed under the three headings of monetary measures; fiscal measures; and trade reforms.

The monetary measures targeted high levels of inflation caused by profligate government spending. High inflation was considered a serious and threatening condition which eroded business confidence and signaled that the market was not performing to its full potential. Consequently, anti-inflationary policies formed the bedrock of the reform agenda, without which the reform measures were unlikely to succeed. Anne Krueger explained, "When public sector deficits are large, and/or inflation is proceeding at annual rates in excess of, say, 100 percent, major reduction in the size of the public sector deficit is a virtual necessary condition for the success of the reform effort".[30] IMF conditionality required a drastic reduction in government spending and increase in domestic interest rates to control and bring down inflation levels. Higher domestic interest rates had the additional advantage of encouraging private savings, reducing consumption, and discouraging capital flight.[31]

The fiscal measures concentrated around reducing the size of the public sector within the economy. This was the most painful aspect of structural adjustment because of withdrawal of various governmental services and subsidies. On the positive side, this curtailed investment in "white elephant" projects and retrenched state involvement in inefficient public enterprises through forced privatization. Apart from reductions in government expenditure, structural adjustment also entailed reforms in the tax structure. Instead of relying on export and import taxes for revenue, IMF reforms required states to raise revenue by taxing domestic sales and excise taxes, or income tax. This was not very successful given the inadequacies of the administrative bureaucracy to monitor and collect taxes from a broad domestic base.

The trade measures were largely designed to encourage exports and reduce barriers to imports. This involved liberalization of tariff schedules, tariffication of trade restrictions, and exchange rate adjustments. Many developing countries had introduced exchange restrictions and also maintained an overvalued exchange rate on the dual assumption that export demand for their products was unlikely to expand significantly and that import demand was constant and the essential imports could not be reduced. Under these assumptions, countries tried to minimize their total import bill by maintaining overvalued currency rates. Unfortunately, an overvalued currency also made imports cheaper and it created a dependency on imports. Between 1977 and 1981, for example, Mexican imports grew at 35 percent each year. Nigel Harris wrote that, "For an import substituting economy, this was poor performance. Some saw it as intrinsic to the imperfect structure of the economy, its 'dependency', but a simpler explanation related it to the value of the peso; dollar denominated imports were generally cheaper than domestic produced goods. Thus, the advantage of protection was nullified by the exchange rate".[32]

At the same time, cheaper imports, of at least capital and intermediate producer goods, was considered desirable for the domestic industrialization program. To prevent luxury imports from benefiting from overvalued exchange rates, many countries introduced dual or multiple exchange rate system such that a lower rate applied for non-essential luxury imports.[33] Overvalued exchange rates were a tax on exports and while multiple exchange rates solved the problem of luxury imports flooding the domestic market, such a system also produced negative externalities.

Under structural adjustment programs, countries were forced to adopt a unitary exchange rate and one that did not penalize exports but rather encouraged it. They were also forced to remove quantitative import restrictions. A measure of the importance of exchange rate changes in IMF lending practices can be seen in the fact that while exchange rate actions were required in only 31 percent of the Fund programs during 1963–1972, such actions were part of 64 percent of the programs during 1981–1983.[34] For a group of 15 developing countries undergoing reform, the exchange rate by 1987 had depreciated by around 40 percent compared to the 1965–1981 levels.[35]

On specific trade restrictions Krueger argued that non-prohibitive import restrictions and rent seeking activities eroded people's confidence in the market mechanism because of the perception that the rich benefit or were successful as rent seekers "whereas the poor are those precluded from or unsuccessful in rent seeking...".[36] This set off a political vicious circle where the government was "forced" to intervene to correct market distortions which only further distorted the economic payoff structure. A logical corollary of this, not pointed out by Krueger, was that such a system should lead to political instability whereas a transition to liberal trade and freeing up of the market mechanism should restore faith in the market and enhance political legitimacy.

Structural adjustment programs were for fixed periods and both the IMF and the World Bank provided special structural adjustment loans to make the transition easier for developing countries. The World Bank classified its financial assistance programs as Structural Adjustment Loans (SALs) and Sectoral Adjustment Loans (SECALs). The latter was narrowly focused but both had the same objective of improving market efficiency and resource allocation. Between 1980 and 1987, the World Bank provided a total of US$15 billion to 51 countries under the two loan programs.[37]

Social Impact of Structural Adjustment Policies

The developing countries shouldered a disproportionate share of the cost of stabilizing the international financial system. Rather than receive foreign aid and capital, debt servicing, in the 1980s, meant a perverse flow of capital from the developing to the rich countries. In 1981, the developing countries' net receipt (new debt less total debt repayment) was US$36.5 billion but by 1986 this had turned into a deficit of US$19.7 billion and to a deficit of US$42.9 billion in 1989.[38] Within the developing countries, the worst affected was the poorer segment of the population because governments pared welfare spending to meet interest payments.

Structural adjustment policies imposed a regime of openness on developing countries and thrust them into the global economy. The result was to enhance the degree of integration of the developing economies into the global economy. Most developing countries, except Latin America and the Caribbean, substantially increased the ratio of their trade to GDP between 1985 and 1995 and also benefited from vastly expanded inflow of foreign direct investment. In 1990, FDI brought US$24.2 billion of investment to developing countries but by 1995 this had increased to US$91.8 billion.[39]

The economic consensus was that liberalization would enhance growth prospects in developing countries. The World Bank's own assessment was that the reforms had been generally successful in promoting growth. According to the World Bank, between 1985 and 1987, economic growth in countries with a strong reform program averaged 3.8 percent a year whereas economic growth in countries with weak or no reform was only 1.5 percent a year.[40] Another World Bank study of 29 Sub-Saharan African countries reached similar conclusions, that countries that persevered did better than countries which vacillated on the implementation of reforms. The study acknowledged that growth had failed to meet expectations but, according to Christine Jones and Miguel Kiguel, the inability to generate growth was because reforms had not been sustained, and not a failure of the reforms themselves.[41] Another study by Lawrence Summers and Lant Pritchett found that those countries that underwent "intensive structural adjustment", that is those countries which had at least two structural adjustment loans between 1986 and 1990, "...enjoyed faster growth, higher export and savings shares, and lower fiscal deficits in the second half of the 1980's, both compared with other countries and compared with their own earlier performance".[42]

Critics of greater integration into a global economy, however, argue that it will lead to large western transnational corporations dominating the economies of the third world. According to Martin Khor, the developing countries, by hitching into a system over which they have little control, risk losing their "indigenous skills, their capacity for self-reliance, their confidence, and, in many cases, the very resource base on which their survival depends".[43]

Apart from the introduction of inappropriate technologies, many developing countries have also become dumping grounds for pollutants generated elsewhere. These are essentially problems that result from institutional weaknesses and structural inadequacies, such as in legal systems, to deal with the forces of globalization. If true, then the developing countries may be under-prepared to partake of the benefits of economic globalization. For developing countries, the putative advantage of participating in the global economy is the prospect of eventual convergence of incomes and standards of living. By the late 1990s, however, no convergence had taken place, even if some developing countries had narrowed differentials against developed countries.

Whether this was a conceptual failure or one of implementation, structural adjustment programs, following the 1980 debt crisis and the Indonesian debt crisis of 1997, were criticized for their neglect of political and social considerations. The burden of structural adjustment was placed squarely on the developing countries, much as the Bretton-Woods agreement placed the onus for adjusting to payment difficulties squarely upon the deficit countries. Structural adjustment also imposed tremendous hardships on the poorer segment of the population because cutbacks in government services meant the withdrawal of social safety net.

When structural adjustment programs began in the early 1980s, it was assumed that the adjustment would take no more than a few years and that the hardship too, would be a short-term phenomenon, before the benefits started flowing in. However, the process of adjustment continued longer than expected with little relief for the worst-affected. It resulted in significant decline in the standard of living in many countries. In Peru, for example, from 1985 to 1990, average consumption declined by over 50 percent but the poorest decile (10 percent) was the worst affected. Its monthly per capita consumption declined by 62 percent.[44] Indeed, the 1980s was a decade that was lost to development in that, according to Hans Wolfgang Singer and Sumit Roy, "attention shifted to debt settlement, stabilization, adjustment, structural change, liberalization, and so on — often at the expense of everything that had previously been understood as development, whether growth, employment, redistribution, basic needs or reduction of poverty".[45]

With the emphasis on fiscal discipline and cutbacks on welfare programs, the poor were left to fend for themselves. Likewise, the emphasis on producing cash crops for exports rather than food crops for domestic consumption added to the people's misery and, when global agricultural prices declined, contributed to the crisis of hunger and famine in Africa. For these people, the possibility that structural adjustment would lead to long-term economic prosperity was cold comfort, considering their immediate hunger and impoverishment. The failure of structural adjustment to quickly reverse declining economic fortunes of the developing countries led to new criticisms from dependency theorists that structural adjustment programs merely reproduced dependent development by emphasizing international economic linkages and that such programs were unlikely to alleviate poverty or produce autonomous development. In Nigeria, according to Julius Ohinvbere,

"As at the end of 1989, students, workers, peasants, market women, bankers and indigenous entrepreneurs have pronounced the adjustment package a total disaster. Only transnational corporations, speculators, drug pushers, currency traffickers, consultants and middlemen, as well as top army officers and bureaucrats, are full of praise for the SAP [structural adjustment program]".[46]

In 1988, after the collapse of the Egyptian structural adjustment program because of domestic political repercussions, President Mubarak likened the IMF to an unqualified doctor who prescribed life-threatening dosages of medicines.[47] Because structural adjustment programs affected the poorest segment of the population, it became necessary to search for ways to alleviate their immediate hardships. In Ghana, the government in 1987, was forced to adopt a Program of Action to Mitigate the Social Costs of Adjustment (PAMSCAD), and alleviate the suffering caused by rising unemployment. The government allocated US$90 million to the PAMSCAD in an effort create employment, improve health care, nutrition and other basic needs. Commenting on the economic crisis in Ghana, John Loxley stated that "It is a sad reflection on Fund/Bank thinking that such considerations were not, and generally, still are not, built directly into adjustment programmes. PAMSCAD was tacked onto the end of the body of the reform package as a reluctant afterthought, under pressure from UNICEF and concerned bilateral donors. The IMF did not even see fit to send a representative to the meetings in which PAMSCAD was developed".[48]

Because of the socio-political costs, many developing countries were forced to amend and temper the pace of reform. Countries like Egypt, for example, found it extremely difficult to persist with structural adjustment even if the Egyptian government recognized the importance of economic reform. As a result of structural reform, the Egyptian government was able to reduce its budget deficit from 20 percent of GDP in 1991 to around 4–5 percent of GDP in 1993, and similarly reduce inflation from 22 percent in 1990 to around 11 percent in 1993. Despite these successes, the period 1991–1993 witnessed declining real GDP growth and unemployment at around 20 percent. Such conditions, Bromley and Bush point out, are incubators of social unrest and political instability.[49] The Egyptian government was conscious also of the fact that IMF reform programs and forced austerity had led to food riots in 1977.

As well as the negative impact of structural adjustment programs on the poorer sections of the affected community, these programs took no account of local conditions. Instead, the SAPs followed a "one size fit all approach". The criticisms of this approach to dealing with crises prompted the IMF to change its style, but not so much the substance. As Ha-Joon Chang points out "…the IMF now calls the Structural Adjustment Programme the Poverty Reduction and Growth Facility Program in order to show that it cares about poverty issues, though the contents of the programme have hardly changed from before".[50,51]

Conclusion

The Latin American debt crisis was the single most important source of potential instability in international monetary relations in the 1980s. It was also a crisis of development and the decade of the 1980s is often regarded as a decade lost to development. The western crisis management strategy largely focused on maintaining the viability of the international financial system. The success of this approach was that not a single major financial institution declared bankruptcy as a result of bad loans. Despite the absence of significant debt relief strategies, the structural adjustment programs were designed to relaunch the developing countries onto a more sustainable developmental trajectory.

Table 4.4:   Developing countries' debt indicators.

	Total Debt Stock		Debt Service Ratio	
	1991	1992	1991	1992
All developing countries	1605.9	1662.7	18.6	18.7
East Asia	293.8	320.1	13.4	12.9
Africa and Middle East	386.9	383.1	17.8	25.7
Latin America and Caribbean	488.4	496.3	25.9	29.8

Source: World Debt Tables (1993–1994).

By the early 1990s, it appeared that while the debt problem had not disappeared, it was no longer a compelling issue. The developing countries still remained burdened by high levels of debt, but debt service ratio was more manageable and the danger that debt repudiation might severely stress the pillars of international financial stability had faded. Table 4.4 provides a summary of the debt situation in the early 1990s.

The commercial banks, in the meantime, increased their loan-loss provisions and were in a better position, than before, to absorb loan default. Moreover, since the early 1980s, the commercial banks also increased their equity capital dramatically and reduced their LDC loan assets as a percentage of total bank assets. For the banks, the storm appeared to have passed. With its passing, they returned, once more, as lenders to developing countries. Since the onset of the debt crisis and until 1991, international aid agencies, including the World Bank, were the main donors to developing countries but in 1992 private lenders overtook international agencies. In 1994, private institutions lent well over US$150 billion to developing countries compared to slightly over US$50 billion for the World Bank and other international agencies.

The later crises, such as in Mexico and East Asia, were also crises emanating from the globalization of capital. These two crises were triggered by speculative capital flows and capital flight from the affected countries. They highlighted the vulnerability for countries participating in a globalized system with weak and small domestic financial structures. Certainly there are advantages of participating in the global economy but there are also pitfalls if domestic financial structures are poorly prepared to cope with demands of a global economy. Countries have to be prepared and readied for participation in the global economy and not forced into it simply on ideological considerations. IMF strategies in dealing with these crises included measures that might enhance the resilience of the financial sector in the affected economies but the Indonesian case demonstrated that this was a difficult task to achieve in the context of an on-going crisis. The unfolding of the Indonesian dram revealed also that a transition to a more effective economy required also some prior political liberalization.

Of the four main affected countries in the East Asia, Indonesia's performance in implementing IMF reforms was particularly poor. This was, at least partly, a result of the government's determination to protect economic interests of Suharto and the political cronies who had benefited from the corrupt practices of the regime. The prescribed reform measures were designed to prepare Indonesia to cope with the demands of participation in a global economy but the outcomes were compromised by the irresponsible attempts to preserve entrenched family interests. In the absence of political liberalization and democratic accountability, the Suharto regime was more intent on protecting family interests than national interests. Not surprisingly Michel Camdessus, Managing Director of the IMF, remarked that democracy and effective economics were sisters. As to whether this was unnecessary intrusion into domestic politics, he added that, "...it would be pointless, indeed reckless, and contrary to the IMF's charter, for the IMF to use its members' resources to support these programs unless there were strong reasons to believe that they would be successful in restoring market confidence and economic growth".[52] The concern was that unless Indonesia faithfully implemented the reform measures it would leave itself vulnerable to future crises of a similar nature.

At the same time, however, structural adjustment policies have to take into consideration the issue of political feasibility. The first two IMF rescue packages for Indonesia had to be inevitably abandoned because they were politically impractical. This of course raises the vexed question of whether reform policies should be dictated by what is politically feasible or whether they should be based solely on economic merit, regardless of political and social consequences. With respect to Indonesia, the

Australian government, worried of a tidal wave of refugees, actively lobbied the IMF to reconsider its reform package. It maintained that political instability in Indonesia would have adverse regional consequences and that it was imperative, therefore, not to destabilize the Suharto regime. These are difficult issues that will eventually have to be resolved but there are no easy solutions.

The Asian currency crisis highlighted the importance of good governance in the age of economic globalization. An important lesson of the crisis was that market signals are quickly relayed across the globe and that political failure is punished quickly and ruthlessly. It emphasized the importance of prudential economic management in order to avoid panic in the markets. The crisis also underlined the importance of developing sound and robust financial institutions prior to implementing liberaization of financial markets. While the Latin American debt crisis was an indictment of import substitution policies, the East Asian crisis was not a result of flawed developmental strategy but, in part, of policies high-jacked and derailed by corrupt practices and political cronyism. As a result of increasing corruption, Indonesia pursued many ambitious national projects, such as national car production, but instead of contributing to growth, such investment was detrimental to growth because it channelled capital into sectors with low productivity.[53]

The events surrounding the Mexican and the East Asian crises also revealed flaws in the existing system of international monetary surveillance. The IMF had played a leading part in managing the debt crisis in the 1980s but still had woefully inadequate surveillance powers to ensure sound international financial management. At a minimum, the events of 1995 underscored the importance of establishing a code of conduct to ensure that member governments adhered to standards of transparency. Few countries, however, publish their economic statistics, provide details of foreign exchange operations, or collect important economic information. The East Asian economic crisis highlighted, for example, the basic gaps in understanding the nature of the crisis because there were no aggregate statistics on firms' foreign indebtedness.[54] If the Mexican and East Asian governments had been obliged to publish details of reserve movements and short-term liabilities, financial markets and commercial banks would have been better informed about their overall exposure.

A problem for effective IMF surveillance is that it has no capacity to dictate to members except when they borrow from it. Instead, the members control IMF and even when danger signals are present, IMF cannot force them to alter policies. Prior to the East Asian crisis, the Thai government had ignored policy advice by the IMF when it became concerned with the direction of the Thai economy.[55] Yet when conditions did deteriorate, the Thai government did not shy away from seeking IMF assistance.

Inevitably, IMF's bail-out operations leave the impression that IMF will always step in to fill the breach. Thus, the bail-out of Mexico in 1995 may have added to the poor investment decisions that created the crisis of 1997. Rescue packages carry the attendant risk of diminishing even more the need for prudential and disciplined investment decision when the lesson of a crisis must be to introduce greater discipline. Bail-outs thus create the problem of "moral hazard" by eliminating the risk factor that must be the base of all market based economic activity. The succession of debt and currency crises reveals that there is a fine line between the problem of moral hazard and the need to ensure continued system stability.

Chapter Five

RUSSIA, CHINA AND INDIA IN THE GLOBAL ECONOMY

Economic transformation and the rise of China, Russia, and India has injected new dynamism in the global economy. If they continue their current growth trends, it is certain that these countries will join existing power blocks of the European Union, the United States and Japan at the center of world stage. There are various estimates that, by 2020, China will overtake the United States in size of its GDP or that India will surpass Japan but their per capita GDP is likely to remain a fraction of that of most developed countries for the considerable future. But given their overall size and growth rates, both China and India cast a lengthy shadow over the global economy. Both have been important engines of growth for the global economy and in particular for resource rich countries. Australia and many countries in Africa have benefited from the import demand for energy and resources in both China and India and from Chinese investments in the resources sector.

The process of transition in each of the three countries was markedly different, with each starting from a different baseline but hoping to converge on the advanced industrial model of free markets and decentralized decision-making. Their experiences have also been vastly different. In the post-Soviet era, Russia went through more than a decade of economic and political turmoil but more recently, it has begun to reassert itself on the global stage and this resurgence is underpinned by an economy that has rebounded strongly. The Soviet collapse had been precipitated by lacklustre economic performance but the "new" Russia appears to have overcome that problem. India is a more recent entrant as a major player and its rise has been fuelled by strong economic performance in the period after the 1990s. India has also become an influential player in international economic relations and, in partnership with Brazil in the Group of Twenty (G20), played an important role in Doha Round trade negotiations even though this did not produce any significant breakthrough for developing countries.

In this chapter, I will trace the transitional processes that have led to the rise of China, India and Russia. These three transitional economies embraced globalization after a long association with either central planning or autarkic economic policies. For Russia, the transition was not entirely a smooth and painless journey but all three appear to have benefited tremendously by participating in and seizing opportunities provided by the global economy.

Central Planning and the Transition of China and Russia

During the Cold War, the socialist economies had limited access to GATT and to western markets because, as one US trade official explained, "How can you have a centrally planned economy, in which all the decisions are made by the state, in an organization whose fundamental principle is market economy?"[1] GATT required transparency of national trade regulations and decentralized decision making, whereas command economies had trade rules that were opaque and arbitrary, and centralized decision making. Central authorities pre-determined the level of trade by government fiat and decisions could also be altered arbitrarily or applied selectively with no recourse for a trading partner to verify non-discrimination in trade practices. Denied access to GATT, the socialist countries formed their own economic grouping, the Council for Mutual Economic Assistance (known either as CMEA or Comecon). This completed the political and economic bifurcation of the international system.

Nonetheless, some command economies, such as Poland and Romania, were given conditional GATT membership. The benefits of participating in a liberal trading regime were selectively extended to some East European countries to entice them away from the Soviet Union and to weaken the bloc cohesion. Yugoslavia, the first East European country to join in 1966 was given the easiest entry conditions and allowed to join as if it had a market-type economy. Its only commitments were in the realm of tariff reduction. In the case of Poland, however, GATT required that it expand annual imports by 7 percent to compensate "... for a similar annual increase in exports anticipated out of Poland's participation in the GATT".[2] This was done to ensure that in the absence of an operating and effective market, Polish imports would increase at least as fast as projected increase in exports. Hungary's accession also was conditioned on a similar commitment. Romania benefited from being accorded the status of a developing country and was only required to give vague commitments to increase imports.

In the 1980s, economic difficulties forced East European countries to initiate economic reforms. The process of reform culminated in the dissolution of the CMEA in June 1991. Reform was an admission that central planning in complex and large economies could not anticipate and respond to the needs of the people.[3,a] Poland led the reform movement in East Europe with the objective of establishing a market based economy within a short span of 2–3 years. A key architect of the Polish model, incorporating the three features of economic liberalization, macroeconomic stabilization and privatization was Professor Jeffrey Sachs of Harvard University.[4] Economic liberalization was designed to introduce market competition, macroeconomic stabilization to create a stable and functioning monetary system, and privatization to transfer ownership of state corporations to the private sector. Because of the rapid pace of transition from command to a market economy, the Polish model is variously described as the 'big bang', 'shock therapy', or 'cold turkey' approach. It was a derivative of neo-classical economic theory, which assumed that it was better to unshackle markets from state regulations and to revive profit/utility maximizing behavior as quickly and as thoroughly as possible. The rapidity of change was justified also as necessary to prevent a subversion of the reform agenda.

---

[a] The collapse of communism was neither foreseen nor is there any consensus on what caused it. Explanations range from the inability of central planners to manage a complex economy; the failure of communism to satisfy the self-recognition needs of individuals (Francis Fukuyama); the arms race and its deleterious consequences; to economic stagnation caused by the non-substitutability of capital for labor. The last factor explains the collapse of command economies in terms of extremely low returns on capital investments.

By contrast, the 'gradualist' approach, adopted by China, assumed that any transition from state to market mechanisms had to be gradual and contingent on the development of appropriate market based institutions. If the big bang approach was grounded in neoclassical economics, the roots of the gradualist model can be traced to institutional economics. The main insight of the institutional approach is that economic performance is dependent on institutional efficiency to lower transaction costs. Rather than risk the possibility of an institutional vacuum, and attendant instability, China opted to transition in a long gradual process on the assumption that institutions take time to establish and become resilient. In short, the Russian approach was to dismantle existing rules and institutions and to proceed *tabula rasa* to the development of new rules and institutions, whereas China adopted a gradualist approach of "developing" alternative market based institutions before dismantling existing structures.

Each school claimed superior outcomes for its model of transition but these claims have yet to be verified. It should be emphasized that divergent Russian and Chinese reform experience should not be interpreted as evidence for or against either the radical or the gradualist approach. It is easy to fall into this logical trap but the initial conditions in each of the two countries were so different as to make meaningless a comparative assessment. While under-performing, the Chinese economy was not, at the time of the reforms, in fundamental macroeconomic imbalance as was the Russian economy. Nor did Chinese reformers have to contend with political vacuum and instability, except for a brief period in 1989, whereas the Russian reform agenda was adversely affected by the collapse of political authority and effective governance. In China, the transition was managed by the Communist Party whereas in Russia the transition was buffeted by a power struggle between the communists and the reformers.

China

The impetus to reform, as mentioned above, was poor economic performance in China. Chairman Mao's erratic economic policies had created serious economic difficulties and after his death in 1976, the new leaders were anxious to discard campaign-driven economic policies. Starting in the late 1970s, Chinese leaders introduced greater reliance on market mechanism and decentralized decision-making. The government introduced measured reforms to promote entrepreneurial activity rather than outright privatization of state owned enterprises. The state sector was not immediately dismantled but its position weight in the national economy declined with the emergence of private entrepreneurial activity. In 1980 the state sector contributed 76 percent to total industrial output but by 1990 this had declined to 54.5 percent.[5] By the late 1990s, state owned enterprises (SOEs) were contributing less than 30 percent to the country's industrial output.[6] In the late 1990s, there were approximately 340,000 state owned enterprises employing more than 110 million workers. The number of SOEs had declined to 150,000 by 2003. However, by avoiding large-scale privatisation from the very outset unemployment was kept to a minimum, and state enterprises assisted by state subsidies, continued to employ excess workers and provide a social safety net. Although subsidies distorted the industrial structure, they also provided a safety net without which reforms might not have been so readily accepted.

The government did introduce measures to make the state sector more efficient and profitable such as allowing them to withhold part of their profits, instead of remitting it all to the state. Such measures could not turn around the under-performing SOEs and these remained a drag on the Chinese economy. A substantial proportion of SOEs were loss making ventures and in 1996 approximately 6200 SOEs declared bankruptcy. In September 1997, the government announced plans to turn around the SOEs by around the end of the century. The plan included mergers to form more internationally competitive and viable units as well as privatization. Reform of the SOEs had become imperative because domestic commercial banks, with extensive loans to SOEs, could not be expected to carry the burden of inefficient industries indefinitely into the future. Privatization has been carried out through a number of avenues, including employee buyout programs and foreign direct investments.

Despite some economic difficulties, China's economic transition is regarded as a success. This is evidenced by impressive increases in export levels and GNP growth. In 1992, the Chinese economy grew by 13 percent.

Over the period 1978–1990 real per capita GNP growth was 7.2 percent a year and export growth was 10 percent a year.[7]

Critical to the success of reforms was the flow of foreign investment into China. Since the start of the reform process China has been a major beneficiary of foreign direct investment and in 2003 it was the leading destination for FDI, followed by the United States. The level of investment reflected investor confidence that the new openness was not a transient phenomenon. Between 1979 and 1992 the authorized level of total direct foreign investment in China was US$109.8 billion, of which US$34.5 billion had actually been invested. Approximately 70 percent of total foreign investment was from Hong Kong, Macao, Taiwan and the ASEAN countries.[8]

The tremendous economic achievements since the early 1980s have, however, created some unsettling problems. While poverty levels have fallen markedly there is growing income inequality between the coastal and urban regions where growth is largely concentrated and the inland and rural areas, which appear to have been left behind, in relative terms. The Gini coefficient, a measure of income disparity ranging from 0 (perfect equality) to 1 (perfect inequality), for China was 0.447 in 2001, considerably worse than Japan at 0.249, and even worse than the United States at 0.408. This two-dimensional inequality problem is problematic because it contains the potential for substantial popular unrest and agitation. Inequality has also contributed to internal migration from rural and inland areas to the coastal and urban centers of China. Unfortunately many of the migrants have not been able to tap into economic opportunities and only added to the pool of surplus workers to keep wages down. It is interesting to note that wages as a percentage of GDP has fallen from 53 percent in 1998 to only 41 percent in 2005, well below the United States at 56 percent. With less of the national wealth being paid out in wages, domestic consumption levels have also fallen from 47 percent in the early 1990s to 36 percent in 2006.[9] The Chinese economy is ever more reliant on the foreign trade sector to generate growth but a sustainable growth trajectory requires a larger reliance on domestic consumption and less on foreign trade. The fragility of trade based growth was underscored by concerns about the American economy in 2007 and the potential of the housing market collapse to trigger a general slowdown in economic growth. That would inevitably have a chain effect on Chinese economic performance and, further upstream, on the exporters of resources and minerals to China, such as Australia.

Having committed to global economic engagement, the People's Republic of China applied, in June 1986, to resume its GATT membership after having opted out of the GATT following the communist revolution. For China an important advantage of GATT membership was that it would create a stable trade environment at a time when China's foreign trade and exports were increasing rapidly. In 1982, for example, total Chinese exports were only about US$22 billion whereas by 1993, this had increased to around US$92 billion. In 1997, following the reversion of Hong Kong from British rule, China further enhanced its status as one of the world's five largest trading nations. GATT membership would also obviate the need for separate bilateral trade treaties with its principal trade partners.[10] In the absence of GATT membership, China had to negotiate MFN access to other countries on a bilateral basis, which tended to be steeped in uncertainty, could be easily revoked, or extended only on conditional terms. The United States, for example, granted MFN status to China in 1980 and renewed it on an annual basis but on numerous occasions threatened to revoke it, expressing dissatisfaction with the government's human rights record.

With the formal application, GATT set up a working party in 1987 to negotiate the terms of membership. Negotiations were suspended after a brutal suppression of the democracy movement in China in June 1989 but resumed in December 1989. In order to strengthen its membership application, the Chinese government progressively reduced the level of state intervention and expanded the scope of market forces in the economy. The state monopoly and privilege in foreign trade was ended and in 1987, 22 ministries/departments and 77 other associations, enterprises and organizations were given the right to engage in foreign trade.[11] The Party, in February 1993, decided to write these into the 1982 Constitution and removed a clause in Article 15, which stated that the "country will practise a planned economy on the basis of a socialist public ownership".[12] Further, China abolished a dual currency system in January 1994, which disadvantaged foreign investors by requiring them to purchase Chinese Yuan at an artificially high rate.

On the merit of China's GATT application, it was clear, according to McKenzie, that denial "… would be close to an admission that GATT is not capable of dealing effectively with economies other than those of western industrial democracies. Moreover, the disruptive threat of the Chinese economy is greater outside the GATT than within it".[13] Similarly, the Director General of GATT, Peter Sutherland, during a visit to China in May 1992, stated that keeping China out of GATT and the proposed World Trade Organization (WTO) would cast doubts about the universality of the WTO.[14] Nonetheless, western governments remained reluctant to extend GATT membership to China, expressing doubts about the openness of Chinese market despite import liberalization programs that had been adopted and which did have the desired effect of reducing China's growing trade surplus from US$9 billion in 1991 to US$4.4 billion in 1992. To allay western doubts and strengthen its membership application, the Chinese government submitted a report on new developments in its foreign trade and associated reforms to the GATT working party on China's membership but in February 1992 the working party, noting the improvements, still withheld recommending Chinese membership.[15]

The Chinese government worked strenuously to have GATT approve its membership in 1994 so that it could join the WTO as a founding member from January 1995. Instead, western governments again rejected the application on grounds that economic and legal reforms were inadequate to protect property, and intellectual property rights. GATT members were concerned, for example, that Chinese trade rules still lacked transparency and uniformity, with different rules applying at different Chinese ports.[16]

Expansion of WTO membership will have significant impact on international trade patterns, both positive in terms of welfare gains, and negative in terms of regime management.

It is true that expansion of membership will have consequences for internal decision making within the WTO, but on the positive side, WTO inclusiveness will enhance its status and prestige and transform it from a discriminatory to a universal institution. It would, moreover, give recognition to the fact that China was a large economy and a major trading country. Finally, after more than 15 years of intensive negotiations, China became a WTO member in December 2001. The legal text granting membership extended to more than 900 pages and included a lengthy list of conditions that China had to implement over a three-year transition period. These conditions included the following:

- China will provide non-discriminatory treatment to all WTO members. All foreign individuals and enterprises, including those not invested or registered in China, will be accorded treatment no less favorable than that accorded to enterprises in China with respect to the right to trade.
- China will eliminate dual pricing practices as well as differences in treatment accorded to goods produced for sale in China in comparison to those produced for export price controls will not be used for purposes of affording protection to domestic industries or service providers. The WTO Agreement will be implemented by China in an effective and uniform manner by revising its existing domestic laws and enacting new legislation fully in compliance with the WTO Agreement.
- Within three years of accession all enterprises will have the right to import and export all goods and trade them throughout the customs territory with limited exceptions.
- China will not maintain or introduce any export subsidies on agricultural products.

Russia

Reform in Russia, the birthplace of socialist revolution, had enormous significance for the future of world politics. But for many Russians, who had known nothing but socialism, structural reform was a divisive intrusion and, therefore, resented. The catalyst for reform was economic stagnation but the older generation of Russians did not embrace it and when asked, in 1992, whether they preferred a controlled economy or a market economy, those over the age of 60 supported a controlled economy (82–14 percent) while the younger generation was more evenly divided, 52 percent for a controlled economy and 46 percent for a market oriented economy.[17]

In Russia, economic reforms were initiated by Gorbachev and were, initially, gradual and limited in scope. These however, were unable to stem the economic crisis, and in the first quarter of 1991, for example, Soviet national income declined by an estimated 15–16 percent in real terms.[18] According to Anders Aslund, poor economic performance was a result of several factors, including the neglect of democratic processes, unfound belief in gradualism, inability to conceptualize the market, and excessive confidence in the capabilities of the state apparatus.[19] The importance of the democratization, to legitimize economic reform, was recognized also by Jude Wanniski. He explained that, "The economic structure must change continually to keep pace with changing times in a competitive world economy; an optimum democratic structure provides the foundation for such change, enabling the people to exert their wisdom in guiding the direction and contour of economic change."[20] Essentially, the argument was that democratic decision making processes were better suited to coping with change.

It did not help that the Soviet central government was plagued by political instability. Gorbachev initiated reforms but also desperately struggled to preserve the integrity of the old Soviet Union. His tragedy was the inability to make a fundamental break with the old system and his equivocation alienated both defenders of the old system and proponents of a new order. As Carl Linden argues, "Gorbachev was not radical enough. He failed to follow a public that began to press for a break with, not a reform of, the communist autocracy".[21] The Soviet Union did not survive and was replaced by the Confederation of Independent States (CIS) of which Russia was the largest republic and Gorbachev himself was swept aside by a more reformist Boris Yeltsin. The new President introduced sweeping changes but also left behind a legacy of many social inequities and corrupt practices within the Russian political economy.

The starting point of Russian reform was privatization of state owned enterprises, price liberalization and economic stabilization. Because public enterprises were inefficient and survived only with generous state subsidies, privatization became a key component of the restructuring program. The faith in privatization as a solution to economic problems stemmed from the view that public companies, weaned off governmental subsidies and support, would be forced to accept financial discipline and that exposure to market conditions would force them to achieve allocative efficiency.[22]

Privatization in Russia was to cover state enterprises other than state farms and it was stated that roughly 20–25 percent of state property would be privatized in 1992. Privatization of state owned enterprises could be initiated by workers and employees. The privatization plan announced by President Yeltsin in December 1991 established four categories of firms to be privatized. The first sector where privatization was obligatory included retail and wholesale trade, unprofitable enterprises and construction materials enterprises. The second sector included firms that could be privatized with permission of the Federal government, including defense industry and research, air transport, pharmaceutical, and fuel and power industry. The third category included enterprises that could be privatized with consent of local authorities, such as taxis, municipal services and hotels. The final category included enterprises that could not be privatized and included natural resources, historic and cultural facilities, highways, and power stations.[23] The privatization plan privileged 'insiders' including managers or individuals with close political connection or influence, perhaps on the belief that unless insiders were suitably 'bribed', they would subvert and derail the government's privatization plan. The reformers worried also that unless privatization was implemented quickly, communists in the Russian parliament would block the divestment of state assets to private control. By the summer of 1992 about 2000 state owned enterprises were privatized in a manner that allowed top managers to acquire substantial ownership, either free or at discounted prices. Individual Russians were also allocated vouchers to purchase shares in privatized companies and by the late 1990s more Russians than in any other country of the world had become shareholders. Nonetheless, the various stages of privatization disproportionately benefited insiders and top managers and its practical consequence was to create an instantly wealthy group of industrialists with very close links to the state. The level of income inequality was such that by around 2005, the top 10 percent of Russian society had incomes 15 times greater than those at the bottom of Russian society. The process of privatisation created a very corrupted system, with the economy dominated by a group of oligarchs who had cleverly manipulated privatization to gain enormous wealth for themselves.

Following the departure of the inglorious Boris Yeltsin, President Putin reasserted the authority of the state and either imprisoned many of the oligarchs or forced them into exile. This result was not necessarily a less corrupt economic and political system, and indeed in 2006 Transparency International ranked Russia 121 out of 163 countries in its Transparency Perception Index, co-equal with the Philippines but just ahead of Indonesia. Putin's actions were intended more as a signal to all of the powers of the Kremlin. The Russian state also resumed control of many key sectors of the economy and, in 2005, took over the Yukos oil company, indicating a clear intent to dominate the strategic industries.[24] This was an authoritarian turn of events that did not sit too well with western observers but welcomed by many Russians who welcomed the assertiveness and confidence of the Russian state both within and on the international stage.

Price liberalization in Russia was premised on the belief that unless true relative prices were established, progress on other fronts would continue to be distorted by inaccurate prices. Price decontrol was begun in early January 1992 and the immediate result was high levels of price increases. In the month of January alone, consumer prices increased by 250 percent but the inflationary spiral subsided in later months after the initial surge. The problem with price liberalization was that, in the absence of an open import regime, there was very little effective control on price rises to ensure that prices did not overshoot international market prices. Excessively high prices not only affected individual consumers, but also users of secondary inputs and this may have forced otherwise viable firms into bankruptcy, unable to remain profitable with too high input costs.

Unlike transition in China, which was assisted by a large inflow of foreign direct assistance, the Russian economy received little foreign capital input. The importance of such assistance had increased following downward revision of estimated Soviet gold reserves which were now regarded as inadequate to finance the transition process.[25] According to David Roche of Morgan Stanley International, Russia's total financial needs, including infrastructure, social welfare and balance of payments assistance, were between US$76 and US$167 billion a year.[26] Jeffrey Sachs extrapolated that since western countries had provided eastern European countries, with a population base of 125 million, with approximately US$57 billion between the summer of 1989 and May 1990, the Soviet requirement was likely to be in excess of US$100 billion.[27]

Compared to Russian needs, promised financial assistance was insignificant. Not only was official assistance slow in coming but private sector capital flows, too, did not materialize because of continued political and economic instability in Russia. This was in sharp contrast to China and, Jeffrey Sachs, the leading Western proponent of shock therapy, blamed setbacks in the Russian reform process to Western insincerity and poor strategy of aid disbursement. For example, he pointed out that the West had failed to give even the aid that had been promised. In 1992, US$24 billion had been promised but only US$10 billion was actually delivered and in 1993, US$28 billion was promised and only US$5 billion delivered.[28] Foreign assistance remained limited for a number of reasons.

The United States was burdened by its own fiscal accounts deficits and an improbable source for large-scale financial assistance. Germany, too, was in no position to extend significant aid to Russia considering that the reunification of East and West Germany had already cost the Bonn government more than US$100 billion. Japan, a capital surplus country, was reasonably well placed to provide financial assistance, but was unwilling to assist the Russian economic transition. Jeffrey Sachs observed that the Japanese government played an essentially harmful role in the process of Russian transition,[29] by withholding substantial aid until a resolution of the territorial dispute and return of the four northern islands, Habomai, Shikotan, Kunashiri and Etorofu, occupied by the Soviet Union after the Second World War.[b]

Under US prerssure, the Japanese government relented in April 1993 and declared that it would no longer link aid to Russia with the territorial issue. This turnaround followed a French proposal to convene a special summit to discuss aid to Russia, which the Japanese government feared would sideline the Tokyo summit of the seven industrialized countries in

---

[b] During the height of the Cold War, the Japanese claim had received strong support from the US and encouraged by this, the government adopted a maximalist position and demanded the return of all four islands before concluding any peace treaty with the Soviet Union. However, once the Cold War was over, American support evaporated quickly and the Japanese government found itself isolated but unable to abandon the long-held policy without 'losing face'. The Russian government, too, refused to negotiate a face-saving settlement for fear of reviving irredentist claims by other countries. In 1992, Russian President Boris Yeltsin cancelled, at short notice, a scheduled visit to Japan, concerned that Japan would simply exploit the occasion to press for the return of the islands.

July 1993. The Japanese government finessed over its embarrassment by distinguishing between the territorial dispute, which was a *bilateral* issue, and aid to Russia, which was a *multilateral* policy to encourage Russian economic reforms, and in the interest of world peace and democracy. In April 1993, both the United States and Japan announced separate aid packages to Russia. The G7 finance ministers also agreed on a major aid package totalling about US$45 billion.

Sachs also criticized Western strategy of disbursing aid through the IMF, which acted more like a cautious banker rather than as coordinators of Western aid. His recommendation was for a radical restructuring of the IMF and the World Bank to make these institutions more responsive to Russian needs. One IMF official, however, dismissed Sach's criticisms as misdirected and suggested that the real problem afflicting the Russian economy was a general inability of the political system to fend of sectional interests and their demands for welfare and transfer payments. These, he claimed, had rendered the task of balancing the state budget much more difficult and, consequently, resulted in poor macroeconomic stabilization.[30]

In the area of stabilization policy and budget reform, apart from reducing budget deficits, the plan involved the float of the Russian rouble and currency convertibility from January 1, 1992. Major emphasis was on reducing budget deficits and controlling inflation. The importance of combating inflation was emphasized on grounds that reform would not succeed because inflation, if not kept in check, would sap work incentives and social support for reform.[31] Western aid agencies have, similarly, emphasized the importance of reducing inflation levels. Thus, in 1992, when Russia joined the IMF, it secured loans of US$24 billion, conditioned on drastic cutbacks in budget deficit and strict adherence to fiscal austerity. In the first half of 1992, budget deficit was reduced to only 5 percent of GNP, compared to 20 percent in the previous year. Similarly, in 1995, the government adopted an austere budget in order to secure additional IMF funding.

Economic transition in Russia has been more painful and tortured than in China. One explanation might be that in Russia reformers dismantled existing structures and institutions even before they had put in place alternate functioning institutions. They chose to do this to prevent communist sympathizers from regrouping and mounting a challenge to the reformers but a consequence of this hastily implemented transformation process was a prolonged period of economic instability and chaos. Another contributing factor may have been poor implementation of stated reform policies. The simultaneous occurrence of rampant inflation and negative growth suggested that budget cuts and fiscal austerity were more contrived than real. It was obvious, according to Jeffrey Hough, that "the Gaidar government followed a loose-money policy from the beginning, but put most of the deficit off-budget to create the impression of a balanced budget".[32] This might be explained by the fact that the political system was pulling in different directions. For example, a conservative parliament forced President Yeltsin to include anti-reformers in the government,[c] and it did not help that the Russian Central Bank, under the jurisdiction of the Russian Parliament, was also not very enthusiastic about the pace of economic reform.

In the late 1990s, Russia slowly turned the corner. Interest rate differentials and a stable Russian Rouble led to increased capital inflow which, in 1995, amounted to US$1.5 billion, roughly half of which was FDI capital. Russia's export position also improved compared to the early 1990s. After six years of economic decline, 1997 was the first year of economic growth in Russia. The European Bank for Reconstruction and Development estimated that roughly 70 percent of the Russian GDP in 1997 was accounted for by the private sector. Stanley Fischer, Deputy Managing Director of the IMF confidently predicted that, in the new millennium, if reform policies were implemented as planned, Russian GDP could grow at around six percent with lower fiscal deficits and inflation.[33]

In 2000, Vladimir Putin assumed presidency in Russia and his tenure in office benefited immensely from an oil-induced economic boom. In 1998, for example, Russian exports of energy resources were about US$28 billion but increased to $191 billion in 2006 (Table 5.1). On the

---

[c] Yegor Gaidar himself, was forced out of office by the conservative opponents of President Yeltsin. Following the April 1993 referendum, however, which produced results supportive of continued reform some of the conservative forces within the government were forced out but the conservative Vice-President Alexander Rutskoi continues to defy Yeltsin and shows no indication of resigning.

Table 5.1: Russian economic indicators.

	1992	1994	1996	1998	2000	2002	2004	2006
GDP growth (%)	−14.5	−12.6	−3.6	−5.3	10.0	4.7	7.2	6.7
Inflation (%)	1353	302	47.7	27.7	20.8	15.8	10.9	9.7
Curr. acc. balance ($billion)			10.8	0.22	47.0	29.0	59.5	95.3

back of resources and mineral exports, the economy posted healthy growth, with significant reductions in the number of unemployed and those living below the poverty line.

The oil boom highlighted the importance of foreign trade but Russian membership in the WTO[d] remained mired in lengthy and complicated negotiations. Nonetheless, expectations are that Russia will secure full membership in 2008 and that will add to upbeat sentiments about profitability of foreign investments in Russia.

State Capitalism and Transition in India

India was, for a long time after the Second World War, a case study of missed opportunities and failed potential. Comparing India and Korea, in 1960, Korea was only marginally richer than India and had a domestic savings rate of 1 percent, compared to India's 12–15 percent and, yet, by 1995, Korea had emerged as a high income country while India continued to languish as a poverty stricken, low income economy.[34] The economic success of Korea and other East Asian economies was a result of their foreign trade expansion but India, following independence in 1947, had pursued a policy of self-reliance that limited both foreign trade and foreign direct investment. Successive Indian governments harboured insecurities about allowing foreign capital or foreign products into the economy and Indian businesses, protected from foreign competition within a large domestic market, had little incentive to be efficient and innovative, and expand their export profile. The Indian government, influenced perhaps

---

[d] Russia applied for membership in June 1993.

by the Latin American model, implemented a strong import substitution regime. Behind high tariff barriers, India developed a broad based manufacturing capacity but one that was internationally uncompetitive and unable to generate meaningful export growth.

The state became an active player in the economy, not only because of a large nationalized sector but also because of regulatory controls that stifled entrepreneurial activity. India's transition from state-led to market capitalism began in earnest in the early 1990s under the leadership of Prime Minister Narasimha Rao although some tentative reform oriented measures had been introduced by Prime Minister Rajiv Gandhi in the mid-1980s. It is important to note that economic transition in India was not from central planning to capitalism, as in the case of Russia and China, because India already had well established capitalist institutions, but it was a transition from a regulatory structure that was stifling and detrimental to innovation and entrepreneurial activity to a market based system of risk taking and reward. After decades of pursuing an import substitution industrialization strategy (ISI), Indian leaders abandoned ISI in favour of export-oriented industrialization (EOI), a statergy that had been so successfully employed by East Asian countries.

The catalyst for change, as in the case of Russia and China, was extremely poor economic growth rate in 1990 and a precarious foreign exchange reserve position that, at one point, had dwindled to the equivalent of three weeks supply of imports. The reform agenda focused on deregulation of economic activity, and on the liberalization of trade and investments.

Much has been achieved in the 15 years since reforms were introduced and India has emerged as a new powerhouse in the software and informational technology (IT) industry. It was fortunate that liberalization and reforms were being introduced at a time when the West was growing increasingly concerned about the looming millennium bug (Y2K) crisis, which created an instant demand for the software technicians and manpower that was available in India. Where China has emerged as a leading manufacturing center, Indian economy growth has been underpinned by the services and technology sector. This is reflected in the share of services in the national economy, which has grown from 41 percent at the start of the reform process to 54 percent in 2005. By contrast, share of the industrial sector has been relatively stable, but slightly lower than before.

Despite, success, excessive governmental regulation continues to constrain economic activity in India. For instance, while India has a large and well functioning banking system, government regulations mean that banks can lend a smaller portion of deposits than in other similarly placed countries. This has constrained new investment and growth potential.

Like China, India adopted the gradualist approach in order to minimize internal tensions between advocates and critics of reform.[35] In a democratic setting, Indian policy makers could not ignore the substantial base of opposition to reforms as implying a capitulation to foreign capitalists and multinational corporations.

With an import substitution industrialization strategy tariff levels, until the late 1980s, were as high as 200 percent on average but, as a result of reform, average non-agricultural tariffs were reduced to below 15 percent and there was a similar relaxation of controls on foreign investments. The government also liberalized foreign investment rules and as a result inward foreign investment, which stood at US$103 million (of which FDI was US$97 million) in 1990–1991 had increased to US$8.152 billion (of which FDI was US$6.131) in 2001–2002. In 2006, FDI flows to India totalled US$18.9 billion. The growth in foreign and foreign direct investment has been large but these are still only a fraction of investment into China.[36] Domestic savings, as in East Asia, has been an important source of investment in India and the saving rate has increased to about 30 percent in recent years. Indian firms have also invested overseas and the total outflow of FDI in 2005 was almost US$8 billion.

Trade policy reform and liberalization have boosted levels of trade and trade as a percentage of GDP increased from around 15 percent on average before the reforms to 36.5 percent in 2005. This was still substantially below that of Russia and China at 57 percent and 64.5 percent, respectively, in 2005. Overall economic growth rates have been impressive but less than the double-digit growth rates of the Chinese economy in recent years. Since 2003, average annual growth rate in India has been around 8.5 percent and increased to 9 percent in 2006. India's precarious foreign exchange position has also been reversed and in 2006, India had total reserves of US$180 billion, enough to cover imports for almost one year. In the process, India's industrial structure has been radically transformed with important wealth and welfare gains. Poverty levels were close to 40 percent before the start of the reform process but had declined to about 26 percent at the end of the 1990s. Even though the size of the middle class has expanded rapidly, lingering high levels of poverty is a challenge that governments will have to deal with to avoid rising discontent, particularly in the rural areas.

India's liberalization process has led to some speculation that India will compete with China in manufacturing exports but the two economies have developed, instead, a complementary export profile. Indian exports have concentrated in services and information technology (IT) whereas Chinese exports have been dominated by manufactured goods. The rapid development of the services and the IT industry in India and the growth of service exports, relying on the fiber-optic cable, have allowed industrialists to bypass infrastructural bottlenecks.[37] For that same reason, manufacturing growth in India has been about half that of China. But infrastructural problems can be "easily" addressed and overcome through capital investments. India has not been able to replicate the stellar economic growth performance of the Chinese economy but the Chinese economy faces a number of future challenges that India is likely to be spared, most importantly the issue of political liberalization. India is a large and stable democracy and not likely to experience the sorts of difficulties experienced by Russia during its early transition period. Democracy in India, also provides governments the legitimacy to make tough decisions.[38] By contrast, there remains some uncertainty as to how China will manage likely future claims for a more liberal political regime. India also has a demographic advantage over China, with a growing and relatively youthful workforce.

Conclusion

Despite a broadly similar transition ideology, there are important differences in the way transition has impacted on political realities in China, Russia and India. In China, economic reforms did not extend to political reforms and an incipient democracy movement was brutally crushed in

1989. The Communist Party remains the only legitimate national political authority and it is difficult to envisage a scenario where the Party might be persuaded to give up its stranglehold on power, whether from internal or foreign pressure. In Russia, by contrast, expectations were that collapse of the Soviet Union would usher in a period of democracy. Democracy in Russia, however, was subverted by close links that emerged between the state and business communities largely as a result of the privatization process. Corruption during the years of Yeltsin presidency became the hallmark of Russian politics and continues to affect democratic politics in Russia even today. During the Putin presidency, there was an equally disturbing drift to more authoritarian political practices, including restrictions on media and the press. While Putin restored tarnished Russian pride and pulled the economy out of a tailspin, helped by a fortuitous rise in oil prices, to many western observers this was achieved at the expense of democratic politics. With economic recovery, Russia also emerged as a more assertive and ambitious global player, but married to authoritarian domestic politics, this has reignited concerns that the United States–Russian tensions could escalate to a Second Cold War. This reflects an unhelpful obsession to interpret developments in sharply dichotomous terms but it is clear that economic growth in the three large transition economies, if sustained, will necessitate some political adjustments in the West.

If they do not do so already, each of the three transition countries is projected to increase its economic weight in the global economy, both in terms of share of the global GDP and share of world trade. As Table 5.2 shows, while China occupies a major share of world trade, at close to 13 percent in 2004, Russia's economic presence is only a third that of China and India lags even further behind, at less than a sixth that of China. However, both India and Russia are on a trajectory to increase their relative weight in the global economy.

Of the three, only China and India are members of the WTO. China's economic success has been based on export growth and, in 2007, China's trade surplus was projected to reach US$400 billion, approximately 12 percent of GDP. According to Nicholas Lardy, China's current account surplus as a percentage of GDP is "triple Japan's level in the 1980s when Japan-bashing was at its peak".[39]

Table 5.2:   Chinese, Russian and Indian Economic Indicators.

	GDP (US$, trillion)	Share of world trade (%)	
	2006	2003	2004
China	2.7	11.4	12.8
Russia	1.002	3.3 (2002)	4.1
India	0.814	1.7	1.9

Note: GDP is calculated at market exchange rates, not purchasing power parity.

Given the magnitude of its global trade China was well positioned to play a prominent role in the Doha Round of trade negotiations but, interestingly, it was outplayed by India, which as one of the leaders of the G20 coalition of developing countries was active in agricultural negotiations. China's reluctance to become actively involved, despite being a member of the G20, might be explained by the fact that Chinese exports are dominated by manufactured goods and it has less reason to make common cause on agriculture with developing countries, a primary focus of the G20. Moreover, Chinese leaders may have decided that it would be imprudent to demand greater access to western farm markets at a time when Chinese manufactured exports had increased their market penetration in the West, and produced large trade surpluses.

Politically and diplomatically, despite rapid economic emergence, China and India are likely to be identified more as regional rather than global powers, at least in the short to medium term. Indian ambitions are largely regional in nature and its potential sphere of influence might be defined as extending from Southeast Asia to the Middle East, where there is a large Indian diaspora. China too has pursued an active policy of developing closer links with regional countries in East Asia, through bilateral free trade agreements, seemingly in competition with Japan. The Chinese government also won generous praise from regional countries during the Asian financial crisis when it ruled out a devaluation of the Chinese currency that would have added to the strain on crises affected regional countries.

Militarily, China is not a concern to western government but just as the collapse of the Soviet Union was hastened by economic stagnation, the strength of the Chinese economy has given the government new opportunities to significantly expand its future military potential. The prospect of China as a global superpower, even if unlikely in the immediate future, has led to speculation about China's future in the global economic system. Despite numerous assertions by its leaders that China intends to play a constructive and positive role in global politics and economy, there are many sceptics who are convinced that China's rise poses a threat to the West. This may in part be attributed to the continued dominance of the communist party in China but evidence, such as its role in defusing tensions on the Korean peninsula and membership of the WTO, points to its preparedness to play a constructive role in global politics. Indeed, it is difficult to imagine a China that might chose to destabilize an international regime from which it has derived immense benefits. Certainly, there might be some tinkering of the established rules and norms but that is unlikely to lead to a dismantling of the liberal economic system. A bigger challenge for the West is to engage China in a way that is commensurate to its growing power and influence, such that it does not feel marginalized and without voice in, say, the multilateral institutions and in the rule making processes. This will require more of an adjustment from western powers that have dominated positions of influence within the global political economy. The issue, therefore, is not one of ensnaring China in a web of global economic constraints where it has no independent capacity to destabilize the edifice of global trade and economy but rather of western willingness to accommodate an emerging China within the global power hierarchy.

Chapter Six

POLITICAL ECONOMY OF FOREIGN INVESTMENT

The flow of international capital has, historically, mirrored the flow of goods and services. In the contemporary global economy, however, trade levels no longer provide a guide to the flow of capital, which are substantially larger and determined more by interest rate differentials and by exchange rate movements. This flow is made possible by currency convertibility and removal of exchange restrictions. A substantial proportion of contemporary capital flows can be classified as speculative and short-term, which also have the potential to undermine national monetary and economic objectives and even to destabilize economies by undermining confidence in the local currency. That is what happened in East Asia in 1997, when large-scale capital flight triggered distress in both financial and industrial sectors. Various proposals have been put forward either to restrict the flow of speculative capital or to develop safeguards against their potentially damaging consequences, but the international community has not developed the level of collaboration or cooperation that would be necessary to implement such schemes. Instead, the task is left to prudent national policies.

Unlike speculative capital flows, foreign direct investment (FDI) is long-term commitment to productive activities in a foreign (host) country. There may be some debate about its utility or appropriateness but FDI generally does not have the same destabilizing potential. Foreign direct investment has increased dramatically in recent years, rising from US$220 billion in 1994 to about US$1.3 trillion in 2006, originating mainly in Japan, the European Union and the United States. Developed countries are also the main hosts of foreign direct investments. More recently, however, South Korea, China and Taiwan have emerged as important sources of foreign investment, particularly in Southeast Asia and Africa.

While companies invest in foreign productive activities (and become in the process a multinational company, or MNC), in principle, foreign demand for products and services can be met through exports and there is no logical reason for a firm to consider production in a host economy, unless there are significant costs benefits. The product-cycle theory helps explain why, at a certain point in the life of a product, it may be beneficial to produce in a host country rather than export the product/service from the home country. Essentially, the product-cycle theory explains mobility of businesses from say metropolitan centers in developed countries to the non-metropolitan areas and from non-metropolitan areas to foreign markets. The advantages of foreign investment range from cost reduction and better customer service. According to Ferdows,[1] the various advantages can be ranged from those that are the most tangible to the least tangible. These are:

Most Tangible

- Reduce direct and indirect costs
- Reduce capital costs
- Reduce taxes
- Reduce logistics costs
- Overcome tariff barriers
- Provide better customer service
- Spread foreign exchange risks
- Build alternative supply sources
- Pre-empt potential competitors
- Learn from local suppliers
- Learn from foreign customers
- Learn from competitors
- Learn from foreign research centers
- Attract talent globally

Most Intangible

While most FDI flows are among developed countries, the flow of FDI from developed to developing countries has attracted considerable attention, as to whether such flows are beneficial or detrimental to overall economic performance and growth, and to political stability. In the contemporary period, most developing countries welcome foreign investment but until the 1970s there was considerable hostility to it on grounds that it diminished economic sovereignty or impeded development. In the past, most FDI in developing countries in the earlier period was concentrated in the resources sector and the benefit of foreign investment to resource rich developing countries was small because MNCs, typically, engaged in little value-adding activities in these economies and tended, instead, to export commodities in crude form. Thus, foreign investment failed to stimulate industrial deepening and development.

A common criticism, articulated by Sanjaya Lall and Paul Streeten, is that "host economies do not gain much financial benefit from foreign direct investment, and would be seen to gain even less if hidden remittances in the form of transfer pricing were fully known".[2] Transfer pricing is a corporate tax minimization strategy, which MNCs may engage in by artificially fixing prices for intra-firm trade across borders to shift excess profits out of national jurisdictions with high taxation rates. Multinationals are ideally positioned to take advantage of these strategies because they operate in a number of national jurisdictions and source supplies from subsidiaries in other countries. There are many documented instances of transfer pricing, including cases of rocket launcher exports at US$40, bulldozer exports at US$525, and imports of tweezers at US$4896, and wrenches at US$1089. Ha-Joon Chang argues that transfer pricing is more of a problem today than in the past "...because of the proliferation of tax havens that have no or minimal corporate income taxes. Companies can vastly reduce their tax obligations by shifting most of their profits to a paper company registered in a tax haven".[3] Transfer pricing is beneficial to MNCs but host governments potentially lose out on potential taxation revenue. The revenue losses for governments may be significant, especially in developing countries.

Again, in the past FDI was presumed not to benefit developing countries because of the imbalance of power between a large foreign MNC and a small developing country, such that MNCs were able to extract a favorable deal, including tax holidays, that lowered benefits to the host economy. Another criticism was that MNCs tended to introduce capital intensive and sophisticated technology that was inappropriate to developing countries, which had a comparative advantage in labor intensive manufacturing. MNC technology was usually capital intensive but inappropriate in a developing country, which had surplus labor and high levels of unemployment or underemployment. MNC reputation was tarnished also by a fear that these companies were agents of the home government and intervened in host country politics to advantage the home country. One of the best examples of this was the way the International Telephone and Telegraph Company (ITT), an American multinational, orchestrated a campaign against the democratically elected, but socialist, government of Salvador Allende in Chile in the early 1970s. ITT encouraged capital flight that paralyzed the Chilean economy, and in the end a bloody coup d'etat that toppled the government of Allende.

Finally, dependency theory was inhospitable to FDI and recommended a policy of self-reliance for developing country. Dependency theorists, like Raul Prebisch, and Andre Gunder Frank, argued that underdevelopment was a result of western exploitation and that developing countries should pursue inward-looking and autarchic policies, avoid or minimize economic exchange with western countries, in order to promote development at home. They maintained that, historically, developing countries, with a reliance on primary exports, suffered deteriorating terms of trade which impeded their development and that there were structural constraints to successful industrialization, which was essential for the development. Drawing on the experiences of Latin America, they maintained that it was no coincidence that Latin American industrialization had to await the onset of the First World War, when trade with the western countries was disrupted. Since MNCs, essentially western based, were a source of integration and linkages with developed countries, it was obvious that MNCs had to be controlled and limited in their ability to operate in developing countries. The evidence that MNC activity contributed little to developing countries might be that despite a long history of FDI in developing countries, there had been no appreciable improvement of economic conditions in a majority of the host countries.[4]

Debates about FDI raged through the late 1970s but, in the 1980s, FDI became less of a lightning rod for criticisms because capital flows to developing countries had practically dried up. Following the Latin American debt crisis which ushered in a decade of economic stagnation in most developing countries, there was neither demand nor supply side pressure to expand FDI. The level of FDI had declined to insignificance and consequently did not occupy the mind of potential critics. Moreover, in the 1980s, East Asian countries exemplified the potential of foreign investment to promote development. It was no longer so obvious that FDI was always or necessarily a detriment to development. East Asian economies demonstrated that it was possible to exploit foreign investment to promote industrialization. They successfully implemented an exported oriented industrialization strategy, which relied extensively on foreign capital. It helped also that international developments, such as the appreciation of the Japanese Yen after 1985, forced many Japanese firms to relocate production to cheaper cost countries in Asia in order to remain internationally competitive and service demand in third countries.

In the 1990s, after a long hiatus, FDI flows to developing countries began to increase again. In the early 1980s, for example, developing countries received an annual average of US$12.6 billion, or only 20 percent of global FDI but in 1994 FDI in developing countries had increased to US$70 billion, or 32 percent of total.[5] By 1996, net foreign investment in developing countries had increased slightly to over US$100 billion, nearly 60 percent of which went to Asian countries. In 2006, FDI flows to China alone amounted to nearly US$70 billion, about 5.5 percent of global FDI. The increase in FDI flows to developing countries reflected the passage of Latin America's debt crisis. In the aftermath of that debt crisis, private capital flows to developing countries had declined considerably forcing them to rely mainly on international agencies like the World Bank and the International Monetary Fund (IMF). The return of private sector lenders was an indication that the worst of the debt crisis had been successfully negotiated. The growth in foreign investment can be attributed, in part, to liberalization and the abandonment of import substitution industrialization for export oriented industrialization in developing countries. Not surprisingly, the World Bank, and IMF, take some of the credit for having improved the investment climate in developing countries following structural adjustment programs of the early 1980s.[6]

In contrast to earlier periods, the increase in FDI flows did not trigger the same negative reception. This may perhaps be attributed to the view that in an increasingly globalized world economy, MNCs had become "nationalitiless" commercial entities. Former US Secretary of Labor, Robert Reich, argued that US MNCs had become global citizens,[7] implying that they were less likely to serve narrow US political interests. More likely, the positive appraisal of FDI was the result of a mindshift, reflected in the Washington Consensus that encouraged or forced developing countries to liberalize capital markets and embrace the inflow of foreign capital. Developing countries welcomed FDI as plugging a savings gap, expanding the pool of investment capital, and providing access to technology and management skills. It is incorrect to assume however that all FDI leads to increased economic activity, and instead, when foreign interests simply buy into an existing firm there is no new economic activity. Nonetheless, the welcome mat had been put out and most developing countries, especially China, appeared to have benefitted from inflow of FDI. Admittedly, the link between FDI and growth is correlational but it is not entirely unreasonable to assume that FDI has some positive impact on growth.

Since liberalization in the early 1980s, the Chinese economy had benefited tremendously from Japanese investments and India too, benefited from the inflow of investments following reforms in the early 1990s. Contrary suggestions that investment flows to China and India have failed to narrow the technology gap with developed countries[8] overlook the reality that, even if developing countries did not gain access to cutting edge technology, they still acquired technology that they previously did not possess.

An important development in the foreign investment flows has been the emergence of Japan as a major creditor country.[9] For much of the postwar period, for instance, Japanese companies relied on exports to meet overseas demand. In the United States, in the late 1970s and after, there was a concerted push to force Japan to invest in local production rather than rely on exports. This was premised on the reasoning that local production would create jobs, add to the industrial base and benefit the local economy, whereas exports undermined the target economy by eliminating local competitors. One of the motivations behind the American demand for voluntary export restraints on Japanese cars in the early 1980s was to force Japanese car manufacturers to invest in production in the United States. Indeed, the boom in Japanese investment in the United States began in the early 1980s and was led by investment in auto plants in the United States. Along with export restrictions, which played a part in encouraging Japanese FDI in the United States, the outflow of FDI from Japan received a fresh boost, in the mid-1980s, when exchange rate adjustments made Japanese exports less competitive.

The growth of Japanese FDI began in the mid-1980s and was briefly interrupted when the asset price bubble burst in the early 1990s to plunge the economy into a recession. It, however, recovered a few years later.[10] In overall terms, the bulk of Japanese investment has been in the developed economies of North America and Europe. In 1994, FDI outflows to the United States accounted for 43.7 percent of the total, the European countries received 19.4 percent and the Asian countries 16 percent.[11] Even though most Japanese FDI is in the United States, Japan is a major investor in the East Asian countries. The stock of Japanese FDI in Asia exceeds that of the United States and Japanese corporations loom large in the small economies of East Asia.

While Japan has emerged as a major source of FDI, inflows of FDI into Japan have remained relatively small. In 1993, the stock of FDI in Japan was US$29.9 billion while the stock of Japanese FDI abroad stood at $422.5 billion. In 1996, total Japanese FDI overseas was US$49 billion (Yen 5.5 trillion) whereas overseas FDI in Japan was only US$7 billion (Yen 770 billion). By contrast, the comparative figures for the United States were US$85.6 billion and US$78.1 billion, in 1996. The imbalance in Japanese FDI flows is large but it should be noted that FDI flows into and from the United States were also highly unbalanced in the early post-war period and into the 1970s. In 1970, the United States was the source of nearly 63 percent of FDI outflows and absorbed only about 16 percent.[12]

A number of factors stimulated the growth of Japanese foreign investment, including protectionism in the United States. As the United States, in the early 1980s, forced Japan to exercise voluntary export restraint in automobiles, Japanese car manufacturers began to set up production facilities in the United States in order to retain market shares. Another factor was the currency realignment following the Plaza Accord of 1985, which made Japanese exports less competitive. As the Yen appreciated and pushed up production costs in Japan, Japanese manufacturers began to relocate production to less costly countries. Japanese investments in East and Southeast Asia, according to Hatch and Yamamura, have also been motivated by a strategic vision, formulated by the Japanese Ministry of International Trade and Industry (MITI), to create a regional division of labor and integrate the entire region into a production network in order to pursue a global corporate strategy.[13] It is true that manufacturers in Japan have used East Asia as a production platform not only to satisfy demand in host countries but also in Japan and elsewhere. In 1992, the ratio of exports to total sales of Japanese affiliates in the manufacturing sector in Asia was 45 percent.[14]

The high proportion of exports to local sales for Japanese subsidiaries in East Asia is, however, part of a broader pattern of MNC activity. Studies have shown that foreign firms export a greater proportion of their production than do locally owned firms. This can perhaps be explained by the fact that MNCs are the dominant source of FDI and they trade extensively among their own affiliates. There is evidence that intra-firm trade among MNCs accounts for a third of total world trade.[15] Moreover, to attribute Japanese FDI in East Asia to a grand MITI plan may be an exaggeration because MITI (now renamed Ministry of Economy, Trade and Industry, or METI) had much diminished powers to implement an industrial policy even within Japan.

The rapid expansion of Japanese foreign investment in East Asia produced worrying concerns that it might lead to a "hollowing out" of Japanese industry and ultimately to the erosion of Japanese industrial base. Such concerns were not without precedence. In the United States, in the 1960s and 1970s, the outflow of American FDI had produced similar reactions. A spokesperson for the AFL-CIO stated that the transfer of production overseas was making the United States, "a nation of hamburger stands…a country stripped of industrial capacity and meaningful work…a service economy…a nation of citizens busily buying and selling cheeseburgers and root beer floats".[16]

As foreign direct investment increased, the absence of uniform regulatory standards began to loom large as a hindrance to international capital flows. To simplify the regulatory environment, the Uruguay Round included foreign investment in its negotiations.

Uruguay Round and Trade Related Investment Measures

Developing countries in particular have a history of stipulating conditions, such as local content, or export requirements, on foreign investors. To the extent that domestic investor have no such conditions imposed on their activities meant that there was bias against MNCs. Negotiators in the Uruguay Round sought to rectify this imbalance and the result of this was an agreement on Trade Related Investment Measures (TRIMs). This constitutes one of the main legal instruments of the World Trade Organization. The objective of the TRIMs agreement was to create a more liberal investment climate and remove overt discrimination in the treatment of foreign investments. TRIMS can be classified either as input (local content requirement, local equity requirement, R&D requirement) or output (export performance requirement, export controls) measures. Some such as trade balancing requirements operate both as input and export measure because they require foreign investors to counterbalance imports of parts and raw materials with exports of finished commodities. TRIMs are widely used and, according to David Greenaway, have three objectives.

- Influence the location and pattern of economic activity.
- Ensure benefits to the host country.
- Redistribute part of surplus generated by FDI away from MNCs and towards host countries.[17]

There was initial disagreement between the developed and developing countries as to whether TRIMs should be included as part of an agreement of international trade. Developing countries argued that TRIMs were an investment, and not trade, policy measures, and, therefore, beyond the jurisdiction of the GATT. The gulf, however, was not, according to David Greenaway, "unbridgeable" and could be overcome with preferential treatment for the developing countries through an extended transitional period. Moreover, it is wrong to presume that there is a clear demarcation between developing countries as hosts of FDI and the developed countries as the home countries. In recent years, developing countries, too, have started investing overseas and this has blurred the division between developed and developing countries. In 1989–1990, for example, Taiwan's FDI was US$12 billion and that of South Korea $1.3 billion.[18] Even smaller countries, like Thailand, Malaysia and the Philippines, have been investing in other countries.

Global business corporations were especially keen to see the establishment of standardized rules and regulations that did not arbitrarily restrict their global strategies. TRIMs, like local content requirements, are policy measures used by government to force foreign investors to achieve certain performance criteria. But local content regulations can restrict trade by forcing a company to procure locally what might otherwise be cheaply sourced from abroad. Similarly, minimum export requirements also distort and divert trade by substituting home country exports to third countries, with host country exports to such markets. GATT's involvement with TRIMs was natural given its emphasis on trade creation, as opposed to trade restriction or trade diversion but its significance was not lost on global businesses.

Developing countries, however, resisted the pressure to force them to give up local content requirements, which they regarded as essential to their developmental objectives. By contrast, the OECD countries insisted that such measures distorted trade and should be part of the trade negotiating agenda. The Uruguay Round Agreement recognised the significance of TRIMS and applied the principle of national treatment (Article 3) to prevent discriminatory national policies. It, however, permitted developing countries an extended grace period to eliminate non-conforming TRIMs. The accepted schedule specified that developed countries had to remove all non-conforming TRIMs within two years, the developing countries within five years, and the least developed countries within seven years.[19] The agreement determined that local content requirements violated GATT principles but, interestingly, did not address the question of export performance requirements. The TRIMs agreement was to be reviewed within five years of the establishment of the WTO to assess the need for more general disciplines on investment and the possibility of expanding the list of prohibited TRIMs.[20]

The Uruguay Round took the first step toward achieving a uniform and non-discriminatory regulatory environment in international investments. The inclusion of TRIMs in the negotiating agenda was of particular interest to global corporations, which hoped, thereby, to lower transaction costs and minimize the trade distortionary consequences of host-country investment regulations.

Multilateral Agreement on Investment

In the absence of uniform standards, bilateral investment treaties proliferated and, according to UNCTAD, there were, at the end of June 1996, nearly 1160 bilateral investment treaties, of which about two-thirds had been concluded during the 1990s.[21] This meant that foreign investors confronted a very complex and complicated legal environment and which also provided no certainty about the long-term investment climate.

To simplify and harmonize investment standards, the European Commission initially proposed that the WTO facilitate the development of a global investments treaty. The United States argued instead that the venue for an investments treaty be the Organization for Economic Cooperation and Development (OECD), which comprised the leading industrial countries. The United States had determined that group of similar countries would be more conducive to the formulation of a treaty of very 'high standards'. It was also felt that negotiations on a uniform code for FDI under the auspices of the WTO would be complicated by the divergent interests of developed and developing countries.

To avert a possible deadlock in negotiations along the North–South axis, the OECD countries, in 1995, began the process of negotiating a Multilateral Agreement on Investments (MAI). By negotiating initially within the OECD, it was expected that members would be able to agree on high standards that did not have to be watered down as a result of objections from smaller developing countries. OECD member countries are major players in FDI, accounting for 85 percent of FDI outflows and 60 percent of FDI inflows, or $243 billion and $191 billion, respectively, in 1995.[22] As major players they expect also to be key beneficiaries of a liberal code on investments. A Canadian study, for example, found that an increase of US$1 billion in incoming FDI produced, over a five-year period, an additional 45,000 jobs and added $4.5 billion to gross domestic product. It is understandable, therefore, that the OECD was interested in a liberal and transparent code that is comprehensive and uniform.

Confining negotiations to the OECD countries precluded any consideration of developing country interests. Foreign investment is a significant proportion of total domestic investment in many developing countries but these countries found themselves locked out of the negotiation process. Critics charged that negotiations were motivated primarily by an interest to promote MNCs, a majority of which were headquartered in OECD countries. But if expectations were that confining negotiations to OECD countries would produce easy and quick agreement on final terms of the treaty, such hopes proved unfounded. When the draft text of the treaty became public, consumer and citizens' groups within the OECD countries emerged as leading critics of the MAI, fearful that the outcome would diminish state sovereignty in favor of MNCs. OECD negotiations on MAI began in 1995, with the expectation that an agreement would be achieved by May 1997. When that became unlikely, the deadline was extended to May 1998. The second deadline also passed without agreement but discussions were expected to resume later in the year. The delays pointed to difficulties confronting negotiators amid the many criticisms that such an agreement would infringe national sovereignty and act to the detriment of the national interests of participating countries. The hurdles in the path of an agreement were issues of labor and environmental standards and cultural protectionism. In April 1998, the OECD released a draft of the negotiating text of the MAI treaty listing all the major points of disagreement among the negotiating countries. These ranged from trivial disagreement on specific words and terminology to disagreement on more substantive issues, such as whether agreed upon rights and privileges should extend not only to citizens of contracting countries but also to permanent residents.

The main principles of the MAI guaranteed national treatment and most favored nation treatment to foreign investors, and transparency of regulatory frameworks. The objective was to create a liberal investment climate that facilitated the expansion of global FDI. The draft agreement proposed to eliminate all discriminatory performance requirements, whether on the input or the output side of productive activities. It established clear parameters to discipline state behavior and force compliance with established rules. According to the OECD, the advantage for states and for investors, was that MAI would lead to a more open and transparent investment climate. However, governments were permitted to declare a list of exemptions, identifying industries that would not be subject to provisions of the MAI treaty. Most negotiating countries announced plans to prepare a list of exemptions including, for example, culture industries.

The MAI was to be a free standing treaty among the 29 OECD member countries, with possible accession by non-OECD countries that were able to meet its obligations. Non-OECD countries that wished to accede to the MAI would also be able to negotiate their entry conditions rather than confront a 'take it or leave it' situation. However, the core obligations could not be renegotiated.[23] The ultimate stated objective was that the MAI would, at some stage, be adopted also by the WTO. Indeed, the WTO secretariat, along with several other non-OECD members, attended MAI negotiations as observers.[a]

However, as negotiations progressed, pockets of resistance cropped up even within developed countries. This spread quickly and became more organized with the help of the Internet. Critics charged that negotiations had been carried out in secrecy to benefit MNCs and without adequate safeguard of national interest. The assertion that the treaty privileged MNCs at the expense of states was premised on a widely held belief that, under the terms of the agreement, MNCs had won the right to sue states for damages, a right that they did not then possess and a right that was not granted to local companies. The negotiating text of the treaty elaborated extensively on dispute resolution mechanism and provided for a tribunal to be established to resolve disputes between an investor and a contracting party, if a contracting party failed to honor its commitments to the investor at the time of initial investment. Whether this eroded national sovereignty is extremely dubious and there were, in any case, safeguards provided to states in times of war and other international emergencies. As noted in earlier chapters, similar objections were raised when the

---

[a] Other observers to the MAI negotiations were Hong Kong, Argentina, Brazil, Chile and Slovakia.

International Trade Organization was proposed and, again, when the WTO was established. These objections were really attempts to hold back the tide of globalization in the guise of protecting national sovereignty. In reality, governments remained free to regulate activities in most areas provided regulation was not discriminatory and treated foreign investors equitably.

Critics charged also that the MAI went well beyond establishing a principle of non-discrimination to positive discrimination in favor of MNCs. For instance, it was suggested that states were not permitted to apply discriminatory performance standards (export quota, local content, etc.) on foreign investment, even "if a national government imposed these performance requirements on domestic companies...".[24] This was a misrepresentation of the principle of national treatment, which essentially obligated governments not to selectively discriminate against foreign investors but even so the MAI had created the impression that it was a treaty of "corporate rights and state obligations". Critics expressed concerns also that a signatory country had no easy opt-out clause and was bound by MAI conditions for at least 20 years.

If the MAI was deficient, it is in the fact that contracting parties were not themselves transparent in their negotiations and failed to keep their own citizens adequately informed. This created a situation where critics of the MAI could attack it as an MNC-led conspiracy against the rights of states. Another weakness of the MAI negotiations was the exclusion of developing countries. This may have made sense in terms of the stated objective of achieving a treaty of high standards but it also made it less likely to attract support of a group of countries that had no input in its design, especially in the context of an unstated expectation that the WTO would adopt the treaty for universal coverage. A more inclusive and transparent process might have produced better result.

As criticism mounted, OECD countries became increasingly jittery. When France pulled out, it spelled the end of further negotiations. It is ironic that the treaty, instigated and inspired by globalization, should have fallen victim to one of the tools of globalization. Without Internet, the movement against MAI would not have spread as easily as it did. Critics used this modern means of communication to great advantage, to mobilize public support and outrage, and to pressure politicians to abandon it.

France, always uneasy about the potential impact on the arts and culture industry, was the first country to pull out and that put an end to this attempt at harmonizing investment rules.

Conclusion

The overwhelmingly negative popular perception of MNCs is gradually being replaced by more realistic assessments that MNCs and foreign investment can be harnessed for national economic development. The negative perceptions in developing countries were based on experiences with tax evasion, transfer pricing, exploitation of labor, introduction of inappropriate technologies, and their negative impact on domestic competition and indigenous entrepreneurs, and poor safety standards relative to home countries. This last aspect of MNC investment in developing countries was most vividly highlighted by the large number of deaths in India resulting from a poison gas leak in the local Union Carbide factory. More recently, however, spurred by East Asian experiences developing countries are eagerly trying to attract foreign investment. Another positive development is the gradual removal of the North–South divide in foreign investment, where the former group of countries provided foreign investment and the latter were mainly the host countries. Developing countries have also become foreign investors.

The increased global significance of foreign investment has spurred international efforts to create a uniform regulatory code but globalization of standards will necessarily be a slow and gradual process. The logical place for any future negotiation on a multilateral agreement on investments is the WTO but this is unlikely to happen in the near future, as developing countries are more intent on erasing existing inequities, in agriculture trade, for example, than in expanding the negotiating agenda.

Chapter Seven

ENVIRONMENTAL POLITICS

Environmental pollution and degradation is an inevitable by-product of human activity. Even pre-modern societies had an impact on the environment but since the start of industrial revolution and spread of consumerism, human imprint on global ecology has become much more extensive. Modern history is punctuated with a series of environmental crises, mostly of a localized nature. These crises typically provoked a local reaction and agitation for remedial action, regulation, legislation and compensation for victims. For example, in Japan in the 1960s Chisso Corporation took advantage of lax environmental regulations to regularly dump large quantities of mercury into Minamata Bay. This poisoned a large number of residents and it was local activism that ultimately led to tighter environmental standards and forced Chisso Corporation to provide compensation to victims of mercury poisoning.

Apart from purely localized instances of pollution, we have also witnessed a growing number of cross-national and regional environmental disasters. This is because waterborne and airborne pollutants do not respect national boundaries even if they have national origins. Following an accident at the Chernobyl nuclear plant on April 26, 1986 the immediate area of radioactive fallout was concentrated in the surrounding areas of Ukraine, Belarus and Russia where approximately 5 million were affected. But by May 6, 1986, radioactivity had been detected as far away as East Asia, North Africa and North America. The Chernobyl accident rendered the immediate region uninhabitable and affected the entire European continent by contaminating the food chain. Similarly, in the 1980s, ozone depletion was detected as a serious problem in the southern hemisphere but this was a result of ozone depleting gases being emitted largely by countries in the Northern hemisphere. As a result of wind currents, ozone levels built up over the Antarctic and degraded the ozone layer protecting the surface of the earth from harmful radiation.

In the contemporary period, we confront a number of global environmental crises, but the primary challenge is to respond in a proactive way to climate change and to avert the predicted catastrophic consequences. Regional and global environmental problems demand collaborative measures but international cooperation is difficult to engineer, especially when environmental values conflict with economic interests.

Climate change and global warming are, increasingly, acknowledged to be a result of human intervention and the dependence on fossil fuel as the main source of energy. Fossil fuels produce carbon dioxide (CO_2), a leading greenhouse gas and the atmospheric concentration of CO_2 has increased from around 280 parts per million (ppm) at the start of the industrial revolution to nearly 400 ppm today. Greenhouse gases form a blanket around the earth and prevent heat from being radiated out into space. Among the known greenhouse gases, CO_2 is particularly damaging because it takes a longer time to degrade (measured as half-life) than the others, like methane. The long half-life of CO_2 adds urgency to remedial measures to combat global warming but states have not found it easy to reach agreement on any meaningful plan of action. There is disagreement on how to respond to climate change not only between developed and developing countries but also among developed countries. Climate change sceptics do not dispute the higher atmospheric concentration of greenhouse gases but insist that this might also be explained as part of a natural cyclical process and beyond human control, or are prepared to wait for technological solutions to emerge that would obviate the need for costly investment in abatement measures. Thus, James Schlesinger, a former US Secretary of Energy, wrote in 2003 that there were still a number of unresolved uncertainties about climate change projections and that any policy formation "... should be taken only on an exploratory and sequential basis. A premature commitment to a fixed policy can only proceed with fear and trembling".[1]

While industrialization and intensification of economic activity have added to environmental stress and may even have upset the earth's natural capacity to repair and regenerate itself, on a positive level, there is an increasingly active environmental movement, particularly in the West. This has had some effect at the policy level but policy makers, in general, continue to be torn between the competing goals of economic growth and environmental protection; and between costly investments in carbon abatement technology today in return for better environmental quality in the distant future.

Contemporary global warming and climate change may be a legacy of growth and industrialization in developed countries. But, some developing countries, like China, are also major emitters of greenhouse gases and any viable collaborative strategy must include them as well. Yet, in the industrializing countries, the economy still reigns supreme. They also lack resources and technology to protect environmental quality while pursuing economic development. On the other hand, the environmental record of former socialist economies has improved considerably since the collapse of communism. In East European countries, environmental protection has become an important policy objective. Previously, central planners in East European countries were committed to increasing material output, regardless of environmental impact. The distorted domestic price mechanism and subsidies on energy resources also contributed to a wasteful usage and higher levels of pollution. Pollution indicators improved significantly following the collapse of socialism, initially as a result of a decline in industrial output and later, as a result of both industrial restructuring and modernization,[2] and a decision to join the European Union[3] which required harmonization of environmental standards. For the West European countries, this was a welcome dividend of the collapse of communism. Previously, they had suffered air pollution drifting in from unregulated industries in the East, but had failed to find cooperative solutions to their trans-border pollution woes.

The European experience during the Cold War was not unique. Trans-border pollution problems are difficult to resolve either because of divergent state interests or domestic political constraints. Despite obvious difficulties in co-ordinating state activities, there has been some success in formulating cooperative approaches to deal with specific problems. Multilateral environmental regimes include:

- Convention on Biological Diversity, 1992 (CBD);
- Convention on International Trade in Endangered Species, 1973 (CITES);

- Basel Convention on the Trans-boundary Movement of Hazardous Waste, 1989;
- Vienna Convention, 1985, and Montreal Protocol, 1987 on ozone depletion;
- Convention on Wetlands of International Importance, 1971 (RAMSAR);
- Convention on Protection of World Cultural & Natural Heritage, 1927;
- Law of the Sea, 1982 (UNCLOS); and
- Kyoto Protocol on Climate Change, 1997.

It is difficult to evaluate these conventions and treaties with any great precision. But, as always, some are more important than others. The Vienna Convention is an obvious success case because it eliminated the usage of ozone-depleting gases such as Chloro-Fluorocarbons (CFCs) in order to not exacerbate depletion of the earth's protective ozone belt and to repair damage from past use of CFCs in aerosol cans, etc. Among others, the Ramsar Convention, signed at Ramsar, Iran, includes 157 members. It was signed in 1971 and came into effect in 1975. It requires members to designate at least one wetland site for conservation and obliges countries to commit to a "wise use" policy regarding wetlands. Wise use is not clearly defined and one way is to interpret it to mean sustainable use. At the other end of the spectrum, the Kyoto Protocol was handicapped by American and Australian refusal to accept targets for carbon emissions both because (i) it would be inimical to domestic economic growth and (ii) developing countries were not required to limit their carbon emissions. In late 2007, the Australian government under a new Prime Minister ratified the Kyoto Protocol but the United States remains a major handicap to collaborative global efforts to deal with climate change.

As indicated above, environmental pollution is linked to economic and human activity and we can assess that impact in terms of the following three states/societal forms.

- Developed or developing,
- Open/global or closed, and
- Democratic or Authoritarian.

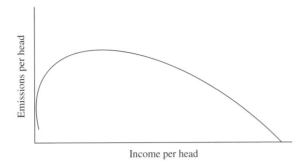

Figure 7.1:   Environmental Kuznets curve.

In economic theory, Kuznets curve is a graphic representation of an initial increase in income inequality before it begins to decline after a certain income level. There is ample evidence of an environmental Kuznets curve (Fig. 7.1) that is also shaped as an inverted-U and plots an initial increase in pollution as income levels rise before declining after a certain, yet undefined, income level.

Pollution may be a function of income levels but contemporary per capita emissions of greenhouse gases are still much greater in the developed countries than in developing countries. Overall, while the United States is the largest single source of greenhouse gases it is estimated that China will exceed total US emissions in the near future. This explains why the United States continues to insist that no binding agreement will have any significant impact unless developing countries are also included in pollution abatement schemes. Nonetheless, while it is true that developing countries, in particular China and India, are major sources of environmental pollution, the current crisis of climate change is largely a result of pollutants emitted by developed countries in the past.

In developed countries the problem is, largely, profligate and conspicuous consumption. But they possess both the technology and resources to improve their environmental performance. On the other hand, developing countries have resource and technology constraints and also, as a matter of national policy, prioritize development over environmental protection, in a repeat of the industrialization pattern of the developed countries. Lack of commitment by the poor has become an excuse for the rich to avoid investment in the environment. A World Bank report in 1992 observed that while the Third World countries were guilty of environmental damage, they were not necessarily the main agents of environmental destruction. It admitted that "those who cause[d] environmental damage ... [were] likely to be the rich and influential, while those who suffer[ed] most [we]re often the poor and powerless".[4]

Broad categorizations, like developed and developing countries, conceal significant differences within each group. For example, the average American consumes twice as much energy (and is responsible for more environmental damage) as the average Japanese.[5] Energy efficiency was a major governmental objective in Japan after the oil crisis of 1973 and while the gains have been significant, it is possible to achieve further improvements. The European countries, too, lagged behind Japan but are now as energy efficient as Japan and more ambitious than Japan in future energy efficiency.

In terms of open or closed economies, it might be argued that since trade expands our consumption frontier and leads to higher levels of production that open economies bear greater responsibility for environmental degradation. Not suprisingly some environmental groups have opposed trade liberalization and were active in the protest movement that disrupted the WTO ministerial meeting in Seattle in 1999. Yet, at the same time, it is clear that trade liberalisation and global competition forces producers to become internationally competitive, and if trade leads to more efficient production of goods and services, then the same output can be produced with fewer inputs and, consequently, less pollution.

A constraint for democracies is that political leaders have a shorter policy horizon and are reluctant to invest in initiatives that will have a payoff in the distant future. It is difficult for elected politicians to impose an immediate cost, higher taxation or slower economic growth and higher unemployment, in return for promised benefit that may only materialize after a considerable time lag. Political leaders are sensitive also to electoral backlash if environmental policies impose pain on the current generation of voters. Authoritarian leaders who do not have to submit to the demands of an electoral cycle may find it easier to implement painful environmental measures. Green policy making may be more difficult in a democratic setting but it is also true that once voters become motivated and mobilized, politicians respond quickly to environmental demand.

Sustainable Development

Historically, development has been achieved through environmental compromises. Notwithstanding the historical reality, an important question is whether development must necessarily be detrimental to the environment. The answer, of course, depends on how development is defined. To break with the tyranny of history, it is necessary not to equate development simply with rapid GDP growth. In practice, as gleaned from development policies of the Third World, development is narrowly defined as growth in income and industrialization. However, development can also be defined to include improvements in the quality of life and welfare. Such a redefinition would elevate environmental protection to a worthy developmental objective alongside material improvements, especially as environmental degradation can be correlated with diseases and a general deterioration in the quality of life indicators. In China it is estimated that 300,000 people die prematurely each year as a result of pollution related illnesses.[6] This is a clear evidence that present production and income growth are being purchased at the expense of future productivity losses. Similarly, while deforestation in Latin America, Asia and elsewhere, may produce immediate and short-term economic gains, in the long-term the loss of forestry cover could be detrimental to economic growth, as result of soil erosion, loss of biological diversity, and desertification.

In recent years, the term "sustainable development" has gained greater acceptance as a way of underscoring the complementarity between income growth and environmental protection. The first usage of the term is credited to the World Commission on Environment and Development (WCED). The WCED, in its 1987 report titled *Our Common Future* (also known as the Brundtland Report, after the Chairperson of the WCED, Norwegian Prime Minister Gro Harlem Brundtland), defined sustainable development as a development that meets the needs of the present without compromising the ability of future generation to meet their own needs.[7] As a concept, it attempted to reconcile environmental and economic logic by emphasizing that environmentally unsustainable development might only exacerbate quality of life rather than improve it. Consequently, it tried to balance the desirability of development with the environmental tradeoffs. The necessary balancing act is not easy, nor carefully defined, but it has at least provided a basis for fuller assessment of the environmental impact of large projects. In a sense, sustainable development highlights the importance of appropriate technologies to achieve a particular objective, or to forego a project, for instance, which cannot adequately safeguard the environment given existing technologies. It, therefore, hinges around "technological appropriateness" and in this context has increased the importance of technology transfer from the developed to developing countries.

As a concept, sustainable development applies to both developed and developing countries and, according to Stephan Schmidheiny, "… sustainable development will require the greatest changes in the wealthiest nations, which consume the most resources, release the most pollution, and have the greatest capacity to make the necessary changes".[8] Developing countries, on the other hand, claim they have a right to be exempt from excessively onerous conditions because they have not yet been able to provide for the needs of the present generation, which as the concept of sustainable development implies, must come before the needs of their future generations.

In its annual report for 1992, the World Bank urged a balanced approach to income growth and quality of life. It suggested that environment should not be sacrificed for income, but pointed also to the reverse danger. According to the World Bank, "… too much environmental quality is now being given up. There is, however, a danger that too much income growth may be given up in the future because of failure to clarify and minimize trade-offs and to take advantage of policies that are good for both economic development and the environment".[9] Evaluating the trade-off between costs and benefits of present and future generations is not easy but sustainable development suggests that environmental costs should be factored into all investment decisions. When such costs are factored in, certain investments may be unwise but, of course, the problem is in assigning values and determining appropriate discount rates for further values. A study of Mexican livestock industry suggested that adjustments for the costs of soil erosion sharply reduced this industry's net value added. The World Bank was cautious in stating that such studies did not in themselves indicate to "… policymakers as to whether Mexico's use of natural capital has been in the country's best interest, but they can be useful in reminding policymakers of potential tradeoffs and can assist in setting sectoral priorities".[10]

The concept of sustainable development also logically leads to the notion of sustainable population. Given that human activity is the cause of pollution and environmental degradation, it is obvious that attempts to restore environmental quality must also include measures of population control. Focusing on one without the other will weaken whatever positive gains are made. Population puts immense pressure on the environment, especially in the conversion of natural habitat for agricultural production. It is obvious, therefore, that environmental policies have to include measures aimed at reducing the population growth rate.

Sustainable development requires, first, an understanding that there has to be some mechanism for technology transfer to the developing countries so that they can use resources more efficiently and pursue development without endangering environmental quality. Developed countries may agree on this practical necessity but have failed to follow through with offers of financial aid or technical assistance. Secondly, economic analysis has to include a consideration of future values rather than only present day costs/benefits. At present, the needs of the present generation take undue precedence over the needs of future generations because in economic analyses the future is heavily discounted. Much of present day economic development in Asia may be unsustainable because of high environmental costs but this is not revealed in existing economic models. In China, the World Bank estimated that every year US$14 billion of industrial output is lost; annual crop losses are about US$24 billion (acid raid, soil degradation) and that the health costs of industrial pollution will rise to US$98 billion a year by the year 2020.[6]

It is obvious that there is a direct and negative correlation between environment and economic progress and yet we still largely disregard the costs of environmental pollution in making economic decisions. We have notions of environmental impact studies but these still do not internalise the cost of damage to the environment. Environmental damage is considered as an externality and what really needs to happen is to internalise the costs in the economic calculus. The cost of cleaning up the environment as a result of damage caused in the production of a certain commodity should be included in the cost price so that consumers and producers pay for environmental damage. At present, we do not do that and appear content to let future generations deal with the consequences of our actions and inactions, just as we are forced to deal with those of past generations. This cycle, however, cannot be continued into the furture if we are to avert potential planetary overload.

Multilateral Environmental Initiatives

In terms of global initiatives for environmental management, there have been three so-called Earth Summits, the first was held in Stockholm in 1972, the second in Rio De Janeiro in 1992 and the third in Johannesburg in 2002. The first conference led to the establishment of the United Nations Environment Program (UNEP) in 1972 to identify gaps where nothing or too little was being done and to stimulate and catalyze the necessary action; to pinpoint overlaps in the UN system's efforts to protect and improve the environment, and to seek to coordinate those efforts both inside and outside the system. The UNEP is the leading global environmental agency under the UN and together with the World Meteorological Agency it established the Intergovernmental Panel on Climate Change (IPCC) in 1988. The IPCC is the scientific arm of the UNEP and produces, periodically, estimates of global warming and climate change. The first IPPC projection on climate change was published in 1990 and since then the issue has been at the forefront of global environmental agenda.

Between the first and second Earth Summits, the UN established the World Commission on Environment and Development in 1983 under the Norwegian Prime Minister Gro Harlem Brundltand which released its report in 1987 calling for a focus on sustainable development. The report highlighted the danger of continuing with existing practices, which included global warming.

It was to discuss the WCED report and explore ways of advancing sustainable development and combat global warming that the Rio conference was convened in 1992. The organizers of the Rio summit hoped to go beyond the limited achievements of the Stockholm summit. The summit itself was a grand occasion and attended by 175 countries, more than 100 heads of government, about 1500 officially accredited non-governmental organizations (such as the Greenpeace), and 7000 journalists. The summit adopted an 800 page document (40 chapters) titled *Agenda 21*, on measures to clean up the environment. Agenda 21 was the name given to the action plan for sustainable development and intended as a guideline for future national and international action in the field of environment and development.[11] Agenda 21 specified measures required by member countries to combat global poverty, protect the environment, etc. and provided also a full costing of each of the planned agenda items and the funding requirements of developing countries which was presumably to come from developed countries.

Most people are dismissive of what was achieved at Rio because apart from rhetorical declarations in support of environmental protection there was little discernable evidence of a real shift in policy response among the member countries. Still Rio was not insignificant. It led to a number of initiatives and the establishment of a new agency, the Commission for Sustainable Development (CSD), which had the responsibility of working on a series of thematic issues on a two-year cycle. Its thematic cluster in 2004/2005 was sanitation, water and human settlement and for 2008/2009 the CSD agreed to focus on issues of agriculture, rural development, drought and desertification. These are all important issues but when the CSD was established in December 1992, there was some disquiet that it would diminish the UNEP and compete with UNEP for scarce funding resources, leading to an overall diminution of what the UN could achieve in environmental management. The CSD remains a very small body.

Climate Change and Global Warming

There is general agreement among scientists that global warming is human induced. There have been periods of climate change in the past and we have had ice ages and global warming before but most scientists agree that contemporary global warming is not part of a natural cycle because it is too steep to be attributable to natural causes. Over the last

100 years, Australia has experienced a 0.7 °C increase in average temperature readings, compared to 0.6 °C globally. This may seem as a small increment but small changes do have big impact. It is important to note that during the last ice age, approximately 10,000–20,000 years ago, average global temperatures were only 8–10 °C cooler than today. It took at least 8000 years after the ice age for temperatures to increase 8 °C but in the last 50 years alone the temperature has increased by more than half a degree Celsius. By current trends, the next 8 °C increase will take less than 800 years. The evidence for global warming includes the following.

- CO_2 concentration has increased from 280 ppm (parts per million) at the start of industrial revolution to about 380 ppm in the current period. The Earth is on a trajectory to double its atmospheric CO_2 concentration (above 700 ppm) by the year 2065.
- Ice cover is in retreat in places like Uganda, New Zealand, Peru, and most other places. Many river flows are regulated by glaciers and if these disappear, riparian health will be severely jeopardized.
- Scientists have discovered that from 1993 through 1997 average Arctic sea ice thickness was six feet. This represents a significant reduction in Arctic sea ice from 1958 through 1976 when average thickness measured 10 feet. Melting ice cap has reduced the salinity of northern seas.
- The Antarctic Peninsula has seen an increase in average temperatures of almost 5 °F in the last 50 years. Six of the seven warmest years on record occurred between 1980 and 1990.[12]

Global warming is largely the result of greenhouse gases, including carbon dioxide, methane and nitrous oxide, in the atmosphere. These gases trap heat causing surface temperatures to rise. The primary greenhouse gas is carbon dioxide (CO_2) and about 95 percent of CO_2 is produced when we burn fossil fuels to generate electricity, and to power cars, planes and other engines. Total global emission of CO_2 in 2004 was 7910 million metric tons and the United States was the single biggest source of CO_2 emissions (Table 7.1), followed by China. On a per capita basis, however, Chinese CO_2 output is considerably less than the US emissions.

Table 7.1:   Current and projected carbon dioxide emissions.

Year	(1999)	2005	2015	2030
United States	1519.9 mt	5.8bt	6.4bt	6.9bt
China	668.7 mt	5.1bt	8.6bt	11.4bt
Russia	400.1 mt	1.5bt	1.8bt	2.0bt
Japan	306.7 mt	1.2bt	1.3bt	1.2bt
India	243.3 mt	1.1bt	1.8bt	3.3bt
Germany	220.9 mt			
Australia	93.9 mt			

Source: 2007 World Energy Outlook, International Energy Agency.

As mentioned above, the Intergovernmental Panel on Climate Change (IPCC), an agency of the UN Environment Program (UNEP) prepares estimates of global warming. Table 7.2 presents some of the findings.

Table 7.2:   Global warming estimates.

Year of forecast	Rate of warming (°C/decade)	Greenhouse effect by 2030/end 2100	
		Temp. rise (°C)	Sea level rise (cm)
1988	0.8	3.0	20–150
1990 (IPCC)	0.3	1.2	15–40
1995 (IPCC)	0.2	0.8	5–35
2001 (IPCC)		1.4–5.8 (2100)	
2006 (IPCC)		2.0–4.5 °C (2100)	14–43

Note: Forecast for 1988 is from the 1988 "World Conference on the Changing Atmosphere: Implications for Global Security", conference in Toronto, Canada. The 1990 and 1995 forecasts are by the UN's Intergovernmental Panel on Climate Change.

Source: "Global Warming Earth Summit Fact Sheet: The Greenhouse Effect and Global Warming", Global Warming Information Center. 2006 figures are from the IPCC draft report released on September 2006.

Global warming is the result of our reliance on fossil fuels as a source of energy. Composition of energy production in selected countries is given in Table 7.3.

Table 7.3: Energy composition in Australia, Japan and South Korea.

	Australia (%)	Japan (%)	South Korea (%)
Coal	44	17.9	21.0
Oil	35	51.8	54.0
Gas	17	13.1	11.0
Renewable/hydro	05	01.7	–
Nuclear	00	12.4	38[a]

[a] Of total electricity generation.

Any transition to renewable sources of energy will require substantial capital investments but a number of developed and developing countries have formulated targets to increase their reliance on renewable energy sources. However, countries with large reserves of fossil fuels, such as Australia and the United States, have found it difficult to embrace targets for renewable energy sources. Table 7.4 lists some of the renewable energy targets.

Table 7.4: Renewable energy targets (% of total energy).

Italy	25 percent (by 2010)
France	21 percent (by 2010)
Germany	12.5 percent (by 2010)
	20 percent (by 2020)
UK	10 percent (by 2010)
	20 percent (by 2020)
China	10 percent (by 2010)
	16 percent (by 2020)
India	15 percent (by 2032)
US	None

Source: Washington Post, December 9, 2007, p. B2.

To combat the challenge of climate change, participants at the Earth Summit in Rio agreed to the UN Framework Convention on Climate Change (UNFCCC). In the preamble of the Framework Convention, developed countries recognized the importance of immediate action [by them] in a flexible manner to deal with greenhouse gases. And Article 3 of the UNFCCC states that "... the developed country Parties should take the lead in combating climate change and the adverse effects thereof." It also cautioned all parties to take precautionary measures to anticipate, prevent or minimize the causes of climate change. The UNFCCC clearly stipulated that developed countries should take the lead in combating climate change and it was logical in that sense that the initial set of targets to reduce GHGs were to apply only to developed countries. This was the basis on which the Kyoto Protocol (KP) was signed in 1997 in Kyoto, Japan. The protocol established emission targets for developed countries and was to become a binding agreement when at least 55 countries responsible for at least 55 percent of global greenhouse gas emissions had ratified the Protocol. That milestone was reached in February 2005 when the Russian government ratified KP. The United States is the main hold-out claiming that acting on KP targets would be against the national interest, impose high economic costs, and unfair because there were no targets for developing countries. In the US skeptics argued that there was no incontrovertible proof of climate change and that is was better to wait for scientific certitude before costly investments to reverse climate change. They pointed to climate change sceptics and even to the varying predictions of the IPCC as evidence that the science of climate change had not been confirmed.

But it is not unusual for estimations to change as knowledge and estimation techniques improve. Moreover, many critics of IPCC are themselves often associated with vested interests. Oil and coal industry has been at the forefront of efforts to discredit IPCC and the scientists behind global warming. In 1989, several large corporations in the US formed the Global Climate Coalition (GCC) to discredit IPCC. The GCC lobbies US politicians and seeks to influence public opinion against global warming. One of its members, Western Fuels, a utility association, published a report which claimed that carbon dioxide, the leading greenhouse gas, emissions will have a net positive impact on agriculture, plant and wildlife. In reality the GCC acted like the tobacco industry, maintaining the fiction that there was no connection between cigarette smoke and cancer. After the Kyoto Accord, the GCC was weakened by several large defections, Boeing, Toyota, BP, Enron, 3M, etc., which then set up the Pew Center on Global Climate Change. This group endorsed newspaper advertisements that "enough is known about the science and environmental impacts of climate change for us to take actions to address its consequences".[13] Today BP-Amoco is one of the world's largest producer of solar panels.

Sceptics remain unconvinced Richard Lindzen, Professor of Meteorology at the Masachussetts Institute of Technology argues that even if there is evidence of increased carbon dioxide concentrations in the atmosphere, it is a "questionable contention ... that those increases will continue along the path they have followed for the past century".[14] Predictions based on current trends may, indeed, be erroneous because they do not account for future technological shifts and other influences on the trend line. Many dire predictions of the past have, consequently and fortunately, fallen well short of target. Some 200 years earlier, Thomas Malthus had predicted famine and starvation in England based on his understanding of population growth and its capacity to feed itself but improved agriculture and lower population growth rates proved him to be very wrong in his conclusions.

But it is foolish not to need the *precautionary principle* in the expectation that climate change predictions will ultimately prove malthusian, or unrelated to human activity. However, in a report prepared in 2007, Nicholas Stern cautioned that:

> Much of the debate over the attribution of climate change has now been settled as new evidence has emerged to reconcile outstanding issues. It is now clear that while natural factors, such as changes in solar intensity and volcanic eruptions, can explain much of the trend in global temperatures in the early nineteenth century, the rising levels of greenhouse gases provide the only plausible explanation for the observed trend for at least the past 50 years.[15]

Nicholas Stern warned that while there are economic costs associated with reduction of greenhouse gases, the costs of not doing anything would be much greater in the longer term. He accordingly recommended, as a matter of urgency, that countries act now to stabilize atmospheric concentration of carbon dioxide equivalent (CO_2e) at a level of 450–550 ppm by 2050 (contemporary carbon dioxide concentrations are around

380 ppm but concentration of all greenhouse gases, represented as carbon dioxide equivalent, is about 430 ppm). Moreover, despite critics, the so-called precautionary principle demands that individuals, corporations, and policy makers all take responsible measures to avert a looming global crisis.

There are two ways of countering projected global warming and temperature increases. One is to invest in carbon sinks, such as forests, to remove atmospheric carbon dioxide or to invest in geo-sequestration technologies, and the second is to reduce greenhouse gas emissions. Geo-sequestration of carbon emissions may become technologically and financially viable at some future date but the promise of "clean coal" is, at present, a "pie in the sky" scheme.

To avert global warming, developed countries have pressed on developing countries, like Brazil and Malaysia, to protect their rain forests. There exists well-documented evidence of the capacity of rain forests to act as a sink for greenhouse gases and the Brazilian rain forests have been likened to human lungs providing clean air to the world. It is obvious that if these rain forests continue to be cleared, quality of human life everywhere, including in Brazil, would be adversely affected. Unfortunately, developing countries have been unprepared to preserve rain forests for the global good, and insisted on their sovereign right to exploit forestry resources for national economic development.

The Kyoto Protocol established binding commitments for greenhouse gas reductions and, in keeping with the UNFCCC, it is best seen as part of process, not simply a one-shot agreement, to reduce greenhouse gases. The Protocol established targets for the reduction of six greenhouse gases during 2008–2012, relative to the level of emissions in 1990. The target reductions of six greenhouse gases (carbon dioxide, methane, nitrous oxide, hydrofluorocarbons, perfluorocarbons, and sulfur hexafluoride) are as follows:

US = 7 percent reduction;
EU = 8 percent reduction;
Canada/Hungary/Japan/Poland = 6 percent reduction;
Russia/NZ = stabilization;

Norway = 1 percent increase;
Australia = 8 percent increase; and
Iceland = 10 percent increase.

Overall, the Kyoto Protocol committed industrialized countries to reduce their GHG emissions by 5 percent compared to the 1990 levels. The UNFCCC, in late November 2007, reported that based on emission figures for 2005, countries that had ratified the KP were on track to achieve emissions reduction of the order of 11 percent in the period 2008–2012, provided "policies and measures adopted by these countries deliver the reductions as projected". Emission figures for 2005 (Table 7.5) revealed

Table 7.5:   Greenhouse gas emissions.

Country	1990–2005 Change of GHG Emissions Excluding LULUCF (%)	1990–2005 Change of GHG Emissions Including LULUCF (%)
Australia	25.6	4.5
Austria	18.0	13.6
Belarus	−40.6	−51.9
Bulgaria	−47.2	−59.3
Canada	25.3	54.2
Czech Republic	−25.8	−27.5
Hungary	−30.7	−32.7
Ireland	26.3	24.9
Japan	6.9	7.1
Latvia	−58.9	−161.5
New Zealand	24.7	22.7
Poland	−32.0	−33.8
Portugal	42.8	40.3
Russian Federation	−28.7	−27.7
Spain	53.3	59.8
Turkey	74.4	75.9
Ukraine	−54.7	−58.7
United Kingdom	−14.8	−15.4
United States	16.3	16.3

LULUCF, Land-use, land-use change and forestry.
Source: "UNFCCC Fact Sheet on 1990–2005 Emissions Trend", November 2007.

that while there had been a substantial jump in GHG emissions in some countries, including the rapidly growing economies of Turkey, Spain and Portugal, there had been substantial drops in the former East European countries and Russia.

If in the past, economic decisions were based largely on a narrowly based cost-benefit analysis, the challenge now is to introduce an environmental calculus into economic policies. This is needed not only at the micro-level of individual investment decisions but also at the macro-level of national accounts. Only by this, we can heighten our environmental awareness. Measuring the environmental impact is not easy but models have been developed jointly by the World Bank and the UN Statistical Office to have the environmental impact reflected in figures for net domestic product (NDP). While not a perfect system, it nevertheless highlighted the significance of the environment. For example, according to its calculations, Mexico's environmentally adjusted net domestic product in 1985 was only 87 percent of NDP.[16] At present, such estimates are no more than conscious-raising exercises and not very useful as a guide to policymakers but their utility cannot be questioned. These may, in the end, prompt a sound environmental management program through a cooperative international regime.

The Kyoto Protocol is the only available global approach to meet the challenge of global warming and climate change. It has been severely undermined by the unwillingness of the United States to become a part of the process to reduce greenhouse gas emissions. Outwardly, the explanation is that a system that excludes India and China from lower emissions target is unfair but the UNFCCC, to which the United States is a signatory clearly stipulated that the first step in combating global warming was the collective responsibility of the developed countries. China has indicated that it is committed to the Kyoto process and which will mean accepting targets on carbon emissions in the second and subsequent stages of the Kyoto process. The real reason for the American refusal to join Kyoto is their unwillingness to accept constraints on economic activity.

The United States stance on Kyoto can be compared to its initial reluctance to participate also in a global regime to safeguard liberal trade at the end of the First World War. Commenting on US retreat into isolationism and resulting global slide towards protectionism, Charles Kindleberger accused the United States of "global economic irresponsibility" for its failure to assume international leadership and safeguard liberal trade practices. In a similar way, we might, today, find the United States guilty of global environmental irresponsibility for its failure to provide leadership to the global campaign to meet environmental challenges.

In 2007, IPCC (joint recipient of the 2007 Nobel Peace Prize) increased the level of urgency by suggesting that evidence pointed to more severe global warming than past projections. It also argued that there was no longer any doubt that global warming was a direct result of human intervention and not part of a natural cycle. The KP targets on GHG emissions constituted the first tentative steps in what is likely to be a long series of targets. Even if the KP targets are met, it will make no more than a marginal difference to global climate change.

To plan for the next stage of attempts to deal with climate change, UNFCCC members (more than 180 countries) met in Bali, Indonesia, in early December 2007 for a two-week strategy meeting to prepare the path for a follow-up to KP. The UN circulated a draft proposal that called for a halt to growth of worldwide carbon emissions in 10–15 years, followed by a reduction of carbon levels to below half of the levels of 2000. These proposals were drawn up in the backdrop of latest IPCC findings, released earlier in the year, that unless there was an effective plan of action, average global temperatures could increase up to 6 °C by the end of the century. The United States objected to the establishment of a target range for carbon emissions. The United States also rejected language that would have committed developed countries to provide financial and technical assistance to developing countries to enhance their capacity to meet target reductions of greenhouse gases. In the end, the United States obtained its preferred option to defer specifics to the actual negotiating phase.

It is expected that negotiations will produce an agreement by 2009 and that the agreement will be ratified and become effective in 2013, one year after the Kyoto Protocol expires in 2012.

Conclusion: National Interest and Global Imperative

As individuals we are certainly aware of, and may even be prepared to modify our behavior in ways that address global environmental challenges, like climate change. But, at the international level, policy makers have found it difficult to reconcile competing demands of national interest and the looming global imperative. The IPCC and climate change scientists warn of a planetary emergency that will not only affect future generations but also a threat to the current generation as well. But political leaders continue to dither about the appropriate response. In a democracy, the ruling elite faces a short-time horizon dominated by the electoral cycle and this tyrannical reality makes it difficult to justify costly investments for long-term returns. The costs for measures to reverse global warming will be high and worse. The costs will have to be borne by present generation while benefits will accrue primarily to future generation. The problem for politicians in a democracy, moreover, is that voters are the present generation; and future generation does not vote. However, in a democracy, politicians are also responsive to their electorate and ultimately the responsibility is upon us, as individuals, to force governments to act prudently to avert future catastrophe. In the 2007 Australian federal election, the environment and climate change were important issues and voters acted to remove the incumbent government that was seen as obstructionist. The new government, led by the Australian Labor Party, moved swiftly to ratify the Kyoto Protocol. This left the United States as the single major source of climate inaction.

Climate change scientists warm that the present generation must sacrifice so that future generations may live. Individually, countries have taken major steps in the past to improve their environmental quality but such improvement has been costly. An OECD report, in 1991, documenting the significant gains over the last 20 years in protecting the environment, reducing particulate emissions and increasing forest cover in the OECD countries, singled out Japan as the exemplar among OECD countries with emissions of sulfur oxides, particulates, and nitrogen oxides as a share of GNP at one-quarter the OECD average. The environmental gains in the OECD countries have come at a price. Annual expenditure, since the 1970s, on anti-pollution policies ranged between 0.8 and 1.5 percent of GNP.[17]

Another problem is the diversity of global community and the fact that countries are at different stages of economic development. For some countries, tackling environmental issues may be important but for most developing countries it is not their first priority. If we were to prioritize their interests, it would be economic growth, followed by domestic environmental protection (overcoming airborne and water pollution for instance) and finally global environmental protection. When we have a large number of countries with diverse interests, it is understandable why it is hard to reach agreement.

There are obvious difficulties for domestic policy makers in committing to cooperative approaches to climate change but at least the scientific community is relatively united on the validity of its projections and on the potential consequences that will follow unless there is policy level intervention to act as a circuit breaker. In the early years of the debate on climate change, it was not uncommon for policy makers to point to scientific uncertainty but that escape route has been largely foreclosed. This allows for some optimism that policy makers in the leading countries will feel compelled to take appropriate counter measures, much as had happened several decades earlier when countries around the Mediterranean agreed to the Mediterranean Action Plan (Med Plan). The Med Plan was signed in 1976 by all 18 littoral states despite strong objections by developing countries of Africa that development took precedence over protection of the Mediterranean. The Algerian President Houari Boumediene, for example, had declared categorically that if improving the environment meant less bread for Algerians, then he was against it.

In the end, scientific evidence convinced policy makers to support measures to improve water quality of the Mediterranean. According to Peter Haas, consensus among the scientific community allowed them to use consensus as a power resource to bolster their policymaking advice.[18] Scientific evidence has been useful in other issue areas as well. For instance international cooperation in disease prevention was in abeyance for nearly a century until scientific consensus provided an impetus to the formation of an international regime.[19]

It would not be unreasonable to assume that sceptical policy makers today will modify their stance on climate change under the weight of scientific evidence, sooner rather than later. With clear scientific evidence on damage to the environment, it might be possible for countries to address climate change on a technical and functional level, rather than as a political issue, and to cooperate in the development of a comprehensive regime. At the Bali Climate Change summit in 2007, former US Vice President and recipient of the Nobel Peace Prize for his environmental advocacy, Al Gore, acknowledged that the United States was the main obstructionist force but urged assembled delegates to move ahead, in the anticipation that US position will change in the next few years.

Chapter Eight

TRADE AND INTERNATIONAL LABOR STANDARDS

A contentious aspect of contemporary global political economy is the attempt to link trade privileges to minimum labor standards. The United States has been a vocal advocate of labour standards and may be motivated by a genuine desire to see trade benefits filter down to improve the lives of the working poor in developing countries. However, developing countries, in general, see the attempts to include a "social clause" in trade agreements as nothing more than disguised protectionism to appease organized labor groups that fear job losses and displacement of some workers as a result of cheap imports. The assumption is that if developing countries are forced to comply with some minimum labor standards it will add to production costs, reduce their competitive edge, and safeguard jobs in the West. There may be some truth to this but it is essentially a one-eyed view of the reality because trade liberalization and globalization also provide opportunities for an expansion of exports and for job creation. Inevitably, however, labor groups tend to be more concerned about threats to declining sectors and job losses than to the potential for growth in new industries.

Organized labor, with its lobbying prowess, has wielded considerable influence over governments and, in the early 1960s for example, when GATT launched the Kennedy Round of trade negotiations, the US government promised to introduce Trade Related Adjustment Assistance (TRAA) to ensure that workers who were displaced as a result of trade liberalization had access to compensation and re-training programs.

These programs have not been as effective as might have been hoped and, in the contemporary period, the focus of attention has shifted to ensure that developing countries are unable to take "unfair" advantage of trade opportunities.

Understandably, developing countries have not embraced the western agenda because of its protectionist connotations and also because of their own domestic constraints, such as inadequate administrative capacity to implement and enforce internationally agreed labor standards. Developing countries argue also that WTO is not the appropriate venue for attempts to improve working conditions and have prevented labor standards from being added to trade negotiating agendas. They fear that if trade privileges are linked to labor standards, it would make it easy to impose trade sanctions against countries that either export goods produced using labor that is denied minimum labor conditions or lack the administrative capacity to enforce minimum agreed standards. They might agree, for instance, on prohibiting slave labor but do not wish to have the WTO used as an instrument for ensuring compliance. The objectives of the United States are: (i) to promote respect for worker rights and the rights of children consistent with the core labor standards of the International Labor Organization (ILO); (ii) to ensure that parties to trade agreements do not weaken or reduce the protections of domestic labor laws in order to encourage trade; and (iii) to promote the universal ratification of, and full compliance with, ILO Convention 182 (adopted in June 1999) concerning the elimination of the worst forms of child labor.[1] At the 1996 WTO ministerial meeting in Singapore, however, it was agreed that ILO was the relevant international body for promoting labor standards. This principle was reaffirmed in 2001 at the Doha ministerial meeting.

The United States, however, has not been keen to take up the ILO option. The United States has only ratified two of the eight ILO core labor standards and there are aspects of US labor laws that are contrary to ILO provisions, such as the use of prison labor to manufacture consumer goods. Instead, the United States has used "forum shifting" to move the agenda forward, relying on regional and bilateral trade agreements to improve minimum labor conditions. Before submitting the North American Free Trade Agreement (NAFTA) for Congressional ratification, the government, under pressure from labor groups, negotiated the North American

Agreement on Labor Cooperation (NAALC), to ensure that Mexico did not use cheap and "exploited" workers to flood markets in the United States and Canada. Similarly, when in 2006, the United States negotiated a free trade agreement with Oman, the Omani government promised to introduce and implement new labor laws that would guarantee the right of collective bargaining and strike to workers. That same year several leading Congressional Democrats wrote to the United States Trade Representative asking that trade agreements with Peru and Colombia be renegotiated and expressing dismay that the administration has consistently declined to take the simple steps necessary to address our key outstanding concern, which continues to be labor standards. It is interesting to note that in free trade agreements the language used does not refer to core "ILO standards" but simply "internationally recognized labor standards", perhaps for the reasons noted above. At the same time, to make labor standards "saleable", both in a domestic and international context, proponents of labor standards have, according to Andrew Stoler, recast the issue as a question of human rights.[2]

In general, labor standards in many developing countries are either non-existent or inadequately enforced. These countries also have abundant supplies of low-cost labour and a competitive advantage in labor-intensive industries, such as textiles and garments manufacturing. Consequently, they are concerned that the issue of labor standards is a western "Trojan horse" to undermine the export capacity of developing countries. This is not without some justification since labor groups, such as textiles workers in the United States, have, in the past, successfully obtained protection from cheap imports.

One source of the variance in labor standards is the restriction on labor mobility across borders. In a global era, where the flow of capital, merchandise and technology is relatively unrestricted, there remain extensive restrictions on international labor movements. Developing countries have argued for a relaxation of restrictions on short-term movement of labor that, if accepted by developed countries, would boost their available pool of savings and investment capital as a result of remittances of workers in foreign countries. Globally, in 1998 remittances resulted in an income flow of US$52.8 billion to developing countries, well above the US$50 billion in foreign aid given to developing countries that year, of which only about $2.3 billion was grant aid. Remittances are important because they do not have to be repaid or serviced, and there are no stings or conditions attached to these flow of funds.[3]

Without restrictions, labor standards would inevitably move towards some convergence, either up or down, as labor migrated from areas of poor conditions to where work conditions were superior. However, even in the absence of labor mobility, the labor market has been effectively globalized as a result of intensifying economic exchange. Bloom and Brender ask us to consider, for example, "a British entrepreneur who hires an Italian company to design a new line of clothing, then has those designs sent for production in southern China, and has a shipping company in Hong Kong send the finished product for sale in the United States. Without the entrepreneur or any worker having to cross a national border, this example involves the labour services of workers in five countries being exchanged".[4]

Thus, despite restrictions on labor mobility, effective globalisation of labor markets can, according to proponents of labor standards, lead to a decline in labor standards globally as capital migrates from high labor cost countries to low cost countries, where labor standards are either rudimentary or where the enforcement of it is lax. The greater the differential in labour standards and costs, the greater the temptation for firms to shift capital to exploit those conditions. This is not to suggest that investment decisions are based on labor cost considerations alone but they are one important factor in the decision matrix of foreign investors. Capital flight may put pressure on wages and labour conditions in the developed countries and produce a movement toward convergence but at the lower end of the spectrum. The "race to the bottom" might accelerate if governments in developed countries try to attract and retain capital investments by weakening labour standards. In the context of a heightened quest for trade competitiveness, there is concern that low standards in developing countries inevitable put pressure on wages, social benefits, and labour standards in developed countries. Ray Marshall, a former US Secretary of Labor, pointed to census data that suggested that, in the United States, the median hourly wage of men was 14 percent less in 1989 than it was in 1979.[5] Consequently, if a race to the bottom is a distinct possibility, and increased productivity difficult to achieve, then available options are to secure universal acceptance and compliance with a "minimum package of labour standards",[6] and "upward harmonisation"[7] of labour standards.

A North–South Divide on Labor Standards

The debate on labour standards cannot be neatly, or exclusively, segmented along the North–South axis. While the United States has been its leading advocate not all western governments are equally passionate about it. The American position on labor standards has been supported by some European countries but there has been no progress in placing the issue firmly on the WTO agenda, by leading to the establishment of either a working party or a committee. The lack of progress can be attributed to a lack of consensus on how to proceed with establishment of labor standards and whether this is at all desirable. Universal minimum labor standards have been rejected by developing countries and by many western multinational corporations,[8] which suspect that their operations in developing countries could be adversely affected by universal standards.

Proponents of linking labor standards to trade believe this will help raise standards in developing countries. Labor unions in developed countries may regard such moves as a way of demonstrating their concern for working conditions in poorer countries and as a way of expressing solidarity with workers in those countries. There is, according to Torres, evidence to support this proposition based on past experience with the American Generalised System of Preferences (GSP). The GSP was introduced by developed countries to provide easy market access to exports from developing countries, at low or zero tariffs, to assist with their development objectives. The American scheme included a social provision which favoured those developing countries which respected minimum labor standards. According to Torres, an analysis of the American "...GSP suggests that the system has played a part in improving core labour standards in some countries".[9] The GSP is not part of the GATT system and each country has its own GSP program but the demand now is to include respect for labor standards as part of the WTO system.

The United States placed the issue of labor standards on the agenda of world trade at the Marrakesh Ministerial Meeting which concluded the Uruguay Round negotiations. The United States however, is not a new convert to labor standards nor is the idea of linking labor standards to trade a recent phenomenon. The issue of labour standards has been debated since the 19th century and gained prominence especially in times of high levels of international trade, or interdependence. For example, the establishment of the International Labor Organisation (ILO) in 1919 followed "...a hundred years of proposals and conferences",[10] and came at the end of a period of "rapid growth of international trade and the associated demand for international labour standards".[11] The mandate of the ILO is to lead to improved labor standards among member countries. The American commitment to improved standards was reiterated by President Roosevelt in 1937 when he argued that "Goods produced under conditions which do not meet a rudimentary standard of decency should be regarded as contraband and ought not to be allowed to pollute the channels of interstate commerce".[12] In the GATT, however, the only labour standard to be included was a prohibition on the export of goods produced with prison labor.

Multinational corporations (MNCs) may not be enthusiastic about labor standards but it is their activities in developing countries that has added to demands for such standards. MNCs have been criticised for exploiting cheap labor and low regulatory standards in developing countries to produce goods for markets in developed countries. It is not unreasonable to speculate as to whether the poisoning of workers in Bhopal, India would have occurred if Union Carbide had been forced to accord its workers in India the same safety and protection that is available to workers in the West. Nonetheless, it is also true that even if multinationals exploit cheap labor in developing countries, they still pay their workers more than local companies.

The push for labor standards can be attributed also to a western interest in preventing any exodus of manufacturing to developing countries US pressure for labor standards stems partly from a concern that MNCs, by relocating their production to low wage countries were displacing workers and creating unemployment at home.

Another motive may be a belief that in global economy without universal standards, labour conditions everywhere will be whittled away as MNCs relocate productive activities to low cost areas. The resulting army of unemployed can be expected to put pressure on existing labor conditions in developed countries and initiate a race to the bottom. Labor will be the ultimate loser if, in the process, hard won labor conditions are placed in jeopardy. Understandably, therefore, labour unions in the West have been vocal in demanding adoption of universal standards in order to protect work conditions for workers. For example, the "International Confederation of Free Trade Unions (ICFTU), and notably one of its members, the International Metalworkers Federation (IMF), which represents 165 engineering and metalworking trade unions in 70 countries worldwide, have spearheaded a campaign to link trade preference agreements to the maintenance of labour standards".[13] Organised labour may be concerned about losing its gains but governments in many western countries were, in the 1980s and 1990s, engaged precisely in a campaign to curtail the rights and privileges of labour groups.

·   Supporters of international labor standards acknowledge the diverse motives of states, including expressing solidarity with workers in developing countries, achieving minimum human rights, and protecting domestic working conditions. There may be even a more base protectionist motive underpinning the demand for labor standards, especially from those sectors of the economy that are unable to compete with developing countries' exports. However, regardless of the motives, Langille says that the message of improved labor standards ought to be universally welcomed, that we should not ignore the message because of the messenger. The demands, he argues, are ethical standards that should apply everywhere. According to Langille, "...it is necessary to focus on the validity of the arguments, not the motivations of those advancing them".[14] The difficulty, however, is that the validity of the argument for international standards is not beyond question.

Developing countries argue that labor standards, like human rights, are the products of specific historical and cultural experiences and western demands are a veiled attempt to export their notions of appropriate labor standards to other countries. Western demands are based on a supposition that labor standards are universal values and should be upheld everywhere. By contrast to this universalist liberal approach, communitarians maintain that value systems are a derivative of each community's social and cultural heritage and cannot be universalised. This disagreement is reminiscent of the debate between proponents of liberal democracy on the one hand, and advocates of 'Asian democracy' on the other. Southeast Asian advocates of Asian democracy, where the individual is subordinate to the group and where individual rights take second place to societal rights and privileges, insist that it is inappropriate for western government to push liberal democracy on these countries because liberalism is not a part of their cultural tradition. Westerners, however, reject these arguments as self-serving defence of the privileges enjoyed by the ruling authoritarian regimes in several of these countries.

Even if there is no clear resolution of the communitarian and liberal approaches, developing countries are on firmer grounds when they reject uniform and minimum standards as a surreptitious attempt to protect western markets and to exclude cheap exports from developing countries. They maintain that western demands amount to denying developing countries their legitimate international trade advantage in labor intensive manufacturing. Having obtained significant concessions from developed countries in the Uruguay Round of trade negotiations, developing countries fear that gains, in textiles, for example, could be undermined through the imposition of labour standards and the threat of trade sanctions. The fears are not entirely unwarranted as it is entirely reasonable to assume that the withdrawal of MFA quotas on LDC export of textiles will impose severe pain on textile industries in the western countries.

Relatedly, the rejection of universal, and higher, labour standards is also premised on the assumption that high standards would jeopardise trade expansion and their developmental objectives by undermining their comparative advantage. Developing countries characterize the western push as a way of denying developing countries export opportunity to achieve economic development. They claim the West is interested only in obstructing developing country exports. From their perspective, the northern countries should provide better market access rather than threaten to restrict access on grounds of poor labor standards. And they might point to the experiences of East Asian Newly Industrialising Countries that have achieved remarkable economic development, and in the process improved labour standards, through a policy of export oriented industrialisation. Developing countries are wary also of the perceived hypocrisy whereby having restructured their economy, under IMF and

World Bank guidance and encouragement, to become more internationally competitive and outward looking, they are now being threatened with potentially reduced market access.

That would be the case if higher standards became a negative influence on capital inflows and reduced the levels of investment in productive activities. Many developing countries have relatively low savings rate and foreign capital inflow is an important supplement to available domestic resources for investment purposes. If higher labour standards reduced that inflow of capital, it would have the inevitable effect of dampening their growth prospects. There have also been arguments that low standards attract foreign capital because it enhances managerial autonomy and guarantees labour peace and stability. These arguments are also often made by governments in developing countries as reasons why they cannot afford higher standards. However, Linda Lim found that, at least in the case of Singapore, growth and export competitiveness was not significantly explained by restrictions on labour and that controls on labour served a political rather than an economic function. Control on labour was a part of the overall government policy to limit political freedoms and democratic participation. She argues that labor controls are not necessary either for industrial peace or for attracting foreign capital.[15]

As well, developing countries argue that labor standards should be a matter for the International Labor Organisation (ILO) to deliberate rather than be brought under the purview of the World Trade Organization, where it would be easy to link the social clause to trade benefits. Further, they argue that if the West wants to use trade to promote social justice in developing countries, they should liberalize trade rather than threaten trade sanctions, because trade can be the engine of growth to improve welfare for all.

Apart from the appropriateness of labour standards, developing countries also point to the difficulty of enforcing standards given the nature of standards and the institutional capacities of governments. Standards are often devised with factory type production organizations but actual production may take place in unorganized structures or on self-employed basis.[16] Enforcement of standards in such diverse production processes can be difficult and developing countries also point out that institutional capacities of government are inadequate to police and enforce standards. Institutional weakness may be one reason why developing countries have been relatively disinterested in accepting the various ILO conventions on labour standards.

As a subtext to the above, it might be mentioned, as well, that the capacity of developing countries to existing ILO Conventions have been eroded by the structural adjustment requirements imposed by the IMF and the World Bank following the debt crises. Structural adjustment programs have typically included public sector cutbacks resulting in increased unemployment and a worsening of labour conditions, even in those instances where developing countries have ratified ILO Conventions. Roger Plant argues that the early structural adjustment programs of the World Bank were also based on a fundamental theoretical hostility to labour standards as unnecessary interference with market principles. He writes that, "The theoretical assault on labour standards as 'distortions' to the market can find expression in overall adjustment policies, and in some cases in specific structural adjustment programmes. Some criticisms are that excessive regulations…can raise labour costs…restrictions on hiring and firing can impede economic restructuring…and minimum wage-fixing machinery can impede macro-economic stabilisation, facilitating an inflationary spiral.[17] If early structural adjustment programs were anti-thetical to high labour standards, the World Bank and the IMF, in the 1990s, appeared more prepared to accept the importance of state regula-tory intervention in facilitating economic growth and it would be inap-propriate to say that the hostility to labour standards had remained high. Nonetheless, it must be acknowledged that the capacity of developing countries to fulfil the intent of ILO Conventions was severely impaired during the 1980s.

However, if labour standards are eventually introduced, the "institutional capacity" escape route may only be available to the least developed coun-tries. The Marrakesh Agreement of 1994 which established the WTO stipu-lated that least developed countries, as recognized by the United Nations will "only be required to undertake commitments and concessions to the extent consistent with their individual development, financial and trade needs or their administrative and institutional capabilities" (Article 11, para 2).

Core Labor Standards

One of the main shortcomings of the debate on labour standards has been the difficulty in identifying which standards deserve inclusion. To be meaningful, the standards have to modify behavior, otherwise it will be an exercise in futility. But because a basic agreement on the desirability of labour standards and linkage to trade is missing, there has been no collective effort to try and identify some of the possible standards.

To clarify the debate about labor standards and trade, the OECD has tried to identify core labor standards that presumably would be acceptable to all countries. These include:

- the elimination of exploitative child labor,
- the abolition of forced labor,
- non-discrimination in employment, and
- freedom of association and collective bargaining.[18]

These core rights are not inconsistent with Charter of the United Nations or the Universal Declaration of Human Rights but not all countries abide by all of the identified core rights. Children, for example, continue to work in hazardous factory jobs or in the mining industry or in industries such as carpet making. Most countries have no difficulty in supporting the principle of eliminating child labor but according to ILO estimates, there are 120 million children engaged in gainful commercial work.[19] Many developing and emerging economies have also not found it acceptable to them to grant workers the right to free association and collective bargaining. Importantly, the core rights identified by the OECD are process rights rather than substantive outcome, on the presumption that if workers acquire, for example, the right to collective bargaining they will be able to achieve suitable outcomes in wages and other conditions of employment.[20] In the end, therefore, even if the core demands are process conditions, the expectation must be that through, for example, the right to collective bargaining, labor cost in developing countries will rise and that, consequently, wage differentials will be reduced to deny developing countries a comparative advantage in labor intensive production. This may not necessarily be the case if employers succeed in trading-off higher labor standards for lower wages. But where labour costs are already low, there is a limit to further reductions. Without a rise in wages in developing countries, standards will offer no relief to developed countries and this must be the expected outcome of universal standards.

The question remains whether trade policy should be used to enhance social justice in an intrusive manner. From an economic point of view, sub-standard labor conditions in developing countries are not a product of deliberate policy choice but a result of the overall context of poverty and backwardness. Developing countries do not have inferior standards in order to gain an unfair trade advantage and to single out labor standards as requiring elevation might be inappropriate. It could be argued that if the West was concerned, it should be concerned with poverty alleviation in general. Andre Sapir argues that if social clauses were introduced in trade agreements and used to deny trade opportunities, it would exacerbate poverty rather than benefit the poor.[21] Similarly, Chris Milner emphatically asserts that a social clause in trade agreements is undesirable because it would only discipline conditions in traded goods sectors and because it would be much better to try and improve labor standards through improved (rather than restricted) trade access and foreign aid.[22]

Conclusion

The issue of formulating international labour standards has created a sharp divide between the developed and developing countries. There are no easy solutions to the problems and recognizing the intractable nature of the dispute, the Director General of the ILO proposed that instead of taking the route of codifying universal labour standards in legalistic terms, a better way might be to institute a system of dispute resolution using agencies like the ILO. The ILO has in fact been involved in dispute resolution between countries, as between France and Panama, and according to Servais, such an approach "would allow for flexibility and pragmatism in seeking solutions to these thorny problems".[23] However, ILO, despite its long history since establishment in 1919, is a relatively weak international institution and its Conventions, which might become guidelines for dispute resolution, have a poor record of ratification by member countries.

As of 2000, the ILO had adopted 182 conventions but the United States had only ratified 12 of these and the United Kingdom, less than half.

Developing countries insist that their labour standards are appropriate to existing social conditions and that any attempt to impose higher standards would only create domestic social dislocations. It cannot be denied that labor conditions were tightly regulated by governments in the newly industrialising Asian countries, such as South Korea, Taiwan and Singapore, and that their economic miracle provided for a relatively equitable economic growth. In these societies, an organized and independent labor movement did not develop until much later but labor conditions did improve progressively. Countries at a lower level of development argue that they, too must be permitted to regulate labor conditions in order to generate growth.

Nonetheless, a social clause need not be seen only as a brake on development. Higher labor standards can also be a source of opportunity and dynamism. Even if neo-classical economic theory is less convinced of the merits of regulation, according to neo-institutional economics labor standards could become a catalyst for progress and development. In this alternative perspective, "...insufficient labor standards regulation in the international economy will lock some firms and countries into low-productivity production methods that not only deprive workers of basic rights but also produce poor economic outcomes".[24]

Here the example of the East Asian economy is worth keeping in mind. The East Asian economies progressively moved up the technology spectrum as they became proficient in low level manufacturing and as their low cost labor intensive product exports increasingly came up against protectionist restrictions in developed countries. While such protectionism was undesirable, it at least provided opportunities to progressively do more value adding to cross the bar. It is also unlikely that labor regulations will erode the trade competitiveness of any single developing country, provided that the standards are universally applicable. External pressure impeding the retention of existing competitive advantage can become a catalyst for further economic development. When Singapore, for example, was no longer able to compete internationally with low cost labor intensive manufacturing, "the government made extensive investment to upgrade Singapore's technology and services to attract higher, value-added activities".[25]

If developing countries do exploit labor standards to move up the technology ladder, it can be expected to create some domestic dislocation. Given their comparative advantage in labour intensive manufacturing, given a large pool of cheap and abundant labour force, they can expect an immediate worsening of unemployment unless there is compensating growth in the other trade sectors of the economy. For off-setting increase in the growth sectors they will require open trade opportunities rather than sanctions of the threats of sanctions. Without that assistance to restructuring, developing countries will find it hard to vacate labour intensive manufacturing. At the same time, this will also require restructuring in developed countries. Therefore, restructuring is imperative in both developed and developing countries if there is to be much headway in the universal acceptance of international labour standards.

What the developing countries should instead focus on is to ensure that the social clause does not become a pretext for protectionism. Equally, developed countries need to consider the possibility that it is not cheap imports produced by inadequately protected workers in developing countries that is a cause of distress for the unskilled workers in developed countries. According to the Australian Chamber of Commerce and Industry, there is substantial evidence to show that:

> ...the problems that developed-country advocates of trade and labour-standard linkages are seeking to address are not readily attributable to poor labour standards in developing countries. In other words, the 'cure' does not reflect the 'complaint'.
>
> Contrary to these claims, it is technological change rather than unfair international trade that has been the driving force behind the decline in demand for lower skilled workers in developed countries over the past two decades...[26]

Chapter Nine

THE FUTURE OF GLOBALIZATION

Contemporary economic globalization is an evolutionary process rather than a condition and it is, arguably, the second time states have developed such close trade, investment and economic linkages. The first period of globalization extended from the mid- to late 19th century, when Britain introduced free trade by repealing the protectionist Corn Laws. The two periods of globalization are similar in the high levels of trade dependence, in 1913 total global exports were 13 percent of global GDP and in 1992 it was 14 percent. Another similarity between the two periods relates to the role of hegemonic leadership. Nineteenth century free trade was associated with the British hegemony and contemporary globalization may, likewise, be associated with American hegemony and the free trade regime that was introduced under US leadership after the Second World War.

The first period of globalization began with British hegemony and ended with British economic decline that resulted in a resurgence of protectionism. It is possible to envisage a scenario where contemporary globalization is rolled back should the United States lose its pre-eminent position in the global economy. The point to note is that globalization was not permanent in the past and there may be no reason to assume that the contemporary period will be necessarily different. Indeed, we may point to the fragility of globalization by observing that protectionism remains a potent force in national economic policy making.

Neoprotectionist measures were used regularly by the United States in an attempt to reverse chronic and worsening trade deficits. The rules of international trade that had been devised at the end of the Second World

War were designed to favor interests of the United States that expected to be a surplus country for some considerable time. However, trade deficits emerged in the late 1960s, fuelled by expenditures associated with the Great Society Program and by the war in Vietnam. In the 1970s, the problem of trade deficit was compounded by new threats to core industries in the United States, such as automobile and steel, as a result of Japan's export surge. The prospect of de-industrialization and growing protectionist sentiments forced the US government to respond with new "gray area" measures to limit imports from Japan.

In the mid-1970s, the US government negotiated an Orderly Marketing Agreement (OMA) to limit Japanese exports of color television sets. This failed to provide much of an assistance to US manufacturers and most were forced to relocate to other countries where production costs were less. This was followed by the Trigger Price Mechanism (TPM) to provide American producers of steel some relief from increasing Japanese imports. Early in the 1980s, a protracted and somewhat acrimonious trade dispute over Japanese exports of cars was resolved when Japan agreed to a Voluntary Export Restraint (VER). An inadvertent consequence of the VER, in combination with the Plaza Accord of 1985 that re-valued the Japanese currency, was the transformation of production structures.

Prior to the VER agreement in 1982, Japanese car manufacturers had been reluctant to invest in manufacturing facilities overseas, preferring to meet foreign demand with exports. They may have been concerned that their just-in-time inventory control system and quality control practices could not be transplanted to a foreign location but with quantitative restrictions on exports, car manufacturers had a choice of either establishing production facilities in restricted markets or relinquishing market share. Rather than cede market shares, all major car manufacturers quickly established plants in North America. Indeed, this was one of the intended objectives of the United States in demanding export restraint from Japanese car manufacturers.

And yet, despite latent or overt protectionism, contemporary globalization is significantly different from 19th century free trade. The reality is that protectionism rather than being a threat to globalization in the contemporary period was actually a force for its emergence. Contemporary globalization is, at least partially, a response to the neoprotectionism of in the 1970s and 1980s. For instance, as noted above, export restraint agreements forced Japanese manufacturers to relocate production facilities overseas and this became the first step toward the formation of global production networks that is the hallmark of contemporary globalization.

The second important step followed the Plaza Accord of September 1985, which led to a substantial and sustained revaluation of the Japanese Yen. As exports from Japan suddenly became more expensive, manufacturers shifted production and procurement of parts, often produced by Japanese subsidiaries, to low cost production centers in other East Asian countries. Japanese manufacturers not only used production platforms in East Asia to supply markets in Japan and other countries but also exported parts produced in East Asia to manufacturing facilities in Japan and elsewhere. This culminated in the establishment of global manufacturing and the practice spread to other industries and countries. Global production structures make it harder for national governments to limit trade flows or to curtail economic globalization. With the spread of globalization, multinational corporations have become a dominant economic force in the on-going process of global economic integration.

Another important difference between the two periods is that contemporary globalization is underpinned by technological change and that may make it harder to wind back the scale of global economic activity. Certainly, contemporaries in the 19th century must also have marvelled at the technological revolution of the time, such as the invention of the telephone and telegraph, but unlike e-mail and the Internet, 19th century communications technology was expensive and still not as instantaneous as it is today.

Moreover, contemporary globalization is different also in the nature of trade liberalization and openness. Nineteenth century free trade was characterized by agricultural liberalization but today trade liberalization has largely covered only manufactured products, with high levels of protection granted to primary products. The G20 coalition of developing countries has not had much success, as yet, in overcoming the constraints of selective liberalization and farm liberalization, in the West, is unlikely to happen in the near future.

Finally, while 19th century free trade was a product of unilateral liberalization, today free trade and globalization are the result of a negotiated process with a strong emphasis on reciprocity. For all the reasons stated above, we cannot extrapolate that because globalization failed before, it may do so again. And if contemporary globalization fails, it may do so for a different set of reasons.

We cannot ignore that there is considerable global hostility toward globalization, in both developed and developing countries. In developed countries, there is a fear that globalization will initiate a race to the bottom; whereas, in the developing countries, there is a fear that globalization will lead to a form of recolonization where their economies become dominated by western MNCs serving western financial interest. Left groups also criticize globalization for adding to global inequalities, environmental degradation, exacerbation of third world debt, etc. The protest movement in Seattle and other large cities like Melbourne and Genoa highlighted these concerns. This protest movement may develop further to derail globalization just as a citizen's movement had derailed the initiate by developed countries to negotiate the Multilateral Agreement on Investments. The Seattle protests were instigated by a perception that globalization was not a beneficial development either for the developed or developing countries. Certainly some globalized developing countries have done better but income inequalities between the richest and the poorest 10 percent of countries are wider than ever before. Globalization is also seen as having a disastrous consequence for the developing countries and for the poor as became evident during the 1997 Asian finacial crisis. Protestors at Seattle and critics of globalization would want nothing better than to return the genie back in the bottle, perhaps through the imposition of a 'Tobin tax' on capital transactions. The idea of such a tax has been around for a long time but is unenforceable unless all countries join in and tax havens are closed down. Without this capital will simply move to international tax havens and continue to operate as before. At present, the Tobin tax is unlikely to be introduced.

At the same time, we know that the dynamics of protest have changed since the September 11 terrorist attack. Before September 11, the protest movement against globalization had been gaining momentum but protest is now seen as unpatriotic behavior. In early October 2002, when the

World Bank–IMF held their annual meetings in Washington there was hardly any formal protest although the expectation of protest still managed to disrupt the daily routine in Washington. Following September 11, globalization faces less of a challenge from citizens' movements.

Does this mean that globalization will continue its march forward. Thomas Friedman, author of The Lexus and Olive Tree certainly thinks so and asserts that those countries will be successful which display flexibility to cope with global demands and challenges than those countries which remain wedded to old ideologies, including countries, say in the Middle East which are fighting and squabbling over who owns which olive trees (land disputes). Far from reducing the importance of national and local governments, Friedman sees globalization as making governments very important in somewhat new and different ways. "The ability of an economy to withstand the inevitable ups and downs of the herd depends in large part on the quality of its legal system, financial system and economic management — all matters still under the control of governments and bureaucrats. Chile, Taiwan, Hong Kong and Singapore all survived the economic crises of the 1990s so much better than their neighbors because they had better-quality states running better-quality software and operating systems." Yet he points out that no country, no leader or big investor, can control the system. Even if we wanted to stop further globalization, there is no one we could call upon to bring the process of globalization to a halt, not the President of the United States, not the chairman of the Federal Reserve Board, not some gnome in Zurich or big investor in London, Berlin or Tokyo. Friedman characterizes this new globally decentralized system with the neologism, "DOScapital 6.0".

The opposing viewpoint is articulated by Danii Rodrik in terms of what he identifies as the "political trilemma of the global economy". The political trilemma is depicted in Fig. 9.1.

Rodrik asserts that the nation state system, deep economic integration or globalization, and democracy are mutually incompatible and that we can have, at most, two of these three. If we push global integration further, we may have to give up either the nation state or mass, democratic politics. If, on the other hand, we wish to maintain and deepen democracy, we may have to choose between the nation state and international economic

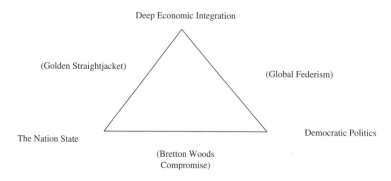

Figure 9.1:   The political trilemma.

Source: Rodrik, D., "Feasible Globalizations", NBER Working Paper Series, Working Paper 9129. Cambridge, MA, September 2002.

integration. And if we choose to keep the nation state, we may have to decide between democracy and international economic integration.

To see the logic in this, consider a hypothetical perfectly integrated world economy in which national borders do not interfere with the exchange of goods, capital or services. Transactions costs and tax differentials would be minimal and there would be a convergence of prices and factor returns. Is this possible? Yes, if nation states become singularly focused on becoming attractive to international markets. To do so domestic regulations will have to be harmonized to international standards. States would be able to provide only those public goods that are compatible with international markets. These are policies that have been identified by Thomas Friedman (1999) as the Golden Straightjacket, which will force countries to constrain politics in order to achieve economic growth. Governments will be forced to respond more to international pressures than to domestic pressures and democratic politics will get crowded out.

An alternative to the "Golden Straightjacket" is "Global Federalism", which is possible in the combination of deep economic integration and democratic politics but we will have to give up the nation state. Democratic politics will not shrink but simply relocate to the global level. This may appear a little too far fetched at present but the European Union appears to be headed in this direction.

The third option would be to sacrifice deep economic integration and this can be termed the "Bretton Woods" compromise. The essence of the Bretton Woods-GATT regime was that countries were free to regulate their domestic economy as long as they removed a number of border restrictions on trade and did not discriminate against or among their trade partners. Under the Bretton Woods system, despite overall trade liberalizations there were a large number of exceptions, on services, textiles, and agriculture. The GATT system also permitted countries to raise trade barriers under some conditions.

These are not choices that we are likely to confront in the immediate future but Danii Rodrik has opened up interesting possibilities as to how the future may evolve.

BIBLIOGRAPHY

Books and Monographs

Abegglen, J. C. and George Stalk, Jr., *Kaisha: The Japanese Corporation* (Charles E. Tuttle, Tokyo, 1988).

Agmon, T., Robert Hawkins and Richard M. Levich (eds.), *The Future of International Monetary System* (Lexington Books, DC Heath and Co., Lexington, 1984).

Aslund, A. (ed.), *The Post-Soviet Economy: Soviet and Western Perspectives* (Pinter, London, 1992).

Axelrod, R., *The Evolution of Cooperation* (Penguin Books, New York, 1984).

Baldwin, R. E., *Trade Policy in a Changing World Economy* (Harvester-Wheatsheaf, London, 1988).

Banerjee, B. *et al.*, *Road Maps of the Transition: The Baltics, the Czech Republic, Hungary and Russia*, IMF Occasional Paper No. 127 (Washington, DC, September 1995).

Bartlett, C. J. (ed.), *Britain Pre-Eminent: Studies of British Influence in the Nineteenth Century* (Macmillan, London, 1969).

Barnet, Richard J. and Ronald E. Muller, *Global Reach: The Power of the Multinational Corporations* (Jonathan Cape, London, 1975).

Bergsten, C. Fred and Marcus Noland (eds.), *Pacific Dynamism and the International Economic System* (Institute for International Economics, Washington, DC, 1993).

Bhagwati, J. and Hugh T. Patrick (eds.), *Aggressive Unilateralism: America's 301 Trade Policy and the World Trading System* (University of Michigan Press, Ann Arbor, 1990).

Blackhurst, R. and Jan Tumlir, *Trade Relations Under Unfair Exchange Rates*, GATT Studies in International Trade, No. 8 (Geneva, 1980). Block, F. L., *The Origins of International Economic Disorder: A Study of United States International Monetary Policy from World War II to the Present* (University of California Press, Berkeley and Los Angeles, 1977).

Boyer, R. and Daniel Drache (eds.), *States Against Markets: The Limits of Globalization* (Routledge, London, and New York, 1996).

Brock, W. E. and Robert D. Hormats (eds.), *The Global Economy: America's Role in the Decade Ahead* (W. W. Norton, New York, 1990).

Chan, S. (ed.), *Foreign Direct Investment in a Changing Global Political Economy* (Macmillan, Houndmills, 1995).

Chang, H-J., *Bad Samaritans: Rich Nations, Poor policies & the Threat to Developing Countries* (Oxford University Press, Oxford, 2007).

Chechile, Richard A. and Susan Carlisle (eds.), *Environmental Decision Making: A Multidisciplinary Approach* (Van Nostrad Reinhold, New York, 1991).

Choucri, N. (ed.), *Global Accord: Environmental Challenges and International Responses* (MIT Press, Cambridge, Massachusetts, 1993).

Cipolla, C. M. (ed.), *The Fontana Economic History of Europe: The Sixteenth and Seventeenth Centuries* (Collins/Fontana, Glasgow, 1974).

Cline, William R., *Debt and the Stability of the World Economy* (Institute for International Economics, Washington, DC, September 1993).

Conybeare, J. A. C., *Trade Wars: The Theory and Practice of International Commercial Rivalry* (Columbia University Press, New York, 1987).

Cooper, R. N., Peter Kenen *et al.*, *The International Monetary System Under Flexible Exchange Rates: Global, Regional and National* (Ballinger, Cambridge, 1982).

Corbridge, S., Ron Martin and Nigel Thrift (eds.), *Money, Power and Space* (Blackwell, Oxford, 1994).

Corden, W. M., *Economic Policy, Exchange Rates, and the International System* (Oxford University Press, Oxford, 1994).

Dam, Kenneth W., *The Rules of the Game: Reform and Evolution in the International Monetary System* (University of Chicago Press, Chicago and London, 1982).

Dauvergne, P., *Shadows in the Forest: Japan and the Politics of Timber in Southeast Asia* (MIT Press, Cambridge, Massachusetts, 1997).

De Cecco, M., *The International Gold Standard: Money and Empire* (Pinter, London, 1984).

De la Motha, J. and Gilles Paquet (eds.), *Evolutionary Economics and the New International Political Economy* (Pinter, 1996).

De Vries, M. G., *The IMF in a Changing World, 1945–1995* (International Monetary Fund, Washington, DC, 1986).

Destler, I. M., Haruhiro Fukui and Hideo Sato, *The Textile Wrangle: Conflict in Japan–America Relations, 1969–1971* (Cornell University Press, Ithaca, 1979).

Dieren, Wouter van (ed.), *Taking Nature Into Account: A Report to the Club of Rome* (Springer-Verlag, New York, 1995).

Dornbusch, R. and Stanley Fischer, *Macroeconomics*, 3rd ed. (McGraw-Hill, Singapore, 1985).

Drummond, I. M., *The Gold Standards and International Monetary System 1900–1939* (Macmillan, Basingstoke, 1987).

Dunkley, G., *The Free Trade Adventure: The Uruguay Round and Globalism — A Critique* (Melbourne University Press, Carlton, Victoria, 1997).

The East Asian Economic Miracle: Economic Growth and Public Policy, A World Bank Policy Research Report (Oxford University Press, New York, 1993).

Eichengreen, B., *Elusive Stability: Essays in the History of International Finance, 1919–1939* (Cambridge University Press, Cambridge, 1990).

Feldstein, M. (ed.), *International Economic Cooperation* (University of Chicago Press, Chicago, 1988).

Fellner, W., *Emergence and Content of Modern Economic Analysis* (McGraw Hill, New York, 1960).

Funabashi, J., *Managing the Dollar: From the Plaza to the Louvre*, 2nd ed. (Institute for International Economics, Washington, DC, 1989).

Furubotn, E. G. and Rudolf Richter (eds.), *The New International Economics* (J. C. B. Mohr, Tubingen, 1991).

Goddard, C. Roe, John T. Passe-Smith and John G. Conklin (eds.), *International Political Economy: State-Market Relations in the Changing Global Order* (Lynne Rienner, Boulder, 1996).

Goddin, Scott R., "Safeguards," *Business America* (1994).

Grilli, E. and Enrico Sassoon (eds.), *The New Protectionist Wave* (New York University Press, New York, 1990).

Haggard, S. and Chung-in Moon (eds.), *Pacific Dynamics: The International Politics of International Change* (Westview, Boulder, Colorado, 1989).

Hajnal, Peter I. (ed.), *The Seven Power Summit: Documents from the Summits of Industrialized Countries 1975–1989* (Krauss, New York, 1989).

Hansson, G., *Social Clauses and International Trade: An Economic Analysis of Labour Standards in Trade Policy* (Croom Helm, London and Canberra, 1983).

Harris, N., *The End of the Third World: Newly Industrializing Countries and the Decline of an Ideology* (Penguin, London, 1986).

Hatch, W. and Kozo Yamamura, *Asia in Japan's Embrace: Building a Regional Production Alliance* (Cambridge University Press, Cambridge, 1996).

Haus, Leah A., *Globalizing the GATT: The Soviet Unions' Successor States, Eastern Europe, and the International Trading System* (The Brookings Institution, Washington, DC, 1992).

Hellmann, Donald C. and Kenneth B. Pyle (eds.), *From APEC to Xanadu: Creating a Viable Community in the Post-Cold War Pacific* (M. E. Sharpe, New York, 1997).

Herzenberg, S. and Jorge F. Perez-Lopez (eds.), *Labor Standards and Development in the Global Economy* (US Department of Labor, Bureau of International Labor, Washington, 1990).

Hilf, M., Francis G. Jacobs and Ernst-Ulrich Petersmann (eds.), *The European Community and GATT* (Kluwer, The Netherlands, 1986).

Hoekman, B. and Michel Kostecki, *The Political Economy of the World Trading System: From GATT to WTO* (Oxford University Press, Oxford, 1995).

Hunter, David B. and Michelle Billig, "International economy and the environment," *Yearbook of International Environmental Law*, Vol. 7 (1996).

Jackson, John H., *Restructuring the GATT System* (Pinter, London, 1990).

Jackson, John H. and Alan O. Sykes (eds.), *Implementing the Uruguay Round* (Clarendon, Oxford, 1997).

Johnson, Stanley P., *The Earth Summit: The United Nations Conference on Environment and Development (UNCED)* (Graham and Trotman/Martinus Nijhoff, London, 1993).

Jones, G., *The Evolution of International Business: An Introduction* (Routledge, London and New York, 1996).

Kahler, M. (ed.), *The Politics of International Debt* (Cornell University Press, Ithaca, New York, 1986).

Kapstein, Ethan B., *Governing the Global Economy: International Finance and the State* (Harvard University Press, Cambridge, Massachusetts, 1994).

Keohane, R. O., *After Hegemony: Cooperation and Discord in the World Political Economy* (Princeton University Press, Princeton, 1984).

Keohane, R. O., Joseph S. Nye and Stanley Hoffmann (eds.), *After the Cold War: International Institutions and State Strategies in Europe, 1989–1991* (Harvard University Press, Cambridge, 1993).

Kitamura, K. and Tsuneo Tanaka (eds.), *Examining Asia's Tigers: Nine Economies Challenging Common Structural Problems* (Institute of Developing Economies, Tokyo, 1997).

Krauss, M. and R. D. Liebowitz (eds.), *Perestroika and East-West Economic Relations: Prospects for the 1990s* (New York University Press, New York, 1990).

Krueger, Anne O., *Economic Policy Reform in Developing Countries: The Kuznets Memorial Lectures at the Economic Growth Center, Yale University* (Blackwell Publishers, Massachusetts, 1992).

Krugman, P., *Peddling Prosperity: Economic Sense and Nonsense in the Age of Diminished Expectations* (W. W. Norton, New York, 1994).

Lall, S. and Paul Streeten, *Foreign Investment, Transnationals and Developing Countries* (Macmillan, London, 1977).

Leidy, M., "Antidumping: Unfair trade or unfair remedy," *Finance & Development*, Vol. 32, No. 1 (March 1995).

Leong, L., *The Chinese Economy in Transition: From Plan to Market* (Edward Elgar, Cheltenham, 1997).

Lieberman, S., *The Economic and Political Roots of New Protectionism* (Rowman and Littlefield, New Jersey, 1989).

Liew, Leong H., *The Chinese Economy in Transition: From Plan to Market* (Edward Elgar, Cheltenham, 1997).

Linden, C. and Jan S. Prybyla (eds.), *Russia and China on the Eve of a New Millenium* (Transactions, New Jersey, 1997).

Mander, J. and Edward Goldsmith (eds.), *The Case Against the Global Economy: And for a Turn Toward the Local* (Sierra Club, San Francisco, 1996).

Mastel, G., *The Rise of the Chinese Economy: The Middle Kingdom Emerges* (M. E. Sharpe, New York, 1997).

Maswood, S.J., *The South in International Economic Relations: Whose Globalization?* (Palgrave Macmillan, Basingstoke, 2006).

Mathias, P. and Sidney Pollard (eds.), *The Cambridge Economic History of Europe*, Vol. 8 (Cambridge University Press, Cambridge, 1989).

McMichael, T., *Planetary Overload* (Cambridge University Press, Cambridge, 1993).

Meier, G. M., *Problems of a World Monetary Order*, 2nd ed. (Oxford University Press, New York, 1982).

Mikdashi, Z. (ed.), *Bankers' and Public Authorities' Management of Risk* (Macmillan, London, 1990).

Milward, A. S., *The Reconstruction of Western Europe, 1945–1951* (Metheun, London, 1984).

Mokyr, J., *The Economics of the Industrial Revolution* (George Allen and Unwin, London, 1985).

Mungall, C. and Digby J. McLaren (eds.), *Planet Under Stress: The Challenge of Global Change* (Oxford University Press, Toronto, 1990).

Musson, A. E., *The Growth of British Industry* (Batsford, London, 1981).

Neelankavil, James P. and Yong Zhang (eds.), *Global Business: Contemporary Issues, Problems and Challenges* (McGraw Hill, New York, 1996).

Nester, William R., *Japan's Growing Power Over East Asia and the World Economy* (Macmillan, Basingstoke and London, 1990).

Nicholson, D. F., *Australia's Trade Relations: An Outline History of Australia's Overseas Trading Arrangements* (F. W. Cheshire, Melbourne, 1955).

Nolan, P., *China's Rise, Russia's Fall: Politics, Economics and Planning in the Transition from Stalinism* (Macmillan, Houndmills, 1995).

Odell, J. S., *US International Monetary Policy: Markets, Power and Ideas as Sources of Change* (Princeton University Press, Princeton, New Jersey, 1982).

Ohmae, K., *The Borderless World: Power and Strategy in the Interlinked Economy* (Fontana, London, 1990).

Oppenheim, P., *Trade Wars: Japan Versus the West* (Weidenfeld and Nicolson, London, 1992).

Our Common Future, The World Commission on Environment and Development (Oxford University Press Melbourne, Australia, 1990).

Pearson, Charles S. (ed.), *Multinational Corporations, Environment, and the Third World* (Duke University Press, Durham, 1987).

Peck, Merton J. and Thomas J. Richardson (eds.), *What is to be Done? Proposals for the Soviet Transition to the Market* (Yale University Press, New Haven and London, 1991).

Petersmann, E-U. (ed.), *Reforming the World trading System: Legitimacy, Efficiency, and Democratic Governance* (Oxford University Press, Oxford, 2005).

Pitchford, R. and Adam Cox (eds.), *EMU Explained: Markets and Monetary Union* (Kogan Page, London, 1997).

Plant, R., *Labour Standards & Structural Adjustment* (International Labour Office, Geneva, 1994).

Porter, G. and Janet Welsh Brown, *Global Environmental Politics* (Westview, Boulder, Colorado, 1991).

Private Capital Flows to Developing Countries: The Road to Financial Integration, A World Bank Policy Research Report (Oxford University Press, New York, 1997).

Putnam, R. D. and Nicholas Bayne, *Hanging Together: The Seven Power Summits* (Heinemann, London, 1984).

The Results of the Uruguay Round of Multilateral Trade Negotiations: The Legal Texts (The GATT Secretariat, Geneva, 1994).

Robb, Caroline M., *Can the Poor Influence Policy?* 2nd Ed., International Monetary Fund, Washington DC, 2002.

Rode, R. (ed.), *GATT and Conflict Management: A Transatlantic Strategy for a Stronger Regime* (Westview, Boulder, Colorado, 1990).

Rosenblatt, J. *et al.*, *The Common Agricultural Policy of the European Community: Principles and Consequences*, The International Monetary Fund, Occasional Papers No. 62 (Washington, DC, November 1988).

Sachs, J. and Andrew Warner, *Economic Convergence and Economic Policies*, NBER Working Paper No. 5039 (National Bureau of Economic Research, Massachusetts, 1995).

Salvatore, D., *The New Protectionist Threat to World Welfare* (North Holland, New York, 1987).

Scammell, W. M., *International Monetary Policy: Bretton-Woods and After* (Macmillan, London and Basingstoke, 1975).

Schlagenhof, M., "Trade Measures Based on Environmental Processes and Production Methods," *Journal of World Trade*, Vol. 29, No. 6 (1995).

Schmidheiny, S., *Changing Course: A Global Business Perspective on Development and the Environment* (MIT Press, Cambridge, Massachusetts, 1992).

Schott, Jeffrey J. (ed.), *Completing the Uruguay Round: A Results Oriented Approach to the GATT Trade Negotiations* (Institute for International Economics, Washington, DC, 1990).

Semmel, B., *The Rise of Free Trade Imperialism: Classical Political Economy, the Empire of Free Trade and Imperialism, 1750–1850* (Cambridge University Press, Cambridge, 1970).

Sengenberger, W. and Duncan Campbell (eds.), *Creating Economic Opportunities: The Role of Labour Standards in Industrial Restructuring* (International Institute for Labour Studies, Geneva, 1994).

Shelton, J., *Money Meltdown: Restoring Order to the Global Currency System* (Free Press, New York, 1994).

Shepherd, W. F., *International Financial Integration: History, Theory and Applications in OECD Countries* (Avebury, Aldershot, 1994).

Smith, D. (ed.), *Business and the Environment: Implications of the New Environmentalism* (Paul Chapman, 1993).

Steele, K. (ed.), *Anti-Dumping Under the WTO: A Comparative Review* (Kluwer, London, 1996).

Sterner, T. (ed.), *Economic Policies for Sustainable Development* (Kluwer, Dordrecht, 1994).

Stevis, D. and Valerie J. Asetto (eds.), *The International Political Economy of the Environment* (Lynne Rienner Publishers, Boulder, 2001).

Strange, S., *States and Markets: An Introduction to International Political Economy* (Pinter, London, 1988).

Stubbs, R. and Geoffrey R. D. Underhill (eds.), *Political Economy and the Changing Global Order* (Macmillan, London, 1994).

Sung, W. and Rosaria Troia, *Developments in Debt Conversion Programs and Conversion Activities*, World Bank technical Paper No. 170 (The World Bank, Washington, DC, 1992).

Suzuki, Y., Junichi Miyake and Mitsuaki Okabe (eds.), *The Evolution of the International Monetary System: How Can Efficiency and Stability be Attained?* (University of Tokyo Press, Tokyo, 1990).

Thomas, Kenneth P., *Capital Beyond Borders: States and Firms in the Auto Industry, 1960–1994* (Macmillan, Houndmills, 1997).

Thurow, L., *Head to Head: The Coming Economic Battle Among Japan, Europe and America* (William Morrow, New York, 1992).

Todaro, Michael P., *Economic Development in the Third World*, 4th ed. (Longman, New York and London, 1989).

Tolba, Mostafa K., Osama A. El-Kholy *et al.* (eds.), *The World Environment, 1972–1992: Two Decades of Challenge* (Chapman & Hall, London, 1993).

Tuchman, B., *The Guns of August* (Macmillan, New York, 1962).

Van Dormael, A., *Breton Woods: Birth of a Monetary System* (Macmillan, London and Basingstoke, 1978).

Walter, A., *World Power and World Money: The Role of Hegemony and International Monetary Order* (Harvester Wheatsheaf, Hertfordshire, 1991).

Williamson, J. and Marcus H. Miller, *Targets and Indicators: A Blueprint for the International Coordination of Economic Policy* (Institute for International Economics, Washington, DC, 1987).

Woods, N., *The Political Economy of Globalization* (Macmillan Press Ltd., London 2000).

World Trade Organization, Annual Report (Geneva, 1996).

Yang, X., *Globalization of the Automobile Industry: The United States, Japan and the People's Republic of China* (Praeger, Westport, 1995).

Articles

Aggarwal, V. K., Robert O. Keohane and David B. Yoffie, "The dynamics of negotiated protectionism," *American Political Science Review*, Vol. 81, No. 2 (1987).

Andrews, S., "Slouching towards forgiveness," *International Investor*, Vol. 23, No. 6 (1989).

Auer, James E., "The imperative of US–Japanese Bond," *Orbis* (1995).

Bacani, C., "Ground zero in Asia's crisis," *Asiaweek* (February 6, 1998).

Barenberg, M., "Law and labor in the new global economy: Through the lens of United States federalism," *Columbia Journal of Transnational Law*, Vol. 33, No. 3 (1995).

Bhagwati, J. N., "Regionalism versus multilateralism," *The World Economy*, Vol. 15, No. 5 (1992).

Blackhurst, R., "The WTO and the global economy," *The World Economy*, Vol. 20, No. 5 (1997).

Blaine, M., "Déjà vu all over again: Explaining Mexico's 1994 financial crisis," *The World Economy*, Vol. 21, No. 1 (January 1998).

Blay, S. K. N., "New trends in the protection of the Antarctic environment: The 1991 Madrid protocol," *American Journal of International Law*, Vol. 86 (1982).

Bohnet, A., Zhong Hong and Frank Muller, "China's open-door policy and its significance for transformation of the economic system," *Intereconomics*, Vol. 28, No. 4 (1993).

Boltho, A., "The return of free trade," *International Affairs*, Vol. 72, No. 2 (1996).

Bonturi, M. and Kiichiro Fukusaku, "Globalization and intra-firm trade: An empirical note," *OECD Economic Studies*, Vol. 20, No. 1 (1993).

Bowles, P. and Brian MacLean, "Regional trading blocs: Will East Asia be next?" *Cambridge Journal of Economics*, Vol. 20, No. 4 (1996).

Bradshaw, Victoria W. and Ana-Maria Wahl, "Foreign debt expansion, the international monetary fund, and regional variation in Third World poverty," *International Studies Quarterly*, Vol. 35 (1995).

Bromley, S. and Ray Bush, "Adjustment in Egypt?: The political economy of reform," *Review of African Political Economy*, Vol. 21, No. 6 (1994).

Campanella, M. L., "The effect of globalization and turbulence on policy making processes," *Government and Opposition*, Vol. 28, No. 2 (1993).

Carlisle, Charles R., "Is the world ready for free trade?" *Foreign Affairs*, Vol. 75, No. 6 (1996).

Chowdury, A., "Soviet implosion paves the way for market economy," *Asian Finance*, Vol. 17, No. 9 (1991).

Clarke, T., "Mai-Day! The corporate rule treaty," http://www.nassist.com/mai/mai(2)x.html.

Collingsworth, T., J. William Goold and Pharis J. Harvey, "Time for a global new deal," *Foreign Affairs*, Vol. 73, No. 1 (1994).

Cooper, Richard N., "External adjustment: The proper role for the IMF," *Challenge* (1993).

Crabbe, L., "The international gold standard and US monetary policy from World War I to the new deal," *Federal Reserve Bulletin*, Vol. 75, No. 6 (1989).

Davies, B., "A balancing act on the road to reform," *Asiamoney*, Vol. 18, No. 10 (December 1997/January 1998).

Dorn, James A., "Economic liberty and democracy in East Asia," *Orbis*, Vol. 37, No. 4 (1993).

Dunning, John H., "How should national governments respond to globalization?" *The International Executive*, Vol. 35, No. 3 (1993).

Easterly, W. and Stanley Fischer, "What can we learn from the Soviet collapse?" *Finance & Development*, Vol. 31, No. 4 (1994).

Edwards, S., "The Mexican peso crisis: How much did we know? When did we know it?" *The World Economy*, Vol. 21, No. 1 (January 1998).

Ehrlich, P., "Too many rich people," *Our Planet*, Vol. 6, No. 3 (1994).

Etzioni, A., "How is Russia bearing up?" *Challenge* (1992).

Feinerman, J. V., "The quest for GATT membership," *The China Business Review*, Vol. 19, No. 3 (1992).

Fieleke, Norman, S., "One trading world, or many: The issue of regional trading blocs," *New England Economic Review* (Federal Reserve Bank of Boston) (1992).

Guitian, M., "The IMF as a monetary institution: The challenge ahead," *Finance & Development*, Vol. 31, No. 3 (1994).

Haas, Peter M., "Do regimes matter? Epistemic communities and the Mediterranean pollution control," *International Organization*, Vol. 43, No. 3 (1989).

Hardin, G., "The tragedy of the commons," *Science*, No. 168 (1968).

Hare, P., Saul Estrin, Mikhail Lugachyov and Lina Takla, "Russia's foreign trade: New directions and western policies," *The World Economy*, Vol. 21, No. 1 (January 1998).

Harris, R. G., "Globalization, trade and income," *Canadian Journal of Economics*, Vol. 26, No. 4 (1993).

Hart, M., "The WTO and the political economy of globalization," *Journal of World Trade*, Vol. 31, No. 5 (1997).

Henkoff, R., "Service is everybody's business," *Fortune*, Vol. 129, No. 13 (1994).

Hirst, P. and Grahame Thompson, "The problem of 'globalization': International economic relations, national economic management and the formation of trading blocs," *Economy and Society*, Vol. 21, No. 4 (1992).

Hoekman, Bernard M., "New issues in the Uruguay Round and beyond," *The Economic Journal*, Vol. 103, No. 421 (1993).

Hogbin, G., "Global warming: The mother of all environmental scares," *Policy*, Vol. 14, No. 1 (Autumn 1998).

Hough, J., "On the road to paradise again? Keeping hopes for Russia realistic," *The Brookings Review*, Vol. 11, No. 1 (1993).

Hutton, W., "Relaunching western economies: The case for regulating financial markets," *Foreign Affairs*, Vol. 75, No. 6 (1996).

Ipsen, E., "The Brady plan's enforcer," *Institutional Investor*, Vol. 23, No. 8 (1989).

Islam, S., "A deal, of sorts," *Far Eastern Economic Review* (1993).

Jager, H., "The global exchange rate system in transition," *The Economist* (The Netherlands), Vol. 139, No. 4 (1991).

Kapstein, Ethan B., "We are US: The myth of the multinational," *The National Interest* (1991–1992).

Katz, S. I., "Balance of payments adjustment, 1945–1986: The IMF experience," *Atlantic Economic Journal*, Vol. 17, No. 4 (1989).

Kawaharada, S., "Shin Jidai o Mukaeru Jidosha Kaigai Jigyo," *Tekko Kai*, Vol. 35, No. 9 (1989).

Kennedy, K. C., "The accession of the Soviet Union to GATT," *Journal of World Trade Law*, Vol. 21, No. 2 (1987).

Kostrzewa, W., Peter Nunnenkamp and Holger Schmieding, "A marshall plan for Middle and Eastern Europe," *The World Economy*, Vol. 13, No. 1 (1990).

Krueger, Anne O., "The political economy of the rent-seeking society," *American Economic Review*, Vol. 64, No. 3 (1974).

Krugman, P., "Is free trade passé?" *The Journal of Economic Perspectives*, Vol. 1, No. 2 (1987).

Krugman, P., "Does the new trade theory require a new trade policy?" *The World Economy*, Vol. 15, No. 4 (1992).

Krugman, P., "Competitiveness: A dangerous obsession," *Foreign Affairs*, Vol. 73, No. 2 (1994).

Krugman, P., "The myth of Asia's miracle," *Foreign Affairs*, Vol. 73, No. 6 (1994).

Langille, Brian A., "Eight ways to think about international labour standards," *Journal of World Trade*, Vol. 31, No. 4 (1997).

Lawrence, R. Z., "The reluctant giant: Will Japan take its role on the world stage?" *The Brookings Review*, Vol. 9, No. 3 (1991).

Lee, E., "Globalization and employment: Is anxiety justified?" *International Labour Review* (1996).

————, "Globalization and labour standards: A review of issues," *International Labour Review*, Vol. 136, No. 2 (1997).

Leong, L., "Chinese reform strategy: A unity of opposites," mimeo (February 1998).

Lindbaek, J. and Jean-Francois Rischard, "Agility in the new world economy," *Finance & Development*, Vol. 31, No. 3 (1994).

Lindzen, Richard S., "Global warming: The origin and nature of the alleged scientific consensus," *Regulation: The Cato Review of Business & Government* (http://www.cato.org/pubs/regulation/reg15n2g.html).

Loxley, J. "Structural adjustment in Africa: Reflections on Ghana and Zambia," *Review of African Political Economy*, Vol. 47 (1990).

Lipson, C., "International cooperation in economic and security affairs," *World Politics*, Vol. 37, No. 1 (1994).

Lustig, Nora C., "NAFTA: Setting the record straight," *The World Economy*, Vol. 20, No. 5 (1997).

Lutz, James M., "GATT reform or regime maintenance: Differing solutions to world trade problems," *Journal of World Trade*, Vol. 25, No. 2 (1991).

Main, Ann. M., "Dispute settlement understanding," *Business America* (1994).

Marrese, M., "CMEA: Effective but cumbersome political economy," *International Organization*, Vol. 40, No. 2 (1986).

McCleary, W. A., "Policy implementation under adjustment lending," *Finance & Development* (1989).

McCulloch, R., "Investment policies in GATT," *The World Economy*, Vol. 13, No. 4 (1990).

McKenzie, P. D., "China's application to the GATT: State trading and the problem of market access," *Journal of World Trade*, Vol. 24, No. 5 (1990).

McMillan, J. and Barry Naughton, "How to reform a planned economy: Lessons from China," *Oxford Review of Economic Policy*, Vol. 8, No. 1 (1992).

Meyer, J. W., David John Frank, Ann Hironaka, Evan Schofer and Nancy Brandon Tuma, "The structuring of a world environmental regime, 1870–1990," *International Organization*, Vol. 51, No. 4 (1997).

Milner, C., "New standards issues' and the WTO," *The Australian Economic Review*, Vol. 30, No. 1 (1997).

Milner, H. V. and David B. Yoffie, "Between free trade and protectionism: Strategic trade policy and the theory of corporate trade demands," *International Organization*, Vol. 43, No. 2 (1989).

Neikirk, William B., "Mexico dropped like a bombshell," *Asian Finance* (1987).

Noren, J. H., "The Russian economic reform: Progress and prospects," *Soviet Economy*, Vol. 8, No. 1 (1992).

Norton, R., "Back to Bretton-Woods," *Fortune* (1994).

Oberthur, S., "Montreal protocol: 10 years after," *Environmental Policy and Law*, Vol. 27, No. 6 (1997).

Prestowitz, Clyde V., "Playing to win," *Foreign Affairs*, Vol. 73, No. 4 (1994).

Qureshi, Z., "Globalization: New opportunities, tough challenges," *Finance and Development*, Vol. 33, No. 1 (1996).

Reich, R. B., "The economics of illusion and the illusion of economics," *Foreign Affairs*, Vol. 66, No. 3 (1987/1988).

Reich, R. B., "We need a strategic trade policy," *Challenge* (1990).

Robertson, D., "The global environment: Are international treaties a distraction?" *The World Economy*, Vol. 13, No. 1 (1990).

Roncesvalles, O. and Andrew Tweedie, "Augmenting the IMF's resources," *Finance & Development* (1991).

Ruggiero, R., "Growing complexity in international economic relations demand broadening and deepening of the multilateral trade system," *WTO Focus*, No. 6 (1996).

Ruggie, John G., "Multilateralism: The anatomy of an institution," *International Organization*, Vol. 46, No. 3 (1992).

Ruggie, John G., "Territoriality and beyond: Problematizing modernity in international relations," *International Organization*, Vol. 47, No. 1 (1993).

Ryrie, Sir William, "Where do we go from here?" *Euromoney* (1994).

Sachs, J., "The economic transformation of Eastern Europe: The case of Poland," *Economics of Planning*, Vol. 25, No. 1 (1992).

Sachs, J., "Strengthening western support for Russia," *International Economic Insights*, Vol. 4, No. 1 (1993).

Sapir, A., "The interaction between labour standards and international trade policy," *The World Economy*, Vol. 18, No. 6 (1995).

Schnoor, Jerald L., James N. Galloway and Bedrich Moldan, "East Central Europe: An environment in transition," *Environmental Science and Technology*, Vol. 31, No. 9 (1997).

Schonhardt-Bailey, C., "Lessons in lobbying for free trade in 19th-century Britain: To concentrate or not," *American Political Science Review*, Vol. 85, No. 1 (1991).

Servais, J. M., "The social clause in trade agreements: Wishful thinking or an instrument of social progress?" *International Labour Review*, Vol. 128, No. 4 (1989).

Simon, Dennis F., "The international technology market: Globalization, regionalization and the pacific rim," *Business & the Contemporary World*, Vol. 5, No. 2 (1993).

Soros, G., "The capitalist threat," *The Atlantic Monthly*, Vol. 279, No. 2 (1997).

Stegemann, K., "Policy rivalry among industrial states: What can we learn from models of strategic trade policy?" *International Organization*, Vol. 43, No. 1 (1989).

Summers L. H. and Lant H. Pritchett, "The structural adjustment debate," *American Economic Review*, Vol. 83, No. 2 (1993).

Tanzi, V. and Hamid Davoodi, "Roads to nowhere: How corruption in public investment hurts growth," *Economic Issues*, No. 12 (International Monetary Fund, Washington DC, 1998).

Tita, A., "A challenge for World Trade Organization: Toward a true transnational law," *Journal of World Trade*, Vol. 29, No. 3 (1995).

Torres, R., "Labour standards and trade," *The OECD Observer*, No. 202 (1996).

Tsang, S. K., "Against 'Big Bang' in economic transition: Normative and positive arguments," *Cambridge Journal of Economics*, Vol. 20, No. 2 (1996).

Van Bael, I., "The GATT dispute settlement procedure," *Journal of World Trade*, Vol. 22, No. 4 (1988).

Wachtel, Howard M., "Taming global money," *Challenge* (1995).

Wang, Xinhua, "Trends towards globalization and a global think tank," *Futures*, Vol. 24, No. 3 (1992).

Wanniski, J., "The future of Russian capitalism," *Foreign Affairs*, Vol. 71, No. 2 (1992).

Wesson, R., "Wrapping up the debt problem," *PS; Political Science and Politics*, Vol. 23, No. 3 (1990).

Wiarda, Howard J., "The politics of Third World debt," *PS: Political Science and Politics*, Vol. 23, No. 3 (1990).

Witherell, William H., "An agreement on investment," *The OECD observer*, No. 202 (1996).

Zeitz, J., "Negotiations on GATT reform and political incentives," *The World Economy*, Vol. 12, No. 1 (1989).

END NOTES

Chapter 1

1 Harris, RG (November 1993). Globalization, trade, and income. *Canadian Journal of Economics,* 26(4), 755.

2 Marrese, M (Spring 1986). CMEA: effective but cumbersome political economy. *International Organization,* 40(2), 290–291.

3 Marrese, M (Spring 1986). CMEA: effective but cumbersome political economy. *International Organization,* 40(2), 299.

4 McKenzie, PD (October 1990). China's Application to the GATT: state trading and the problem of market access. *Journal of World Trade,* 24(5), 141.

5 Simon, DF (Spring 1993). The international technology market: globalization, regionalization and the Pacific rim. *Business & The Contemporary World,* 5(2), 53.

6 Lindbaek, J, JF Rischard (September 1994). Agility in the new World economy. *Finance & Development,* 31(3), 34.

7 Strange, S (1988). *States and Markets: An Introduction to International Political Economy,* p. 63. London: Pinter Publishers.

8 Dunning, JH (May/June 1993). How should national governments respond to globalization? *The International Executive,* 35(3), 192.

9 Chang, H-J (2007). *Bad Samaritans: Rich Nations, Poor Policies & the Threat to the Developing Countries,* p. 29. London: Random House Business Books.

10 Qureshi, Z (March 1996). Globalization: new opportunities, tough challenges. *Finance & Development,* 33(1), 30–32.

11 Harris, RG (November 1993). Globalization, trade, and income. *Canadian Journal of Economics,* 26(4), 758. These 35,000 TNCs own or control about 150,000 foreign affiliates. See, Dunning, JH. (May/June 1993). How should national governments respond to globalization? *The International Executive,* 35(3), 188.

12 Harris, RG (November 1993). Globalization, trade, and income. *Canadian Journal of Economics,* 26(4), 773.

13   Bairoch, P (1996). Globalization myths and realities: one century of external trade and foreign investment. In *States Against Markets: The Limits of Globalization*, Boyer, R, D Drache (eds.), p. 180. London, New York: Routledge.

14   Krugman, P (1994). *Peddling Prosperity: Economic Sense and Nonsense in the Age of Diminished Expectations*, p. 258. New York: W.W. Norton and Co., Inc.

15   Boyer, R, D Drache (eds.), (1996). *States Against Markets: The Limits of Globalization*, p. 130. London, New York: Routledge.

16   McCulloch, R (December 1990). Investment policies in GATT. *The World Economy*, 13(4), 344.

17   Blackhurst, R (August 1997). The WTO and the Global Economy. *The World Economy*, 20(5), 531.

18   Ruggie, JG (Winter 1993). Territoriality and beyond: problematizing modernity in international relations. *International Organization*, 47(1).

19   Ruggie, JG (Winter 1993). Territoriality and beyond: problematizing modernity in international relations. *International Organization*, 47(1), 155.

20   Ohmae, K (1990). *The Borderless World: Power and Strategy in the Interlinked Economy*, p. 16. London: Fontana.

21   Kapstein, B (Winter 1991–1992). We are US: The myth of the multinational. *The National Interest*. See also Kapstein, B (1994). *Governing the Global Economy: International Finance and the State*, Cambridge, Mass: Harvard University Press, Chap. 1.

22   Hirst, P, G Thompson (November 1992). The problem of 'globalization': international economic relations, national economic management and the formation of trading blocs. *Economy and Society globally*, 21(4), 369.

23   http://www.cid.harvard.edu/cidtrade/issues/washingtonlink.html#_2.

24   http://www.cid.harvard.edu/cidtrade/issues/washingtonlink.html#_4.

25   http://www.cid.harvard.edu/cidtrade/issues/washingtonlink.html#_1.

26   http://www.cid.harvard.edu/cidtrade/issues/washingtonlink.html#_1.

27   [F&D, September 2002, p. 26].

Chapter 2

1   Glamann, K (1974). European trade 1500–1750. In *The Fontana Economic History of Europe: The Sixteenth and Seventeenth Centuries*, Cipolla, CM (ed.), p. 430. Glasgow: Collins/Fontana Books.

2   Fellner, W (1960). *Emergence and Content of Modern Economic Analysis*, p. 37. New York: McGraw-Hill Book Co. Ltd.

3   Musson, AE (1981). *The Growth of British Industry*, p. 66. London: Batsford Academic and Educational Ltd.

4   McCloskey, D (1985). The industrial revolution 1780–1860: a survey. In *The Economics of the Industrial Revolution*, Mokyr J (ed.), p. 57. London: George Allen & Unwin.

5   Fielden, K (1969). The rise and fall of free trade. In *Britain Pre-eminent: Studies of British influence in the nineteenth century,* Bartlett, CJ (ed.), p. 81. London: Macmillan.

6   Schonhardt-Bailey, C (March 1991). Lessons in lobbying for free trade in 19th century Britain: to concentrate or not. *American Political Science Review,* 85(1).

7   Stearns, PN (1969). Britain and the Spread of the Industrial Revolution. In *Britain Pre-eminent: Studies of British world influence in the nineteenth century,* Bartlett, CJ (ed.), p. 13. London: Macmillan and Co. Ltd.

8   Semmel, B (1970). *The Rise of Free Trade Imperialism: Classical Political Economy, the Empire of Free Trade and Imperialism 1750–1850,* p. 207. Cambridge University Press.

9   Conybeare, JAC (1987). *Trade Wars: The Theory and Practice of International Commercial Rivalry,* p. 240. New York: Columbia University Press.

10   Kindleberger, CP. The World in Depression.

11   Tussie, D (1987). pp. 9–10.

12   Tuchman, BW (1962). *The Guns of August,* pp. 310–311. New York: The Macmillan Company.

13   Nicholson, DF (1955). *Australia's Trade Relations: An Outline History of Australia's Overseas Trading Arrangements,* p. 140. Melbourne: F.W. Cheshire.

14   Schott, JJ (1990). U.S. policies toward the GATT: past, present, prospective. In *GATT and Conflict Management,* Reinhard Rode (ed.), p. 25. Boulder, Colo: Westview Press.

15   Kousoulas, DG. *Power and Influence: An Introduction to International Relations,* p. 179.

16   Dam, K. p. 150.

17   Kousoulis, DG. *Power and Influence: An Introduction to International Relations,* p. 181.

18   US Congress (1987). *The GATT Negotiations and U.S. Trade Policy,* p. 34.

19   GATT Activities 1990 (July 1991). *General Agreement on Tariffs and Trade, Geneva, Switzerland,* p. 28.

20   Islam, S (December 1993). A Deal, of Sorts. *Far Eastern Economic Review,* p. 54.

21   United States (1991). *World Economic Survey 1991,* p. 63. New York: Department of International Economic and Social Affairs.

22   General Agreement on Tariffs and Trade, Geneva (1991). *GATT Activities 1990,* p. 35.

23   The final act of the Uruguay Round — a summary (1994). *International Trade Forum,* No. 1, pp. 6–8.

24   The GATT Secretariat (1994). The final act of the Uruguay Round: a summary. *International Trade Forum,* No. 1, p. 10.

25   Henkoff, R (June 27, 1994). Service is everybody's business. *Fortune,* 129(13), 33.

26   Lutz, JM (April 1991). GATT reform or regime maintenance: differing solutions to world trade problems. *Journal of World Trade,* 25(2), 112.

27   *The Economist* (1994). Son of GATT: The new World Trade Organization needs the right priorities and the right boss, August 6, 12.

28   Blackhurst, R (August 1997). The WTO and the global economy. *The World Economy,* 20(5), 543.

29 McGovern, E (1986). Dispute settlement in the GATT — adjudication or negotiation? In *The European Community and GATT,* Hilf, M, FG Jacobs, E-U Petersmann (eds.), p. 74. The Netherlands: Kluwer Law and Taxation Publishers.

30 Van Bael, I (1988). The GATT dispute settlement procedure. *Journal of World Trade,* 22(4), 68–69.

31 Main, AM (January 1994). Dispute settlement understanding. *Business America,* p. 21.

32 Ruggiero, R (October/November 1995). Growing complexity in international economic relations demands broadening and deepening of the multilateral trading system. *WTO Focus,* 6, 10.

33 Goddin, SR (January 1994). Safeguards. *Business America,* p. 18.

34 Steele, K (ed.), (1996). *Anti-Dumping under the WTO: A Comparative Review,* p. 3. London: Kluwer Law International Ltd.

35 Leidy, M (March 1995). Antidumping: unfair trade or unfair remedy. *Finance and Development,* 32(1), 29.

36 Blackhurst, R (August 1997). The WTO and the global economy. *The World Economy,* 20(5), 539.

37 *The Australian,* WTO Skating on Thin Ice with Budget Freeze. April 7, 1998, p. 31.

38 Chang, H-J (2007). *Bad Samaritans: Rich Nations, Poor Policies & the Threat to the Developing Countries,* p. 77. London: Random House.

39 Ismail, F (2005). A Developing country perspective on the WTO July 2004 general council decision. In *Reforming the World Trading System: Legitimacy, Efficiency, and Democratic Governance,* Petersmann, E-U (ed.), p. 59. Oxford: Oxford University Press.

40 Maswood, SJ (2007). Developing countries and the G20 in the Doha round. In *Developing Countries and Global Trade Negotiations,* Crump, L, S Javed Maswood (eds.), London: Routledge.

41 GATT Focus, (January–February 1994), 105, p. 6.

Chapter 3

1 Eichengreen, B (1990). *Elusive Stability: Essays in the History of International Finance, 1919–1939,* pp. 19–20. Cambridge: Cambridge University Press.

2 Blackhurst, R, J Tumlir (1980). Trade Relations Under Flexible Exchange Rates, GATT Studies in International Trade, No. 8, General Agreement on Tariffs and Trade, Geneva, pp. 55ff.

3 Ford, AG (1989). International financial policy and the gold standard, 1870–1914. In *The Cambridge Economic History of Europe,* Mathias, P, Sidney Pollard (eds.), Vol. 8, p. 199. Cambridge: Cambridge University Press.

4 Drummond, IM (1987). *The Gold Standard and the International Monetary System, 1900–1939,* p. 15. Basingstoke: Macmillan Education Ltd.

5 Crabbe, L (June 1989). The International Gold Standard and U.S. Monetary Policy from World War I to the New Deal. *Federal Reserve Bulletin,* 75(6), 426.

6   Block, FL (1977). *The Origins of International Economic Disorder: A Study of United States International Monetary Policy from World War II to the Present*, p. 20. Berkeley and Los Angeles: University of California Press.

7   Moggridge, DE (1989). The gold standard and national financial policies, 1919–39. In *The Cambridge Economic History of Europe*, Mathias, P, Sidney Pollard (eds.), p. 306. Vol. 8, Cambridge: Cambridge University Press.

8   Odell, JS (1982). *U.S. International Monetary Policy: Markets, Power, and Ideas as Sources of Change*, pp. 80–81. New Jersey: Princeton University Press. [Taken from IO, (1975). pp. 64–65].

9   Dam, KW (1982). *The Rules of the Game: Reform and Evolution in the International Monetary System*, pp. 77–83. Chicago and London: The University of Chicago Press.

10   Van Dormael, A (1978). *Bretton-Woods: Birth of a Monetary System*, p. 110. London and Basingstoke: The Macmillan Press Ltd.

11   Cohen in Krasner (1983). p. 328.

12   Scammell, WM (1975). *International Monetary Policy: Bretton-Woods and After*, p. 149. London and Basingstoke: The Macmillan Press Ltd.

13   Scammell, WM (1975). *International Monetary Policy: Bretton-Woods and After*, p. 135. London and Basingstoke: The Macmillan Press Ltd.

14   Eichengreen, B (1990). *Elusive Stability: Essays in the History of International Finance, 1919–1939*, New York: Cambridge University Press.

15   Kostrzewa, W (March 1990). Peter Nunnenkamp and Holger Schmieding, "A marshall plan for middle and eastern Europe". *The World Economy*, 13(1), 28.

16   Milward, AS (1984). The Reconstruction of Western Europe, 1945–51, p. 114ff. London: Methuen and Co. Ltd.

17   de Vries, MG (1986). *The IMF in a Changing World, 1945–85*, p. 78. Washington, D.C.: International Monetary Fund.

18   Scammell, WM (1975). *International Monetary Policy: Bretton-Woods and After*, London and Basingstoke: The Macmillan Press Ltd.

19   Block, FL (1997). *The Origins if International Economic Disorder: A Study of United States International Monetary Policy from World War II to the Present*, p. 146. Berkeley and Los Angeles, California: University of California Press.

20   Odell, JS (1982). *U.S. International Monetary Policy: Market, Power, and Ideas as Sources of Change*, pp. 174–175. Princeton: Princeton University Press.

21   Yeager, LB (1984). Opportunities and implications of a return to fixed exchange rates — is gold an answer for international adjustments? In *The Future of International Monetary System*, Agmon, T, Robert G Hawkins, Richard M Levich (eds.), p. 28. Lexington: Lexington Books, D.C. Heath and Co.

22   Katz, SI (December 1989). Balance of payments adjustments, 1945 to 1986: the IMF experience. *Atlantic Economic Journal*, 17(4), 71.

23   Katz, SI (December 1989). Balance of payments adjustment, 1945 to 1986: the IMF experience. *Atlantic Economic Journal*, 17(4), 72.

24   Dam, KW (1982). *The Rules of the Game: Reform and Evolution in the International Monetary System*, p. 177. Chicago and London: The University of Chicago Press.

25   Block, FL (1977). The origins of international economic disorder: a study of United States international monetary policy from World War II to the present, p. 161. California: Berkeley and Los Angeles, University of California Press.

26   Odell, JS (1982). *U.S. International Monetary Policy: Markets, Power and Ideas as Sources of Change*, p. 181. Princeton: Princeton University Press.

27   Crockett A *et al.* (1987). *Strengthening the International IMF*, Occasional Paper No. 50.

28   The Economist London, (January 9, 1988), p. 70.

29   Cooper, RN (1982). Flexible exchange rates, 1973–1980: how bad have they really been? In *The International Monetary System Under Flexible Exchange Rates: Global, Regional, and National*, Cooper, RN, Peter Kenen, *et al.* (eds.), p. 11. Cambridge: Ballinger Publishing Company.

30   Salvatore, D (1987). Chapter 1.

31   The Australian (March 10, 1993). p. 37.

32   Jager, H (1991). The global exchange rate system in transition. *The Economist* (*Netherlands*), 139(4), 477.

33   The Banker, (October 1994). *G–7 Reshapes Bretton-Woods*, p. 38.

34   Blackhurst, R, Jan Tumlir (1980). Trade relations under flexible exchange rates. *GATT Studies in International Trade,* No. 8, p. 13. Geneva: General Agreement on Tariffs and Trade.

35   Dam, KW (1982). *The Rules of the Game: Reform and Evolution in the International Monetary System*, p. 197. Chicago and London: The University of Chicago Press.

36   Cooper, RN (1985). Recent history of world monetary problems. In *The Future of the International Monetary System*, Agmon, T, Robert G Hawkins, Richard M Levich (eds.), p. 16. Lexington: Lexington Books, D.C. Heath and Co.

37   Modigliani, F (1984). Comment. In *The Future of the International Monetary System*, Agmon, T, Robert G Hawkins, Richard M Levich (eds.), p. 52. Lexington: Lexington Books, D.C. Heath and Co.

38   Cooper, R (1982). The Gold Standard: Historical facts and future prospects. *Brookings Papers on Economic Activity, No. 1.*

39   Shelton, J (1994). *Money Meltdown: Restoring Order to the Global Currency System*, p. 6. New York: The Free Press.

40   Judy Shelton (1994). *Money Meltdown: Restoring Order to the Global Currency System*, pp. 196–211. New York: The Free Press.

41   Dam, KW (1982). *The Rules of the Game: Reform and Evolution in the International Monetary System*, p. 197. Chicago and London: The University of Chicago Press.

42   Shinkai, Y (1990). Evaluation of the Bretton Woods regime and the floating exchange rate system. In *The Evolution of the International Monetary System: How Can Efficiency and Stability be Attained?* Suzuki, Y, Junichi Miyake, Mitsuaki Okabe (eds.), p. 132. Tokyo: University of Tokyo Press.

43   Williamson, J, MH Miller (September 1987). *Targets and Indicators: A Blueprint for the International Coordination of Economic Policy*, p. 12. Washington, D.C.: Institute for International Economics.

44   Richter, R (1991). The Louvre accord: from the viewpoint of the new institutional economics. In *The New Institutional Economics*, Furubotn, EG, Rudolf Richter (eds.), p. 278, 284. Tubingen: J.C.B. Mohr.

45   Shinkai, Y (1990). Evaluation of the Bretton-Woods regime and the floating exchange rate system. In *The Evolution of the International Monetary System: How Can Efficiency and Stability be Attained?* Suzuki, Y, Junichi Miyake, Mitsuaki Okabe (eds.), p. 144. Tokyo: University of Tokyo Press.

46   Meier, GM (1982). *Problems of a World Monetary Order*, p. 281. Second edition, New York: Oxford University Press.

47   Funabashi, Y (1988). Managing the Dollar: from the Plaza to the Louvre. Washington, D.C.: Institute for International Economics.

48   Fraser, BW (December 1994). *Central bank independence: what does it mean? Reserve Bank of Australia Bulletin.*

49   Polak, JJ (1989). Strengthening the role of the IMF in the international monetary system. In *The International Monetary Fund in a Multipolar World: Pulling Together*, p. 50. New Brunswick: Transaction Books.

50   The Banker (October 1994). *G–7 Reshapes Bretton-Woods*, p. 42.

51   Cooper, RN (May–June 1993). *External Adjustment: The Proper Role for the IMF.* Challenge, 55.

52   Wachtel, HM (January–February 1995). Taming Global Money. *Challenge*, 36.

53   Cooper, Richard, N (1990). What future for the international monetary system? In *The Evolution of the International Monetary System: How Can Efficiency and Stability be Attained*, Yoshio Suzuki, Junichi Miyake, Mitsuaki Okabe (eds.), p. 291. Tokyo: University of Tokyo Press.

54   Hutton, W (November/December 1996). Relaunching western economies: the case for regulating financial markets, *Foreign Affairs*, 75(6), 12.

55   Kenen, P (1989). The Use of IMF Credit. In *The International Monetary Fund in a Multipolar World: Pulling Together*, p. 87. New Brunswick: Transaction Books.

56   Press Conference of Michel Camdessus on April 14, 1998, Washington: IMF Headquarters.

57   Guitian, M (September 1994). The IMF as a monetary institution: the challenge ahead. *Finance and Development*, 31(3), 39.

58   Hirsh, M (January 23, 1995). All shook up, *Newsweek*, 10.

59   Roncesvalles, O, Andrew Tweedie (December 1991). Augmenting the IMF's resources, *Finance and Development*, 26.

60   The Banker (October 1994). *G–7 Reshapes Bretton-Woods*, pp. 37–38.

61   IMF chief's plans include greater role for himself, (June 12 1995). *The Asian Wall Street Journal*, 1.

62   Cooper, RN (1990). What future for the international monetary system? In *The Evolution of the International Monetary System*, Yoshio Suzuki, Junichi Miyake, Mitsuaki Okabe (eds.), p. 295. Tokyo: University of Tokyo Press.

Chapter 4

1   Cline, WR (September 1983). *International Debt and the Stability of the World Economy*, p. 11. Washington D.C.: Institute for International Economics.
2   Neikirk, WB (October 15, 1987). Mexico dropped like a bombshell, *Asian Finance*, 57.
3   Wiarda, HJ (September 1990). The politics of Third World debt. *PS: Political Science and Politics*, 23(3), 414.
4   Kahler, M (1986). Conclusion: politics and proposals for reform. In *The Politics of International Debt*, Kahler, H (ed.), p. 259. Ithaca, New York: Cornell University Press.
5   Ipsen, E (July 1989). The Brady Plan's enforcer. *Institutional Investor*, 23(8), 179.
6   Kahler, M (1986). *Op. Cit.*, p. 267.
7   Andrews, S (May 1989). Slouching toward forgiveness. *Institutional Investor*, 23(6), 88.
8   Wesson, R (September 1990). Wrapping up the debt problem. *PS: Political Science and Politics*, 23(3), 423 (Italics in original).
9   Clark, J, Eliot Kaltor (September 1982). Recent innovations in debt restructuring. *Finance & Development*, 6.
10 Sung, W, Rosaria Troia (1992). Developments in debt conversion programs and conversion activities, World Bank Technical Paper No. 170, pp. 28–29. Washington, D.C.: The World Bank.
11 Blaine, MJ (January 1998). Déjà Vu all over again: explaining Mexico's 1994 financial crisis. *The World Economy*, 21(1), 34.
12 Edwards, S (January 1998). The Mexican peso crisis: how much did we know? When did we know it? *The World Economy*, 21(1).
13 The Economist (January 7, 1995). p. 36.
14 Lustig, NC (August 1997). NAFTA: setting the record straight. *The World Economy*, 20(5), 607.
15 Shigemitsu Sugisaki (January 30, 1998). Deputy Managing Director of the International Monetary Fund. Economic crisis in Asia. Harvard Asia Business Conference, Harvard Business School (http://www.imf.org/external/np/speeches/1998/013098.HTM).
16 World Bank (1993). *The East Asian Miracle: Economic Growth and Public Policy*, p. 7. New York: Oxford University Press.
17 Krugman, P (November/December 1994). The myth of Asia's miracle. *Foreign Affairs*, 73(6), 70.
18 Private capital flows to the developing countries: the road to financial integration (1997). *A World Bank Policy Research Report*, p. 257. New York: Oxford University Press.
19 Tanzer, A (January 12, 1998). Tight little market. *Forbes*, 52.
20 IMF Survey (December 15, 1997). 26(23), 389.

21   The perils of global capital (April 11, 1998). *The Economist*, p. 62.

22   Capital flow sustanability and speculative currency attacks (December 1997). *Finance & Development*, p. 9.

23   IMF Survey (February 23, 1998). 27(4), 49.

24   Debt on Korea's terms. (February 13, 1998). *Asiaweek*, 46.

25   The Australian (January 31–February 1, 1998). p. 11.

26   The Australian (January 28, 1998). p. 7, (January 31–February 1, 1998), p. 11.

27   Chowdury, A (September 1991). Soviet implosion paves way for market economy. *Asian Finance*, 17(9), 44.

28   Sachs, JD, Andrew Warner (1995). Economic convergence and economic policies. *NBER Working Paper No. 5039*, Massachusetts: National Bureau of Economic Research.

29   Bradshaw, VW, Ana-Maria Wahl (1991). Foreign debt expansion, the International Monetary Fund, and regional variation in Third World poverty. *International Studies Quarterly*, 35, 252.

30   Krueger, AO (1992). *Economic Policy Reform in Developing Countries: The Kuznets Memorial Lectures at the Economic Growth Center*, p. 94. Cambridge, Mass and Oxford: Yale University, Blackwell Publishers.

31   The World Bank (1991). *World Development Report*, p. 124. New York, Washington, D.C.: Oxford University Press.

32   Harris, N (1986). *The End of the Third World: Newly Industrializing Countries and the Decline of an Ideology*, p. 81. London: Penguin Books.

33   Todaro, MP (1982). *Economic Development in the Third World*, p. 447. Fourth edition, New York and London: Longman.

34   Sachs, JD (1987). Trade and exchange rate policies in growth-oriented adjustment programs. In *Growth-Oriented Adjustment Programs*, Corbo, V, Morris Goldstein, Mohsin Khan (eds.), p. 292. Washington, D.C.: International Monetary Fund and The World Bank.

35   Thomas, V, Ajay Chhibber (March 1989). Experience with policy reforms under adjustment: how well have adjustment programs been working? *Finance & Development*, 29.

36   Krueger, AO (June 1974). The political economy of the rent-seeking society. *American Economic Review*, 64(3), 302.

37   McCleary, WA (March 1989). Policy implementation under adjustment lending. *Finance & Development*, 32.

38   Globalization — to what end? (March 1992). Part II, *Monthly Review*, 43(10), 16.

39   Economic trends in the developing world (March 1997). *Finance & Development*, 34(1), 47.

40   Carol Lancaster (1991). Economic Reform in Africa: is it Working? In *The Leadership Challenge of Economic Reforms in Africa*, Obasanjo, O, Hans d'Orville (eds.), p. 95. New York: Crane Russak.

41   Jones, C, Miguel A Kiguel (June 1994). Africa's quest for prosperity: has adjustment helped. *Finance & Development*, 31(2), 2.

42   Summers, LH, Lant H Pritchett (May 1993). The structural-adjustment debate. *American Economic Review*, 83(2), 384.

43   Khor, M (1996). Global economy and the Third World. In *The Case Against the Global Economy: And for a Turn Toward the Local*, Jerry Mander, Edward Goldsmith (eds.), p. 48. San Francisco: Sierra Club Books.

44   World Bank Policy Research Bulletin (November–December 1992). 3(5).

45   Singer, HW, Sumit Roy (1993). *Economic Progress and Prospects in the Third World: Lessons of Development Experience Since 1945*, p. 4. Hants: Edward Elgar.

46   Ihonvbere, JO (1989). Structural adjustment in Nigeria. In *Alternative Strategies for Africa: Debt and Democracy*, Turok, B (ed.), Vol. 3, p. 82. London: Institute for African Alternatives.

47   David Seddon (Spring 1990). The politics of adjustment: Egypt and the IMF, 1977–1990. *Review of African Political Economy*, 47, p. 96.

48   Loxley, J (Spring 1990). Structural adjustment in Africa: reflections on Ghana and Zambia. *A Review of African Political Economy*, 47(21).

49   Bromley, S, Ray Bush (June 1994). Adjustment in Egypt? The political economy of reform. *Review of African Political Economy*, 21(60).

50   Chang, H-J (2007). *Bad Samaritans: Rich Nations, Poor Policies & the threat to the Developing World*, p. 35. London: Random House Business Books.

51   Newsweek (May 29, 1995). p. 20.

52   The Australian (May 6, 1998). p. 6.

53   Tanzi, V, Hamid Davoodi (1998). Roads to nowhere: how corruption in public investment hurts growth. *Economic Issues*, No. 12, Washington D.C.: International Monetary Fund.

54   The Perils of global capital (April 11, 1998). *The Economist*, p. 63.

55   What are the lessons of the Southeast Asian crisis? (December 1, 1997). IMF Survey, 26(22).

Chapter 5

1   Haus, LA (1992). Globalizing the GATT: the Soviet Unions's successor states, Eastern Europe, and the International Trading System, p. 11. Washington, D.C.: The Brookings Institution.

2   McKenzie, PD (October 1990). China's application to the GATT: state trading and the problem of market access. *Journal of World Trade*, 24(5), 141.

3   Easterly, W, Stanley Fischer (December 1994). What we can learn from the Soviet collapse. *Finance and Develpment*, 31(4).

4   Sachs, J (1992). The economic transformation of eastern Europe: the case of Poland. *Economics of Planning*, 25(1), 6.

5   Mark Knell, Wenyan Yang (1992). Lessons from China on Strategy for the Socialist Economies in Transition. In *Socialist Economies in Transition: Appraisals of the*

Market Mechanism, Knell, M, Christine Rider (eds.), p. 220. Aldershot: Edward Elgar. [taken from Statistical Yearbook of China].

6   Painful but inevitable restructuring. (December 1997/January 1998). *Asiamoney*, 8(10), 40.

7   McMillan, J, Barry Naughton (1992). How to reform a planned economy: lessons from China. *Oxford Review of Economic Policy*, 8(1), 131.

8   Bohnet, A, Zhong Hong, Frank Muller (July/August 1993). China's open-door policy and its significance for transformation of the economic system. *Intereconomics*, 28(4), 193.

9   The Economist (October 13, 2007) p. 90.

10 Feinerman, JV (May–June 1992). The quest for GATT membership. *The China Business Review*, 19(3).

11 Balassa, B, Michael P Claudon (1990). Reflections on Perestroika and the foreign economic ties of the Soviet Union. In *Perestroika and East–West Economic Relations: Prospects for the 1990s*, Krauss, M, RD Liebowitz (eds.), p. 114. New York: New York University Press.

12 The Australian (February 17, 1993). p. 12.

13 McKenzie, PD (October 1990). China's application to the GATT: state trading and the problem of market access. *Journal of World Trade*, 24(5), 150.

14 China Daily (May 12, 1994). p. 2.

15 The Straits Times (Singapore) (March 13, 1993). p. 34.

16 The Economist Intelligence Unit (1st quarter 1994). Country Report: China, Mongolia, p. 4.

17 Feinerman, JV (May–June 1992). The quest for GATT membership. *The China Business Review*, 19(3).

18 China and the GATT: reaching an impasse. (August 6, 1994). *The Economist*.

19 Merkl, PH (2000). The Russian prospect: hope and despair. In *Transitions to capitalism and Democracy in Russia and Central Europe: Achievements, Problems, Prospects*, Donald hancock, M, John Logue (eds.), p. 98. Westport, Connecticut: Praeger.

20 Khanin, G (1992). The Soviet economy — from crisis to catastrophe. In *The Post-Soviet Economy: Soviet and Western Perspectives*, Aslund, A (ed.), p. 13. London: Pinter Publishers.

21 Aslund, A (1992). A critique of the Soviet reform plan. In *The Post-Soviet Economy: Soviet and Western Perspectives*, Aslund, A (ed.), p. 168. London: Pinter Publishers.

22 Wanniski, J (Spring 1992). The future of Russian capitalism. *Foreign Affairs*, 71(2), 18.

23 Linden, C (1997). Yeltsin and the Russian Republic's rebirth in a time of troubles. In *Russia and China on the Eve of a New Millennium*, Linden C, JS Prybyla (eds.), p. 118. New Jersey: Transactions Publishers.

24 Hemming, R, AM Mansoor (January 1988). Privatization and Public Enterprises, Occasional Paper No. 56, International Monetary Fund, Washington, D.C.

25 Noren, JH (January–March 1992). The Russian economic reform: progress and prospects. *Soviet Economy*, 8(1), 12.

26   Hanson, P, E Teague (2007). Russian political capitalism and its Environment. In *Varieties of Capitalism in Post-Communist Countries*, Lane D, M Myant (eds.), p. 153. London: Palgrave Macmillan.

27   Khanin, G (1992). The Soviet economy — From crisis to catastrophe. In *The Post-Soviet Economy: Soviet and Western Perspectives*, Aslund A (ed.), p. 12. London: Pinter Publishers.

28   Economist (London), Vol. 324, No. 7766, July 4, 1992, p. 18.

29   Sachs, J (1992). The Grand Bargain. In *The Post-Soviet Economy: Soviet and Western Perspective*, Anslund A (ed.), p. 210. London: Pinter Publishers.

30   Sachs, J (1994). West may be losing critical chance to help advance Russian reforms. *The Straits Times*, 28 January, p. 35.

31   Sachs, J (July/February 1993). Strengthening western support for Russia. *International Economic Insights*, 4(1), 11.

32   Hernandez-Cata, E (September 1994). Russia and the IMF: The Political Economy of Macro-Stabilization. IMF Paper of Policy Analysis and Assessment, PPAA/94/20.

33   Noren, JH (January–March 1992). The Russian economic reform: progress and prospects. *Soviet Economy*, 8(1), 14.

34   Hough, J (Winter 1993). On the road to paradise again? Keeping hopes for Russia realistic. *The Brookings Review*, 11(1), 15.

35   Fischer, S (January 1998). The Russian Economy at the Start of 1998. Address at the 1998 US-Russian Investment Symposium at Harvard University (http://www.imf.org/external/np/speeches/1998/010998.HTM).

36   Hossain, M, Iyanatul Islam, Reza Kibria (1999). *South Asian Economic Development: Transformation, Opportunities and Challenges*, pp. 4–5. London: Routledge.

37   Raj, B (2007). Inida's economic growth miracle in a global economy. In *India and South Asia: Economic Developments in the Age of Globalization*, Siddiqui A (ed.), p. 66. New York: M.E. Sharpe.

38   Anwar, S, Parikshit K Basu (2007). Foreign investment and economic growth: a case study of India. In *India and South Asia: Economic Development in the Age of Globalization*, Anjum Siddiqui (ed.), p. 159. New York: M.E. Sharpe.

39   Restall, H (March 2006). India's coming eclipse of China. *Far Eastern Economic review*, 169(2).

40   Cohen, SP (2001). *India: Emerging Power*, p. 299. Washington, D.C.: Brookings Institution Press.

41   Samuelson, RJ (December 26, 2007). *The End of Free Trade*, p. A21. Washington Post.

Chapter 6

1   Ferdows, K (March–April 1997). *Making the Most of Foreign Factories*, p. 82. Harvard Business Review.

2 Lall, S, Paul Streeten (1977). *Foreign Investment, Transnationals and Developing Countries*, p. 54. London: Macmillan Press Ltd.

3 Chang, H-J (2007). *Bad Samaritans*: *Rich Nations, Poor Policies & the Threat to the Developing World*, p. 89. London: Random House Business Books.

4 Jones, G (1996). *The Evolution of International Business*: *An Introduction*, p. 225. London and New York: Routledge.

5 Bergsman, *et al.* (December 1995). *Finance & Development*, p. 6.

6 Private capital flows to developing countries: the road to financial integration, *A World Bank Policy Research Report*, p. 86. New York: Oxford University Press.

7 Reich, R, Who is us? Harvard Business Review.

8 Anwar, S, Parikshit K Basu (2007). Foreign investment and economic growth: a case study of India. In *India and South Asia: Economic Development in the Age of Globalization*, Anjum Siddiqui (ed.), p. 162. New York: M.E. Sharpe.

9 Witherell, WH (October/November 1996). An agreement on investment. *The OECD Observer*, 202, 9.

10 Bayoumi, T, Gabrielle Lipworth (September 1997). Japanese foreign direct investment and regional trade. *Finance & Development*, 34(3), 12.

11 Hatch, W, Kozo Yamamura (1996). *Asia in Japan's Embrace: Building a Regional Production Alliance*, p. 6. Cambridge, UK: Cambridge University Press.

12 Shepherd, WF (1994). *International Financial Integration: History, Theory and Applications in OECD Countries*, p. 32. Aldershot: Avebury.

13 Hatch, W, Kozo Yamamura (1996). *Asia in Japan's Embrace: Building a Regional Production Alliance*, p. 22ff. Cambridge, UK: Cambridge University Press.

14 World Trade Organization (1996). Annual Report, p. 51. Vol. 1, Geneva.

15 World Trade Organization (1996). Annual Report, p. 44. Vol. 1, Geneva.

16 Barnet, RJ, Ronald E Muller (1975). *Global Reach*: *The Power of the Multinational Corporations*, pp. 305–306. London: Jonathan Cape.

17 Greenaway, D (September 1990). Trade related investment measures: political economy aspects and issues for GATT. *The World Economy*, 13(3), 373.

18 Chan, S (1995). Introduction: Foreign Direct Investment in a Changing World. In *Foreign Direct Investment in a Changing Global Political Economy*, Chan, S (ed.), p. 2. Houndmills and London: Macmillan Press Ltd.

19 The GATT Secretariat (1994). The Final Act of the Uruguay Round: A summary. *International Trade Forum*, 1, 10.

20 Hoekman, B, M Kostecki (1995). *The Political Economy of the World Trading System: From GATT to WTO*, p. 122. Oxford: Oxford University Press.

21 World trade Organization (1996). Annual Report, Vol. 1, Geneva, p. 62.

22 The Multilateral Agreement on Investments, OECD Policy Brief, No. 2, 1997, p. 3. (http://www.oecd.org/publications/Pol_brief/9702_Pol.htm)

23 Witherell, WH (October–November 1996). An agreement on investment, *The OECD Observer*, 202, 7.

24   Clarke, T, "MAI-Day! The Corporate Rule Treaty", http://www.nassist.com/mai/
      mai(2)x.html.

Chapter 7

1   Schlesinger, J (July 2003). Climate Change: The Science Isn't Settled, Washington
     Post, 7, A17.
2   Schnoor, JL, JN Galloway, B Molden (September 1997). East Central Europe: An
     environment in transition. *Environmental Science & Technology*, 31(9), 415A.
3   Levy, MA (1993). East-west environmental politics after 1989: the case of air pollu-
     tion. In *After the Cold War: International Institutions and State Strageies in Europe,
     1989–1991*, Keohane, RO, JS Nye, S Hoffmann (eds.), Cambridge: Harvard
     University Press.
4   Zylicz, T (1994). Environmental policy reform in Poland. In *Economic Policies for
     Sustainable Development*, Sterner, T (ed.), pp. 85–86. Dordrecht: Kluwer Academic
     Publishers.
5   World Development Report (1992). The World Bank and Oxford University Press,
     New York, p. 43.
6   Ehrlich, P (1994). Too many rich people. *Our Planet*, 6(3), 13.
7   Elizabeth Economy (March 1999). Painting China Green, Foreign Affairs.
8   Our Common Future (1990). The World Commission on Environment and
     Development, Australia, Melbourne, Oxford University Press, p. 87.
9   Schmidheiny, S (1992). *Changing Course: A Global Business Perspective on
     Development and the Environment*, p. 60. Cambridge, MA: The MIT Press.
10   World Development Report (1992). The World Bank and Oxford University Press,
     New York, p. 35.
11   World Development Report (1992). The World Bank and Oxford University Press,
     New York, p. 36.
12   Johnson, SP (1993). p. 5.
13   Postel, S (1992). Denial in the decisive decade. *In State of the World 1992*, p. 3.
     New York: W.W Norton & Co.
14   Egan D, Levy David (2001). International environmental politics and the interna-
     tionalization of states. In *The International Political Economy of the Environment*,
     Stevis D, VJ Assetto (eds.), p. 73. Boulder Colo: Lynne Rienner.
15   Lindzen, RS Global warming: the origin and nature of the alleged scientific consensus.
     Regulation: The Cato Review of Business and Government, (http://www.cato.org/pubs/
     regulation/reg15n2g.html).
16   Stern, N (2007). *The Economics of Climate Change: The Stern Review*, p. 8.
     Cambridge: Cambridge University Press.
17   Steer, A, E Lutz (December 1993). Measuring environmental sustainable develop-
     ment. *Finance & Development*, 30(4), 21.

18   World Development Report (1992). The World Bank and Oxford University Press, New York, p. 40.

19   Haas, PM (Summer 1989). Do regimes matter? Epistemic communities and the mediterranean pollution control. *International Organization*, 43(3), 398.

20   Cooper R, cited in Horne, J and Paul R. Masson (June 1988). Scope and limits of international economic cooperation and policy coordination. *Staff Papers, International Monetary Fund*, 35(2), 281.

Chapter 8

1   Stoler, AL (June 2006). Free & fairer trade — protecting workers' right in trade agreements, Remarks to the International Alert Series Session on the Big Issues, Adelaide Town Hall, 6, 2006.

2   Report by the United States to the Trade Policy Review Body, World Trade Organization, Geneva, 3 March 2006, WT/TPR/G/160, p. 26.

3   Hayter, T (2000). *Open Borders: The Case Against Immigration Controls*, p. 166. London: Pluto Press.

4   Lee, E (1996). Globalization and employment: is anxiety justified? *International Labour Review*, 491.

5   Marshall, R (1994). The importance of international labour standards in a more competitive global economy. In *International Labour Standards and Economic Interdependence*, Sengenberger, W, D Campbell (eds.), p. 67. Geneva: International Institute for Labour Studies.

6   Emmerij, L (1994). Contemporary challenges for labour standards resulting from globalization. In *International Labour Standards and Economic Interdependence*, Sengenberger, W, D Campbell (eds.), p. 322. Geneva: International Institute for Labour Studies.

7   Barenberg, M (1995). Law and labor in the new global economy: through the lens of United States federalism. *Columbia Journal of Transnational Law*, 33(3), 449.

8   Collingsworth, T, J William Goold, PJ Harvey (January/February 1994). Time for a global new deal. *Foreign Affairs*, 73(1), 9.

9   Torres, R (October–November 1996). Labour standards and trade, *The OECD Observer*, 202, 12.

10   Hansson, G (1983). *Social Clauses and International Trade: An Economic Analysis of Labour Standards in Trade Policy*, p. 182. London and Canberra: Croom Helm.

11   Milner, C (March 1997). 'New standards issue' and the WTO. *Australian Economic Review*, 30(1), 91.

12   Collingsworth, T, J William Goold, PJ Harvey (January/February 1994). Time for a global new deal. *Foreign Affairs*, 73(1), 10.

13   Sengenberger, W (1994). Restructuring at the global level: The role of international labour standards. In *Creating Economic Opportunities: The Role of Labour Standards in Industrial Restructuring*, Sengenberger W, D Campbell (eds.), p. 410. Geneva: International Institute for Labour Studies.

14   Langille, BA (August 1997). Eight ways to think about international labour standards. *Journal of World Trade*, 31(4), 35.

15   Emmerij, L (1994). Contemporary challenges for labour standards resulting from globalization. In *International Labour Standards and Economic Interdependence*, Sengenberger, W, D Campbell (eds.), p. 323. Geneva: International Institute for Labour Studies.

16   Lim, LYC (1990). Singapore. In *Labor Standards and Development in the Global Economy*, Herzenberg S, JF Perez-Lopez (eds.), pp. 88–89. Washington: U.S. Department of Labor, Bureau of International Labor Affairs.

17   Papola, TS (1994). International labour standards and developing countries. In *International Labour Standards and Economic Interdependence*, Sengenberger, W, D Campbell (eds.), pp. 180–181. Geneva: International Institute for Labour Studies.

18   Plant, R (1994). *Labour Standards and Structural Adjustment*, pp. 192–193. Geneva: International Labour Office.

19   Torres, R (October–November 1996). Labour standards and trade, *The OECD Observer*, 202, 10.

20   Sengenberger, W (1994). Restructuring at the global level: the role of international labour standards. In *Creating Economic Opportunities: The Role of Labour Standards in Industrial Restructuring*, Sengenberger, W, D Campbell (eds.), p. 410. Geneva: International Institute for Labour Studies.

21   Langille, BA (August 1997). Eight ways to think about international labour standards. *Journal of World Trade*, 31(4), 32.

22   Sapir, A (November 1995). The interaction between labour standards and international trade policy. *The World Economy*, 18(6), 802.

23   Milner, C (March 1997). 'New standards issues' and the WTO. *The Australian Economic Review*, 30(1), 91–92.

24   Servais, J-M (1989). The social clause in trade agreements: wishful thinking or an instrument of social progress? *International Labour Review*, 128(4), 430.

25   Herzenberg, SA, JF Perez-Lopez, SK Tucker (1990). Labor standards and development in the global economy. In *Labor Standards and Development in the Global Economy*, Herzenberg SA, JF Perez-Lopez (eds.), p. 4. Washington: U.S. Department of Labor, Bureau of International Labor Affairs.

26   Jones, G (1996). *The Evolution of International Business: An Introduction*, p. 303. London and New York: Routledge.

27   International Labour Standards Should not be Used for Protectionist Purposes, Issues Paper, Australian Chamber of Commerce and Industry, Canberra, Australia, March 2005.

Index